Japan Style

Gian Carlo Calza

JAPAN
STYLE

Table of Contents

Irregular Beauty

Japan Style

We often take cultural phenomena and forms of behaviour that are characteristic of Japanese society as evidence of sensibilities and attitudes that were once alien to us, but which have now become integral to a way of seeing and constructing the physical and social world that is both universal and our own.

They might include appreciation of a single flower, exquisitely arranged and presented, compared with a large bouquet, where it is quantity that counts; the intimate, organic qualities of structures built on a human scale, in contrast to those emphasizing the façade; the importance ascribed to the act of creation rather than to the object manufactured; or the value placed on certain daily actions that have come to symbolize fundamental aspects of existence and which would otherwise simply be part of the monotonous, repetitive cycle of things that have to be done day in, day out. But when we perceive such phenomena, and in some cases assimilate them, we generally attribute to them a common characteristic element, over and above differences in the ways they manifest themselves individually. It is a form of what the Chinese call *qi* and the Japanese *ki* – the spirit inherent in things. It is in some respects an individual property, intrinsic to particular phenomena, but when it is seen in relation to the expressive forms of a given culture it could be said to be what is called style.

Style, of course, is a word that has to be handled carefully and used sparingly, as if it were a precious object, fragile and easily broken. And, in fact, its meaning has recently become somewhat blurred, especially because of the tendency to identify it with its superficial, ephemeral usage, to the detriment of a deeper understanding in the realm of causes. The use of the term 'the severe style' in connection with Greek sculpture refers to a number of works carved in such a way as to express, individually and as a whole, certain spiritual values that the Greeks of the day embodied in forms of personal and social behaviour. In other words, they were creating these values, for themselves and for posterity.

This was clearly an elitist process, but it was one whose fruits were available for all to enjoy, just as the buildings of the Acropolis were elitist in comparison with the jumbled chaos of the *astu*: the city below it. These works and their style in turn became the vectors, individually and collectively, of the values they symbolized, and in that way they acquired the status of archetypal images. This is how I propose to discuss the 'Japan style'. Nowadays, the word 'style' is frequently misinterpreted, since it is used to highlight the formal, even decorative, aspects of various phenomena of mass culture. This confusion has reached the point where the unfortunate term 'stylist' has been coined to refer to a person who could never exist: someone who creates style. In fact, style is the result of a complex process of personal and social transformation (and as such not attributable to a single person), one that gives rise to images capable of representing values that are profound and enduring, not ephemeral like fashion which, by definition, must constantly be changing.

The aim of this book is to trace what it is that gives a characteristic quality to Japan, and especially its arts, and is transmitted as a specific, unique contribution to the development of human values, both individual and social. It is, of course, impossible to give a definitive, unambiguous account of the precise style that defines the essence and the aesthetic achievements of Japanese culture, but we can try to interpret certain categories of feeling that have developed within it and make it unique. These include the relationship with nature, which uses philosophical and religious concepts that are also applied to art and architecture. Closely connected with this is the appreciation of materiality, reflected in a vast range of expressive forms in which what is emphasized is their inherent qualities rather than their ability to embody ideas. Then there is the world of ritual, in the sense both of the aesthetic aspect of religious rites and of secular ritualism – for example, the tea ceremony or the canonization of gesture in drama – and lastly, the appreciation of the material in fashion and graphic art in particular. These phenomena are, in fact, interconnected. The relationship with nature lies behind the love of physical materials and materiality in objects and in design. Hence the close connection with the ways in which these are used and thus with ritualism and, finally, with feelings of care and love for the object and the spirit with which it is imbued, demonstrated by traditions such as the funerals held in Kyoto for needles that can no longer be used for sewing.

It is obvious that all this contradicts assertions that it is impossible for a foreigner or someone who is not an expert in the field to fully understand the art and culture of Japan. I do not see it like that, and believe that appreciation of Japanese art, like anything else perhaps, is a matter of interpretation, closely tied to the viewer's sensitivities and their application. Essentially, it is possible to see the human qualities expressed in that art without being Japanese or a specialist. Of course, without a grounding in the subject it is more difficult to make a work speak, and easier to make it say things not intended by its creator, thus distorting its meaning. It is therefore necessary to acquire some interpretative tools and develop appropriate sensibilities. This is what I propose to do here. At the same time, I believe it is impossible to set precise rules for doing so, although direct experience may often be of help in devising a suitable method. This method will have to be constantly revised, because it is vital that each individual always looks for new routes to his or her way of understanding, even if these routes have been trodden many times before.

One autumn a few years ago, the Chilean painter Roberto Matta, who had just been in Tokyo where he was awarded the Imperial Prize, infected me with his passion for contemporary Japanese architecture, especially the enormous complex of new skyscrapers designed by Tange Kenzo in Nishi Shinjuku for the Tokyo Government House. Matta spent part of his eighty-fourth birthday flying back to France after his two-week stay in Japan, but before he left he felt compelled to revisit the Mingeikan Folk Crafts Museum, to savour its atmosphere, look again at some of its ceramics, and buy examples of the textiles.

I was fired by Matta's enthusiasm, and accompanied him to the museum. I was fascinated by his way of looking at things I had been studying for years, his ability to respond with equal intensity to the vast scale of Tange's architecture and the refinement and simplicity of popular art. Matta deplored the fact that in today's world love has disappeared from work, from human interactions, and, above all, from art; and that people hide behind barriers of bureaucracy, trade union practice or academicism in order to avoid its implications and the risks it carries with it. In Japan, he would say, 'Tu vois – tout le monde aime ce qu'il fait' ('You see – everyone loves what they do'). I wasn't too sure about the presence or absence of love, in Japan or in the West, but Matta has undoubtedly found the key to understanding Japanese or, indeed, any other art: love, passion, dedication.

This made me realize that whenever someone asks me what they should read to begin to understand Japanese art, I would always recommend Fosco Maraini's *Meeting with Japan*.[1] This is not a work of art history, but it is the perfect vehicle for getting in tune with the world of Japan. It doesn't shy away from anything, and every aspect of the subject, pleasurable or painful, attractive or repellent, simple or grandiose, provides the opportunity for the sort of exploration that inspires an interest that always ends as love. And after all, isn't this what artists do? Have not *ukiyo-e* prints, 'pictures of the floating world', turned both high- and low-class courtesans into exemplars of beauty and seductiveness? Have they not made the *demi-monde* of the famous red-light district of Yoshiwara more acceptable, helping to disseminate visually, and thus directly and immediately, the culture from which they emanate? And were *ukiyo-e* not also a crucial factor in the very creation of that culture, which exerted such a strong influence not only on modern Japan but also on nineteenth-century Europe?

However, Maraini's fundamental approach assumes that the penetration of East and West is mutual, and thus he is able to internalize the Japanese way of seeing reality. This is expressed not only through the written word but also through images, in this case photographs. One of his most famous is the charming *Frivolous*

1   Fosco Maraini, *Meeting with Japan*, Hutchinson, London, 1959.

Moment, which shows a woman putting on her lipstick, framed in silhouette in a room overlooking the garden of an inn.

The image has all the seductive charm found in *The Tale of Genji* (*Genji monogatari*), where the beauty of its young girls is half-concealed; readers fall in love not with garishly depicted bodies, but with hair that flows in waves in the shadow, with a profile that can only be guessed at behind a screen-of-state, or with the elegant, barely perceptible movement of an outline. I quote from *The Tale of Genji*:

> He felt embarrassed and angry. Suddenly one of the cords of the screen-of-state behind which she was sitting fell across her zither, making as it did so a kind of casual tune. As she bent over the instrument, he saw her for an instant as she must have looked before his arrival made her stiffen; just as she must look when, carelessly and at ease, she swept an idle plectrum over the strings. He was captivated.[2]

For Japanese art to be better understood in the West, it is important to note the extent to which it has often been appreciated first by Western artists and only later as a result of formal academic study. The contribution the Impressionists made to the appreciation of the print and the art of the *ukiyo-e* is well known, but the Art Nouveau tradition also disseminated interest in, and knowledge of, certain images and themes, especially ones taken from nature, which opened the way for new research, in graphic art and design in particular. Architects like Bruno Taut, Richard Neutra, Mies van der Rohe, Frank Lloyd Wright, Le Corbusier and Walter Gropius adapted and reinterpreted concepts of space, such as organicity, modularity and fusion with nature, that are characteristic of the Japanese architectural tradition.

The circle closes, and at the same moment re-opens with the recent profusion of works dealing with specific aspects of Japanese culture. They go ever deeper and are ever more richly documented, but carry the risk of obscuring from view the larger themes that underlie fundamental transformations in art. I should therefore like to conclude by suggesting that, as an antidote to this tendency, the reader keep within reach a classic work, D. T. Suzuki's *Zen and Japanese Culture*.[3] Nowadays, Suzuki is criticized by some for being the source (especially through the works of his pupils and imitators) of a form of 'Zen' that deviates from the true Zen spirit. This may be so. For myself, I shall leave it to those critics to reveal the true Zen spirit, because I do not know what it is and, as I do not know, I hope to continue to search for it – just as, thanks to the lessons I have received from Suzuki among others, I continue to investigate the spirit of Japanese art in its many guises, hoping that at least one of my readers may think it worth trying to do the same.

2   Murasaki Shikibu, *The Tale of Genji* (*Genji monogatari*), trans. A. Waley, Modern Library, New York, 1960, p. 273.

3   Daisetz T. Suzuki, *Zen and Japanese Culture*, Bollingen Series, New York, 1959 (first published 1938).

Tōrei Enji
Ensō, ink on paper, 18th
century

Tea and the Aesthetics of the Undefined

Foremost among the concepts that Asia has passed to the West are those connected with the world of tea – a short word with a vast and complex range of associations. Even though it is part of everyday life, with the attendant dangers of its consumption becoming automatic and taken for granted, it retains an aura of mystery and inscrutability. The introduction of the tea-bag has, of course, made drinking tea a somewhat sterile experience, interposing a barrier that obscures its reality and prevents the full enjoyment of its essence and all its hidden qualities. Yet, even in a crowded, busy bar, tea is not experienced in the same way as an espresso or any other beverage. Even those whose approach to it could not be more down to earth have a reflective air. Of all drinks it is tea that, even in the West, immediately evokes thoughts of private, exclusive and sometimes ritualized consumption. It is as if it has the intrinsic, natural characteristic of inducing a state of its own, creating a break in the routine in which we are submerged, causing us to distance ourselves from our actions and allowing us to contemplate them from a more rarefied dimension where we can grasp the general significance of an act and its true place in our life. We do not feel the same way about coffee, which comes from sunnier, tropical climes and whose purpose seems to be to whip up our psychic energy and stimulate us to engage even more feverishly in what we are doing. Why, then, this difference? Why is tea always surrounded by an aura of refinement and impenetrability?

A legend tells how Bodhidharma, the founder of Zen Buddhism, was immersed in a profound state of meditation that was supposed to last without interruption for several years. As the end of this time was approaching his body gave way to sleep. When he awoke, his reaction to his weakness was to cut off his eyelids to prevent them closing over his eyes and interrupting his state of meditative wakefulness. For this reason, he is often shown with large, round, lidless eyes that look like searchlights constantly scouring an impenetrable mystery. His eyelids fell to the ground and created the tea plant, which has the power to keep the mind alert; the shape of its leaf is like that of an almond-shaped eyelid. This tradition, like every myth, has great metaphorical resonance and in the East it led directly to the cult of tea, understood not as an aesthetic pastime but as a vehicle created by man to keep himself in a wakeful state, in order to avoid sinking into an automatic repetition of practical activities and thus losing contact with the intrinsic value of his own activity and spiritual reality.

From a metaphorical perspective the myth reveals the presence of archetypal values which, throughout the historical evolution of Japanese civilization, have expressed themselves in the tea ceremony – or, rather, in the inner reasons for its creation and survival. The spirit of this ritual has penetrated the wealthiest as well as the poorest homes, creating an aristocracy of taste that is also an aristocracy of manners. The concept is so central that, to quote Okakura (1862–1913) in his wonderful *Book of Tea* (1906), someone who is unable to see the tragicomic side of events in his life is described as '[a man] with no tea'. The Japanese also say of someone who allows himself to be carried away by his feelings, without due respect for life's tragic aspect, that he is one 'with too much tea' in him.[1]

In east Asia, and above all in Japan, there has grown up over the centuries a precisely determined ritual designed to enable those who follow it to rise above the everyday to the sphere of archetypes. A small act like drinking a cup of tea is transformed into an intense aesthetic experience, which is expressed in a multiplicity of cultural vehicles, and several cultural languages are involved in the performance of the ritual (which demands a detached self-mastery). In this context, to hear what tea is saying it is necessary to draw for help on painting and calligraphy, ceramics and the art of flower arrangement. But it is gesture that is fundamental. In the East – and this can never be emphasized too strongly – the body is considered to be a direct manifestation of consciousness, able to transmit inner states often far more clearly than words. Every moment of the tea ceremony is therefore under the tightest possible control. But we are not talking about a recitation to a watching audience, or about a simple gestural form in the sense that the gesture itself expresses a particular spiritual value. The tea ceremony is the symbol, and at the same time the vehicle, for the man who rises above the frenetic struggle for survival to an awareness that every action is an expression of himself, evidence that he is approaching his ideal world or, conversely, regressing to the brute state.

This is a dimension of existence similar to the one created in primitive societies which, in order to differentiate themselves from the world of phenomena that constantly threaten to overwhelm human reality, entrust themselves to the power of the mana, the totem, the *atai*, and to rituals of the hunt, the harvest and the blessing of food. Consumer society has blinded us to the danger of losing this state of attentiveness, substituting for it a guarantee of material and technological progress and so making the danger even more subtle and pernicious. Technology and mechanization cannot foster personal growth. Therefore, in keeping with the emphasis of Zen philosophy, Japan has created arts that have no practical goal and do not even offer aesthetic pleasure, but which represent a form of training designed to bring the conscious mind closer to ultimate reality.

The tea ceremony is one of these, and in order to act as a vehicle for the development of knowledge it requires the practitioner to be versed in the

1   Okakura Kakuzō, *The Book of Tea*, Charles E. Tuttle, Tokyo, 1964 (first published 1906), p. 5.

many arts that converge in it; and, above all, to be aware of the human value of what he or she is doing and not excessively attached to results. The cult (or, rather, the discipline) of tea is permeated by the spirit of Zen, which finds its highest expression in helping individuals to liberate themselves from the shackles of the mind and the physical world, putting them on their guard even against Zen itself – or, at least, against its doctrinaire aspects. Doctrine may be more constricting than the wildest passion: a prison instead of a road to liberation. No more and no less than all Zen disciplines, the art of tea must therefore be practised with devotion, but also with detachment.

The experience of Eugen Herrigel, who visited Japan between the wars, provides a valuable insight into the importance of this detachment. A professor of philosophy, he tried with tireless devotion and Teutonic determination to penetrate the spirit of Zen, in his case through the practice of archery.[2] Anyone who succeeds in experiencing the way they handle the bow as being comparable to creating a work of art achieves perfect harmony of mind and body, transcending the dissociated state in which the Western psyche has been plunged for centuries. Herrigel reveals the efforts and the patience needed to reach this inner harmony when he describes, sometimes with a fine vein of irony and self-awareness, his endless attempts to enter the symbolic and metaphorical world of the hundreds of arts in which Zen manifests itself.[3] That archery, like the tea ceremony, may be an art is in itself difficult to accept, but the idea that it must be 'aimless' (hitting the target, like ingesting the tea, is not the purpose of the exercise) is liable to test Western mental constructs to the limit. The masters of the art, however, lay great emphasis on the purity of the act itself, on the elegance of its total, absolute naturalness. Just as a flower that falls from a plant does not decide to do so for any particular purpose, so the movement of stretching the bow and relaxing the fingers that hold the arrow must be as harmonious and spontaneous as the gestures that accompany the tea ceremony.

The art of tea does, in fact, have a goal: to change oneself, to enlarge one's human capacities and, above all, to achieve an inner awareness of what it is necessary to undertake or avoid for the sake of one's development. Knowledge as such is not important; technical skill is only the first step. What is demanded of exponents of the art is the willingness to give up their intellectual certainties, so that they become aware of the mutability of the world of phenomena. Everyday gestures elevated into an art (despite the strictures that limit their expressive possibilities) have a range of interpretation that is greater than that of a painting or a sculpture. The ritual is not designed to have spectators; there are only participants, who consciously act as both creators and critics in the ensemble.

2   Eugen Herrigel, *Zen in the Art of Archery*, Routledge & Kegan Paul, London, 1953.

3   Rodney Needham in *Exemplars* (University of California Press, 1985, ch. 9) challenges the originality of Herrigel's thought, exposing influences from eighteenth-century German literature. However, his very interesting analysis on intercultural sources of inspiration does not seem to me to be relevant in this context.

Especially, the tea ceremony reflects different aspects of Far Eastern art, allowing freedom of interpretation and enabling those who take part in it to use their imagination to assimilate the universe of empty spaces and allusive asymmetry in which the art of tea, more than any other, is supreme

Okakura does not say these things explicitly in his *Book of Tea*. His writing, his thoughts, his mission – he worked on that lofty and ambitious scale – are creatures of his times. He lived in an era when Western supremacy was proclaimed with the help of all available media – literature, philosophy, art – and, above all, the battleship. But Japan had just won a spectacular victory over tsarist Russia that had left the world gaping in amazement, and Okakura embarked on the task of making known his country's cultural treasures. In his book tea is only the cue, the subtle opportunity to open readers' eyes to the limitless vistas of an entire civilization. This short, delicate essay also symbolizes Okakura's work, his struggle to penetrate and master the tools of Western culture in order to rescue and disseminate the values of his own. He dedicated his entire life to this task, and the *Book of Tea*, originally a private project, established itself as one of the best-known works on the East and is the most fascinating and influential of all his publications.

Zen is indeed fundamental to an understanding of the cult of tea, as Okakura says at the beginning of one of the chapters, 'Taoism and Zennism', even though he lacked the means of making himself fully understood by his readers; D. T. Suzuki's studies, which made Zen the most widely known branch of Buddhism, were not published until later. For this reason, Okakura was forced to devote maximum space to Taoism and to try, by analogy, to infiltrate the principle of Zen into his vision of life and the world. But the real protagonist in the book is art or, rather, the love of beauty and training in the expression of aesthetic feelings. Okakura has achieved self-realization in this regard. His entire life can be read as a journey towards the ideals of beauty and civility that he was in the process of discovering in the past of the Far East; and which he felt compelled not only to pass on and preserve, but also to communicate to the Western mind in order to provide it with a vital stimulus.

Times have changed. Nowadays the East is almost too fashionable and, for this very reason perhaps, is in danger of losing its power to enrich Western society, which can no longer curb its headlong rush to consume as everything is devoured and nothing is savoured. Nevertheless, Okakura's book, now as before, is one of the best means by which to gain access to the spiritual values of Japanese civilization. For Westerners, who tend to make a science even of art, it offers a stimulus to renew their experience of culture, putting it once again at the service of personal and social growth.

Hasegawa Tōhaku
Sen no Rikyū (tea-master),
colour on silk, 16th century

頭上申兼手中翁依然遺像

旧時姿趙州旦坐喫茶底等不

斯翁尊乃知

利休居士肖像常随信男

宗慶煕之請賀伽陀一絶係

上完香供云

文禄第四乙未歳舎季穐念四日

三玄春屋叟宗園

The *kanji* [character] for 'tea'

The Ritual of Tea, Kyoto, 1951,
photograph by Werner Bischof

Left:
Ippitsusai Bunchō
The Kasamori Shrine,
ink and colours on paper,
c. 1780

Right:
Kitagawa Utamaro
Okita from Naniwaya,
colour woodblock print,
1793

Bamboo tea ceremony
implements (left to right):
feather duster (*chabōki*); tea
whisk (*chasen*); water ladle
(*hishaku*); tea spoon
(*chashaku*); photographs by
Iwamiya Takeji

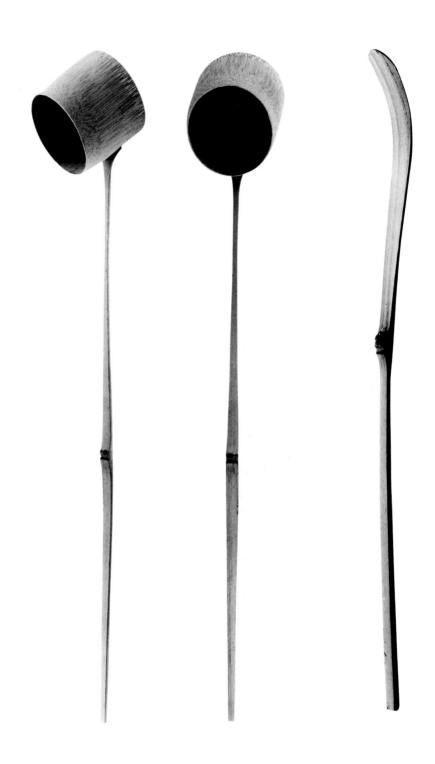

Left:
Anonymous
Tea Time in Japan, c. 1900

Right:
Chōjirō
Black *raku* tea bowl, earthenware,
16th century

Hakuin Ekaku
Daruma (Bodhidharma), ink on
paper, 18th century

Overleaf:
Kitao Masayoshi
'Martial Artists', from *Human
Figures in Abbreviated Drawing
Style*, colour woodblock print,
1799

Images of Emptiness

'Nihon' (Japan) means 'at the roots of the sun', and Japan's national symbol is the rising sun. But the image of the sun, radiating heat and light and triumphing over chaos, is also at the root of stage performance and is related to a very ancient motif in Japanese cosmology. The sun goddess Amaterasu, the chief deity in Shintō, Japan's autochthonous religion, fled from her celestial palace and shut herself up in a cave, plunging the universe into darkness. She had been wounded by the brutal and abusive behaviour of her brother Susano-o, who had contaminated her august abode with the bloodied hide of a horse and had also brought about the death of a servant girl. Faced with the danger of being cast back into chaos, the gods were terrified, and devised a stratagem to make the goddess emerge. A great celebration was prepared outside the cave, and the divine Uzume, celestial dancer and musician, possessed (by a demon), performed an orgiastic dance that drew in the rest of the gods, who joined her in performing it. The din and raucous laughter made Amaterasu curious and she peered out of the cave. Two gods placed a mirror in front of her and told her the feast was in celebration of a more splendid and powerful deity than herself. In her astonishment the goddess took a step forward, and was caught and dragged into the open, forbidden for evermore to enter the cave.

The origins of Japanese theatre are located in Uzume's dance, but this is only a part of the myth, albeit the most dramatic episode and full of pathos. In fact, the entire story can be read as an archetypal expression of the birth of theatre in Japan. A traumatic event (affront, contamination, tragic death) causes a withdrawal from visible presence (the cave, the stage curtain) and yet the life forces, the passions (orgiastic dance and celebration or re-enactment) irresistibly attract the figure who had previously disappeared and force her on to the stage. The spectators (in this myth, the gods) do not play a merely passive role but are witnesses of the event portrayed, which thus becomes sacred and cathartic. In the process of representing this ideal, primeval event on the stage, using various forms of theatre practice, the space that is created in the transition from one gesture to the next is of paramount importance. It is an element that is found equally in the aristocratic nō theatre and the more popular kabuki and *bunraku*, albeit in performative canons that are very different from one another. A moment of high drama and intense emotion is emphasized on the stage by the space created through the medium of silence and stillness, as well as through a feverish musical or gestural rhythm that is allowed to come to an abrupt end.

The same is true of traditional painting, where details are given greater or lesser prominence, not through a hierarchical order based on perspective but by means of isolation using banks of cloud or mist, and by the use of figures of unequal size, foreshortening and scenes viewed 'from an angle'. A given visual narrative may be interrupted by the interposition of an area of cloud, blank and monotone. Beyond it, the scene resumes with an image that is separate from the previous one but related to it. Observers, like the theatre audience, are forced to make their own private and personal connection between the two moments depicted, the two pictures within the painting, the two scenes on the stage. The second, more distant and mysterious, image becomes the focus of attention, the key to understanding the first, to which the viewer returns with renewed interest and awakened senses. This effect is achieved by organizing space in such a way that emptiness serves as a catalyst for the different areas, a method that is fundamentally different to its Western counterpart. In our tradition the concept of emptiness has a predominantly negative value, the sense of something lacking, in contrast with China and Japan where it has a positive role and is represented in various ways.

To understand this positive value, it may be useful to shift our attention away from the concept of emptiness, which may make us feel uncomfortable, away from the *horror vacui*, to a concept with which we are more familiar: silence. This evokes a sense of peace, quietness, serenity, the relinquishment of conscious thought, no ferment of noise or ideas, no anxiety. By oscillating between the concepts of emptiness and silence we will discover that emptiness is no longer a negative; in pictorial terms it may be a bank of mist interrupting the view of a mountain, but it also becomes a way of alluding to a world that exists and which observers may imagine for themselves. And it is by trying to imagine this world that we engage in a process of personal development; we make an effort and become creative.

This appreciation of emptiness has its roots in a number of religious experiences that are alien to Shintō animism, the oldest Japanese tradition. Instead, they are linked with a fusion of Buddhism and Taoism, in which Buddhism developed the concept of meditation and Taoism the aspect of emptiness, which is a vital element in meditation. This is not mental vacuity, but rather a means by which to bring to the surface the most profound part of the self – that is, the nature of the Buddha, the awakened, that is latent in everyone. Later, this concept was also applied to nature as such (with the contribution of Shintō), but perhaps – and I emphasize 'perhaps' – the first movement towards emptiness in Japan came with the introduction of Taoism and Buddhism, and was followed by a return to native traditions. Nature offers many images of emptiness, which we usually fail to see. In Western paintings clouds are primarily visual and allude to nothing else; they indicate themselves alone or, at most, an aspect of the weather, and serve to create solid forms as, for example, in the work of Tiepolo. In China and Japan, however, clouds interpose themselves between the visible and the invisible. They are an interruption of vision and serve to stimulate in observers an attitude of enquiry and creativity.

One of the most famous Japanese paintings, the *Landscape in Broken Ink* (*Haboku sansui*), painted by Sesshū (1420–1506) in 1495 and dedicated to his pupil Sōen, lends itself perfectly to this method of analysis, in that the mist and clouds are a means of representing emptiness.[1] At the same time, it provides important evidence both for the relationship between writing and painting, and for the ethical and aesthetic concept of the Master. The painting occupies the lower part of the scroll, while the upper and middle sections contain various remarks by six monks who were friends of Sesshū. In the central section, there is an autograph text written by Sesshū himself; taking as his starting point the occasion for which he made the painting, he summarizes his pictorial aesthetic and lists those to whom he is indebted as an artist:

The librarian Sōen, born in Sōyō, has long followed my teachings in the field of painting and has already achieved a style of painting of his own. He has devoted himself to this art with deep commitment, and when spring came he said to me: 'I beg you to give me one of your paintings, to hand it on to future generations', and for many days he kept asking me this. I, for all that I could no longer see, was very old and did not know if I would be capable of it, under the pressure of this request took up a worn brush, dipped it in the diluted ink and said to him, 'Long ago I was in the Land of the Song, and crossing the great river in the north, and the states of Qi and Lu, I reached the northern capital. There I searched for a teacher of painting; however, people of quality are rare, but both Zhang Yousheng and Li Zai, from whom respectively I learned the use of colour and the *haboku* method, had gained a certain measure of fame. After some years I returned to Japan, and I have followed to the letter the models and the works of the old masters Josetsu [active 1386?–1428?] and Shūbun [active 1414–63], knowing that I could neither add anything nor take anything away from them. After China I saw [their paintings] many times, I appreciated ever more keenly the quality of their spirit and their skill, and following in their footsteps, I drew without regrets.

1   The painting measures 147.9 x 32.7 cm and is signed 'Sesshū's brush' (*Sesshū hitsu*), with the seal of the artist, SESSHŪ. It is in the Tokyo National Museum and has been designated a national treasure.

2   The traditional Japanese method for calculating the years of a person's life has been followed. According to this, a person is considered to be a year old on the date of his or her birth.

Written at the age of seventy-six[2] by old Sesshū, first position[3] in the Tiantong temple at Siming, at the end of the year of the rabbit of the Meiō period.[4]

In the text Sesshū uses the term 'Land of the Song', probably out of the great respect he had for the paintings produced during the rule of the Song. However, at the time of his journey the dynasty in power was the Ming (1368–1644). Furthermore, the northern capital, the present Beijing, established by the Mongol dynasty of the Yuan (1279–1368), was not the capital at the time of the Song, although it obviously was when Sesshū visited China.

Independently of these historical and geographical considerations, the written text acknowledges those to whom Sesshū is indebted as a painter, above all in learning the *haboku* method (*pomo* in Chinese). But he makes it very clear that this is a debt of respect for the greatness of the Song, since he considers himself a disciple of the Japanese painters Josetsu and Shūbun.

The painting shows how Sesshū applied the theory expressed in his text to the practice of drawing in 'broken ink'. This is a technique or, rather, as defined by Sesshū himself, a method, which in *Haboku sansui* reaches absolute perfection in the use both of the brush stroke and of empty space. Perception of this emptiness is not assisted even by the traditional use of mist or clouds. We know they are there, thanks to our mental ability to perceive on different levels: one way of seeing more actively is stimulated by descriptive elements (even though these are produced using essential traits) in the foreground, and another, more allusive one, is prompted by the mountains in the background. The function of emptiness is to cancel out, or disturb, our sense of distance so that we are per-suaded to read the foreground more clearly, while the mist, which is not depicted but is perceived, exerts an effect that is not meaningful in terms of perspective. As a result, we may feel that the mountains are much closer than might appear at first sight. This is due to the part played by empty space, which allows observers to assign to the objects portrayed spatial positions of relative importance, based on emotion; this creates a hierarchy of relationships that is different from the one we are used to in the West – that is, a composition based on logical, rational pro-gression. Not so here: this approach is more emotional, in the sense that it plays on feelings and sensations, as can happen when we walk through mist, hearing sounds that are distant but seem very close at hand because they are transmit-ted by particles of water suspended in the air.

In some poems fleeting images are created that are similarly immediate , though more dramatic, as in Ezra Pound's 'In a Station of the Metro':

3 *Daiichiza* (literally, the place next to the temple abbot) is a rank and honorific awarded to Sesshū for his merit as a painter.

4 Marcella Marinotti, *La Rivoluzione del Paesaggio in Sesshū*, unpublished dissertation, Milan, 2001.

The apparition of these faces in the crowd
Petals on a wet, black bough

in which a scene – the faces – that appears from an indistinct reality – the crowd – becomes much closer to the observer-reader than one would think. There is a generic, non-descriptive mass of people that all of a sudden is rent apart by the vision of the faces. The first impression is thus given a new reality. In this case no intermediate elements are interposed between the illuminated scene and the reader, as Sesshū's mist cancels out the relationship between foreground and background.

In *Haboku sansui* the same thing is true of the mountains; exposed to view by a gust of wind that has broken up the mist, they suddenly appear very close, because by cutting out the planes between foreground and background the mist makes it impossible to judge how many such intermediate areas there are (one? two? three?), but instantly brings the two planes together and gives the peaks greater prominence. Emptiness thus acts as an amplifier of the images, and is transmitted through the medium of the clouds or mist, which to us would simply be a pictorial element.

Empty space is not seen, but in formal terms it counts for a great deal. The image in the background (the mountains) becomes predominant because it appears to be suspended, not resting on anything, while the density of descriptive detail increases with the height of the peaks. The mountains are hazy at the bottom but gradually become more distinct as they rise, and this has the effect of bringing them even closer. Ones that are in the far distance come very close, just as a detail belonging to a long-past event is triggered by a thought, an incident, and then becomes highly significant, clear and immediate. The mountains are powerful symbols of a universe, a world that each person may interpret according to his or her own sensibility. This process sparks off the observer's creativity.

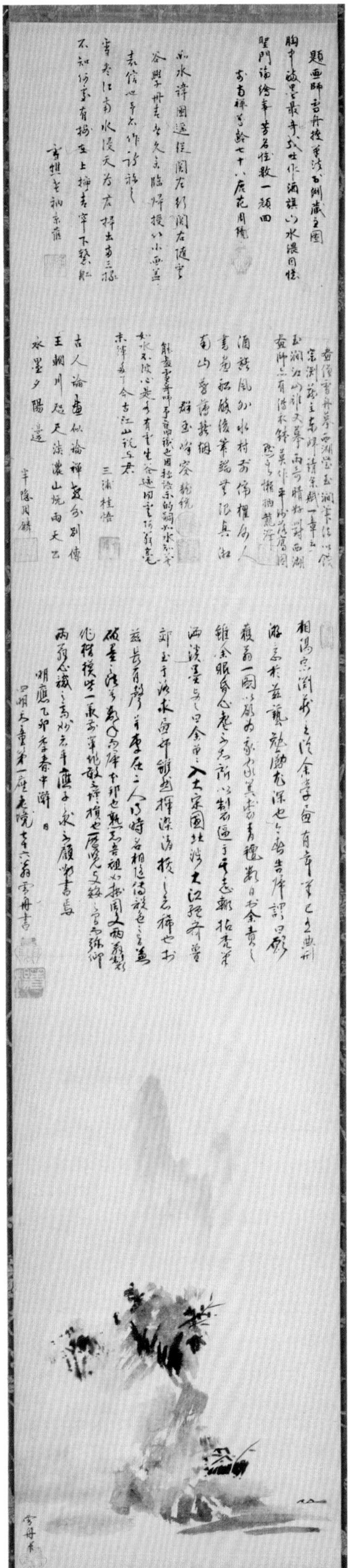

Previous page:
Tōyō Sesshū
Landscape in Broken Ink, ink
on paper, 1495

Zen garden at Ryōsen-an
at Daitoku temple, Kyoto,
Shimoda, 17th century

Spring, Okutama, 1930,
photograph by Fukuhara
Shinzō

Overleaf:
Mori Ransai
'The nine types of leaf and
their placement' from *The
Ransai Picture Album*,
woodblock print, 1782–7

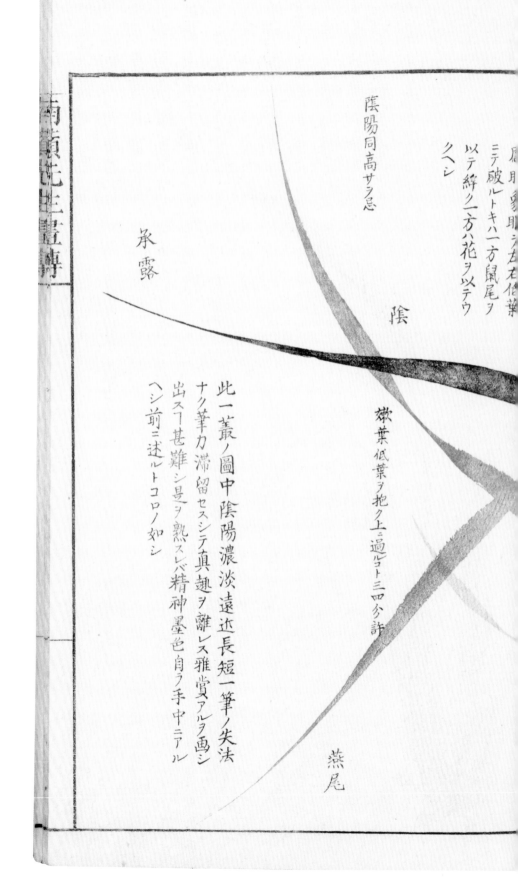

陰陽同高ヲ忌

承露

陰

嫩葉低葉ヲ抱ク上ニ過ルコト三四分許

燕尾

眉月象即ヲ左右ニ佐葉
ニテ破ルトキハ一方鼠尾ヲ
以テ絆ク一方ハ花ヲ以テウ
クヘシ

此一叢ノ圖中陰陽濃淡遠近長短一筆ノ失法
ナク筆力滯留セスシテ眞趣ヲ離レス雅賞アルヲ畫シ
出スコ甚難シ景ヲ熟スレバ精神墨色自ラ手中ニアル
ヘシ前ニ述ルトコロノ如シ

九葉式弁布置法

望雲

陽

鼠尾葉ヲ過ヲ
忌又離ルヲ忌

鳳眼

鼠尾同
高サヲ忌

陽ノ葉同處
ニテ細ク成ヲ忌

嫩葉ノサキ陽ノ葉ニカヽルヲ忌
是ヲ俗ニ離ルノ法ナリ葉サキ
葉ニツクトキハ結ノ病トス

低葉左右同
高サヲ忌

低葉急ニ低ルトキハ嫩
葉是ニソヒテ抱エ葉末
長サ相同キヲ忌

Man and

Left:
Tanaka Ikkō
Man and Writing – Japan 3,
exhibition poster, 1995

Andō Tadao
Forest of Tombs Museum,
Kumamoto, 1992, photograph
by Henry Plummer

Katsushika Hokusai
*Amida Waterfall far in the Distance
on the Kiso Road*, colour woodblock
print, 1834–5

The Seductiveness of Impermanence

Its beak caught firmly
In the clamshell,
The snipe cannot fly away
Of an autumn evening.[1]

Hamaguri ni
hashi o shikka to
hasamarete
shigi tachi-kanuru
aki no yūgure

This humorous poem by Yadoya no Meshimori (1754–1830), with its several double meanings, is written on the fan held by the central figure in one of the most famous woodblock prints of Kitagawa Utamaro (1754–1806). The print, in vivid colours, shows the inside of a house of pleasure. In a room on the upper floor, overlooking a garden of which nothing is seen but the branches of a camellia, a couple embrace, on the point of engaging in intercourse. This is the first and least explicit page (intended for the censors, who were usually not obliged to look any further) of the *Poem of the Pillow* (*Utamakura*), the superb album of twelve erotic scenes published in 1788 by the most highly cultivated publisher of the day, Tsutaya Jūzaburō (?–1797).

No other Japanese artist has succeeded in expressing with comparable intensity – for all that it is barely suggested – the gaze exchanged by the couple depicted in the print. The fine outline of the man's eye, which fits into the curve of the woman's hair, the back of her ear, turned slightly outwards to show the nape of her neck (a part of a woman's body that according to Japanese convention is highly seductive and usually not clearly seen) are details that increase the emotional tension, already heightened by the delicate caress of the young woman's hand against the man's cheek, and of his hand pressing her shoulder. Their limbs, the whiteness of their exposed legs and, in contrast, the exciting red of the garment next to the woman's skin, the sinuous movement of bodies on the verge of intercourse, do not convey so powerful a desire as this gaze that seems to penetrate the flesh. But at the same time, the poem written on the fan the man is still holding in his hand creates an ironic counterpoint that dilutes the intensity of the moment.

Some critics have long claimed to see in the male figure a self-portrait of the artist, on the basis of his transparent outer robe, 'speckled like a fawn', which is also found in another self-portrait authenticated beyond doubt by an inscription. But apart from this hypothesis, which is regarded somewhat sceptically today, the image the general public has of Utamaro, who is universally accepted as the creator of the most evocative portrayals of female beauty in the whole of east

1   Shūgō Asano and Timothy Clark, *The Passionate Art of Kitagawa Utamaro*, 2 vols., British Museum, London, 1995, p. 279.

Asian art, is inseparable from the Bohemian world of 'pleasure districts' such as Yoshiwara in what was then Edo, now Tokyo. They were introduced to Western readers by Edmond de Goncourt in his celebrated *Outamaro: Le peintre des maisons vertes* (Utamaro: the painter of the green houses), published in Paris by Charpentier in 1891. The green houses (*seirō*) are brothels, and Seirō was another name for the pleasure district of Edo, a true city within the city, with its surrounding wall and single entrance designed to prevent the unfortunate women who worked there, whether high or low class, from escaping. In reality, they lived anything but the glamorous lives that writers, figurative artists and dramatists liked to portray.

The Western image of courtesans is derived from a still highly romanticized vision of the 'floating world' – *ukiyo* – the term used, then as now, to refer to the arts and culture of the seventeenth, eighteenth and nineteenth centuries which focused on the ephemeral: the world of popular theatre with its plays, actors and attendant *demi-monde;* the pleasure districts – the 'nightless cities'[2] – and the literature that expressed their new values; the eruption of passions once suppressed by feudal and neo-Confucian tradition. All of this was a world now plunged into crisis by the emergence of new urban classes of artisans and merchants. The writer Jippensha Ikku (1765–1831), in his commentary on the two-volume *Illustrated Annals of the Green Houses* (*Seirō ehon nenjū gyōji*), published in 1804 and illustrated by Utamaro, idealizes the courtesans as genuine 'ladies' living in a cultivated world of fabulous pleasures. This is the image that lies behind the works of Utamaro, one which Edmond de Goncourt popularized in Europe and which still persists, but which modern critics have radically reassessed, revealing the human and social costs that underlay such dazzling splendour.

Utamaro, like Toulouse-Lautrec and Degas after him, also depicted prostitutes of the lowest class. In this he departed from artistic convention (which had in any case been revolutionized in the *ukiyo-e* – pictures of the floating world – and, like his French successors, he discovered in these women a rich vein of humanity to portray. But he still almost always idealizes them, and even in the case of the most wretched prostitutes, the *teppō,* this idealization is achieved by giving them youthful bodies that they would surely not have had at their social level.

A central focus of Western interest in Japan is the multiplicity of artistic and social languages that express the complex, contradictory roles of femininity. It is a femininity that presents itself in a shimmering, multifaceted array of guises. Mythical and historical, heroic and domestic, professional and aristocratic, coquettish and grave, naive and mysterious, all the manifold aspects of the Japanese woman seem to exert the same uniquely powerful allure. It is expressed in

2   See Joseph Ernest de Becker, *The Nightless City; or, the History of Yoshiwara Yūkwaku*, Z. P. Maruya & Co., Yokohama, 1899.

Utamaro's woodcuts, the films of Mizoguchi Kenji (1898–1956) and the descriptions of Kawabata Yasunari (1899–1972), and is present, in reality and myth alike, in the figures of both the geisha and the female pearl fisher. It is a femininity that has always had an indefinable and elusive yet very powerful attraction for the West.

This attraction reached its peak after the Second World War, during the occupation of Japan by the United States, when countless American servicemen were in their turn captivated by the feminine and apparently compliant Cio-Cio Sans in the Land of the Rising Sun. But its roots lie deep in the femininity that had already exerted its fascination in the France of the Impressionists, from where it spread throughout the West. It was an image of woman that drew inspiration above all from the images of the floating world. In medieval times, *ukiyo* referred to the impermanent, melancholy world of daily existence, to which one ought not to 'attach one's own heart' and so chain oneself to it. But from the seventeenth century its meaning, and its pictogram, changed, and the word came to refer to the fleeting pleasures of social gatherings, fashion, the world of theatre and of mercenary and clandestine love, as described for the first time in 1661 by Asai Ryōi (?–1691) in his *Tales of the Floating World* (*Ukiyo monogatari*).

> Living only for the moment, turning our full attention to the pleasures of the moon, the snow, the cherry blossoms and the maple leaves; singing songs, drinking wine, diverting ourselves in just floating, floating; caring not a whit for the pauperism staring us in the face, refusing to be disheartened, like a gourd floating along with the river current: this is what we call the *floating world.*[3]

It was this society that was the context for the new tastes and aspirations that developed in the kabuki theatres and the 'nightless cities', where the great courtesans were creating new mannerisms and forms of etiquette. There was a garish, opulent sense of style based on entertainment, on being fashionable, on attracting and rejecting at the same time. The brothels became true salons, meeting places not only for great merchants but also for actors, men of letters, artists, publishers and even aristocrats in disguise.

The epicentre of the floating world, the nightless city, was also the realm of *iki*. The word denotes more than a concept; it is a mode of behaviour, perhaps even a style, but is made up of allusiveness and levity, based as it is on whatever is its most impermanent aspect. *Iki* refers to the aesthetic quintessence, the sophistication, the grace, the delights of seduction to be found in the refined but cruel world of the pleasure districts. It was there, in the environment of the great

3   Quoted in Richard Lane, *Images from the Floating World*, Oxford University Press, Oxford, 1978, p. 11.

courtesans, the *oiran* (high-class courtesans) of Yoshiwara, Gion and Shimabara, and, even to this day, the geishas of Tokyo and Osaka, the *geiko* and *maiko* of Kyoto, that the etiquette of seduction expressed itself in a set of formal conventions that reached the highest degree of perfection, but at the same time retained great naturalness.

It is impossible to talk about *iki* without referring to a short essay, barely a hundred pages long, by Kuki Shūzō (1888–1941), entitled *The Structure of Iki* (*Iki no kōzō*, 1930), a study in depth of one of the most intriguing concepts in Japanese aesthetics.[4] It was conceived from the start in a cosmopolitan spirit and for a readership with worldwide cultural interests, something that is unusual today, let alone in the Japan of the 1930s, when it was published. The author identifies three basic, inherent characteristics of *iki*, which he defines as 'intensive structure'. Of these three aspects, he seems to privilege the last: renunciation. It is interesting that he believes there is no difference between renunciation caused externally – that is, by the vicissitudes of life – and renunciation as a conscious distancing of the self from attachment. In both cases one may attain *iki*; hence the proverb, 'Under life's knocks, even the boor becomes *iki*.' The author confronts the difficulty of defining *iki* by using an interesting circular approach, consisting of analogy and antithesis, which recalls the philosophy of Nishida Kitarō (1870–1945), under whom Kuki had, in fact, studied.

Kuki does not mention the floating world, and its importance as the principal context in which the various nuances of *iki* manifested themselves seems to have eluded him. He writes that the meaning, the magic, the fascination of Japanese femininity are not static, but are in a state of constant flux. They depend specifically on both separation from the object and the impulse of attraction towards it.

The Japanese woman's ability both to attract and to be remote have been more definitively immortalized in the works of the floating world than in any other pictorial tradition; and intensity of psychological expression reaches new heights in works such the *Series of the Twelve Hours in the Green Houses* (*Seirō jūnitoki tsuzuki*, 1794–5). At the hour of the cockerel, between five and seven in the evening, the moment approaches of encounters in the city that never sleeps, and a maid leans over, preparing a lantern, as she turns towards the *oiran* to ask her something. The *oiran* seems lost in thought, absorbed in a world of her own which no one else is allowed to enter. Her height and the exaggerated slenderness of her body turn her into an other-worldly being. An aspect of her seductiveness is the way she appears to belong to a different sphere from the one inhabited by common mortals, including those who will meet her and possess her, and the background of gold dust[5] emphasizes this, giving the figure a quasi-divine aura.

4 Nara Hiroshi, *The Structure of Detachment: The Aesthetic Vision of Kuki Shūzō with a Translation of Iki no kōzō*, University of Hawaii Press, Honolulu, 2004.

5 A light film of glue on the surface of the print was sprinkled with powdered brass or mica dust and burnished to a high polish to imitate gold dust.

Kitagawa Utamaro
The Hour of the Cock, colour
woodblock print, c. 1794

Boxwood combs (from left to right): a comb for smoothing separations, Shinagawa comb, five-toothed comb, Miyako comb, spatula comb, halberd comb, smaller Shinagawa comb, Genroku comb, rat-tooth comb and clam comb; photograph by Iwamiya Takeji

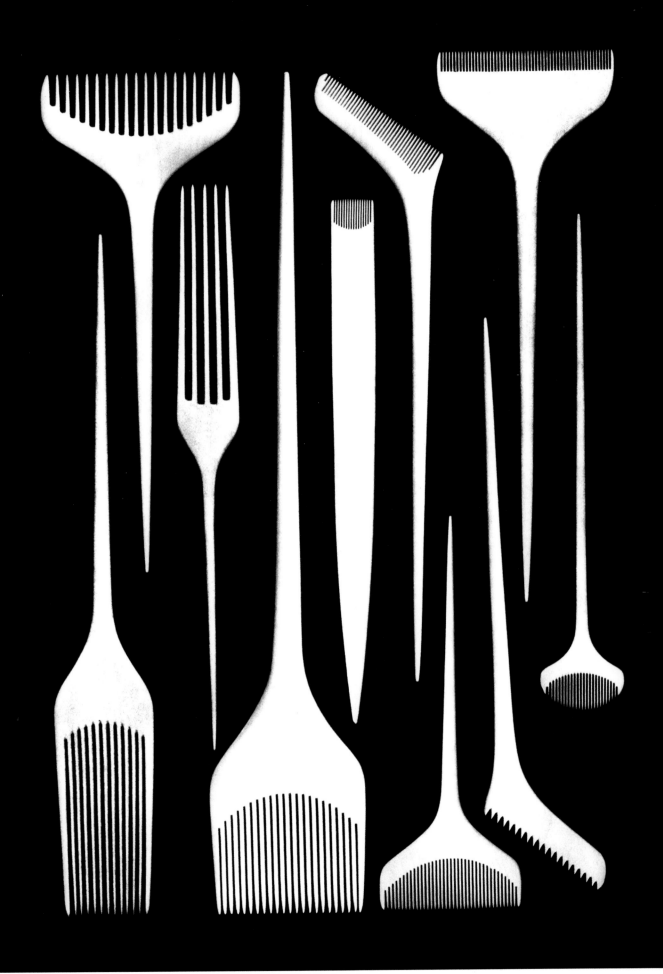

Left:
Geisha hairstyle, c. 1900,
photograph by Tanimoto
Studio

Right:
Kono Takashi
Nippon, poster, 1939

Overleaf:
Yuko sleeping, from
Sentimental Journey, 1971,
photograph by Araki
Nobuyoshi

NIPPON

GOLDEN GATE INTER-
NATIONAL EXHIBITION

GOLDEN GATE
WELT-AUSSTELLUNG

L'EXPOSITION INTERNATIONALE
DE LA PORTE D'OR

17

Yen 1.80

Previous pages:
Kitagawa Utamaro
From *The Poem of the Pillow*, colour
woodblock print, 1788

Geisha playing a *shamisen*, 1890s,
photograph by Michael Maslan

Left:
Sugiura Hisui
Cover, *The Whirlpool*, by Watanabe
Katei, vol. 1, 1913–14

Right:
Kaburagi Kiyokata
Frontispiece, *The Whirlpool*, by
Watanabe Katei, vol. 1, colour
woodblock print, 1913–14

Eccentric? No, Extraordinary

The apogee of elegance is to be found in what is sensed, but does not draw attention to itself, ever. For this reason, it does not follow fashion; it is indifferent to it or, at most, ahead of it. The apogee of culture is what can be recognized in a person, but is not put on display, ever. It is thus far removed from the world of the academy, which, in order to exist, has to demonstrate knowledge. The apogee of religious feeling lies in man's inner dialogue with God, and it cannot be seen, ever; at the very most its presence can be detected in those who practise it. It is thus far removed from ritualism, liturgy and formal practices. The apogee of writing is what happens when, however profound its contents, the text flows along without visible effort, as if the brush (or the pen) were not being held back and slowed down by the effort of thought and the muscular tension demanded by writing.

Thoughts like these (set out here in a somewhat compressed form) come to my mind whenever I consider the significance for Far Eastern culture of the art of the unimportant. In all truth such an art, as I understand it at least, probably does not even exist, and in any case it is an idea that is perhaps too reductive. But it seems to me to be a concept that may well be capable of expressing a certain attentiveness, a care, a way of being, in the person whose temperamental inclinations lie in the directions just indicated. And it is this which may, perhaps, be able to awaken the interest of a society like ours, in which, by contrast, a sense of an individual's own importance is the prevailing attitude and, unfortunately, the one that provides our models of behaviour.

East Asia and Japan have produced wonderfully effective antidotes to excess of this kind. Every social category, but especially the fields of literature and the arts, contains individuals who are thought to stand outside it, who locate themselves in the area of the unpredictable and unprogrammable. Strange, you may say, that categories of the unclassifiable can exist, but so it is. They are clearly deemed to be so important that it is impossible to leave them in the zone of undefinability they have chosen for themselves. A number of Chinese theorists of art managed to draw up criteria by which to rank painters and their styles, only to declare that, above them all, there were unclassifiable ones who therefore belonged to no academy or school; spirits liberated from the conventions of daily life just as they were from those of the world of art and culture. Often dubbed eccentrics, they were and are feared and admired at the same time. Zhuangzi (369–286 BC), one of the founding fathers of Taoism, describes these individuals who, for the first time, in the sixth chapter of his *Zhuangzi*, he calls *jiren* (in

Japanese, *kijin*): extraordinary men. He maintains that they are exempt from the obligation to adhere to conventional norms of behaviour because they are *jiren,* and belong to a transcendent world: 'The extraordinary man is so in comparison with other men, but he is normal in comparison with Heaven. Hence the saying, "a man who is insignificant to Heaven is a great man in the eyes of men; a great man in the eyes of men is a man insignificant to Heaven."'[1]

In Japan, with its passion for the encyclopaedic, there are compendiums that list these men, study them and analyse them: precisely the opposite of the principle they themselves embody. The first, and most famous, is the *Biographies of extraordinary persons of recent times* (*Kinsei kijin den*), written in 1790 by Ban Kōkei (1733–1806), a former merchant turned man of letters. It contains the biographies of about two hundred figures from the seventeenth and eighteenth centuries, who could therefore not easily meet the very demanding criteria set out by Zhuangzi in the fourth century BC; in fact, Kōkei's *kijin* are a mixture of everything: writers, painters, samurai, priests. In short, they belong to almost all social categories and occupations.

In this context, it might also be proposed that the literary style known as *zuihitsu* – the brush that moves over the page of its own accord, leaving behind in elegant, flowing script scattered thoughts that seem to have arrived of themselves, with no apparent effort to think, frame or express them – is to literature what the *jiren* are to the ordinary run of men. In Japan, *zuihitsu* goes back to Sei Shōnagon (965–c. 1017), author of the famous *Pillow Book* (*Makura no sōshi*), who lived at the height of the classical epoch and was a contemporary of Lady Murasaki. This book, which has become one of the monuments of Japanese culture, is mainly a miscellany of prose writings, but also contains poems. The elegance and wit with which the pieces, some only a few lines long, others covering at most several pages, are composed was the crucial influence in creating the *zuihitsu* style, that of the pen entirely free of the shackles of convention.

In writing the *Pillow Book,* Shōnagon filled it liberally with her impressions of Heian court life, describing the events and people of her time, but in such a way as to give her comments, which are often ironic if not caustic, a quality that is not restricted to her circumstances and environment. She has created archetypes, as if the events had taken place and the people had had lives independently of their contingent circumstances. Among her 'Embarrassing Things' there is the timeless description of 'an ignoramus who in the presence of some learned person puts on a knowing air and converses of men of old',[2] while among the 'Hateful Things' there is the man 'one has been foolish enough to invite…

1   *Zhuangzi jishi*, ed. Guo Qingfan, Zhonghua Shuju, Beijing, 1978, vol. I, p. 273.

2   *The Pillow Book of Sei Shōnagon*, ed. I. Morris, Oxford University Press, London, 1967, p. 103.

to spend the night in an unsuitable place – and then he starts snoring', or who while 'one is in the middle of a story...butts in and tries to show he is the only clever person in the room. Such a person is hateful, and so, indeed, is anyone, child or adult, who tries to push himself forward.'[3]

Shōnagon was a haughty, brusque woman, whose sharp tongue earned her many enemies and probably a lonely, miserable old age. But the freedom and limpidity of her thought are faultless, as is her self-awareness, as revealed in the last section of her book, chapter 326:

> I wrote these notes at home, when I had a good deal of time to myself and thought no one would notice what I was doing. Everything that I have seen and felt is included. Since much of it might appear malicious and even harmful to other people, I was careful to keep my book hidden. But now it has become public, which is the last thing I expected.
>
> One day Lord Korechika, the Minister of the Centre, brought the Empress a bundle of notebooks [...] I now had a vast quantity of paper at my disposal, and I set about filling the notebooks with odd facts, stories from the past, and all sorts of other things, often including the most trivial material. On the whole I concentrated on things and people that I found charming and splendid; my notes are also full of poems and observations on trees and plants, birds and insects. I was sure that when people saw my book they would say, 'It's even worse than I expected. Now one can really tell what she is like.' After all, it is written entirely for my own amusement and I put things down exactly as they came to me. How could my casual jottings possibly bear comparison with the many impressive books that exist in our time? Readers have declared, however, that I can be proud of my work. This has surprised me greatly; yet I suppose it is not so strange that people should like it, for, as will be gathered from these notes of mine, I am the sort of person who approves of that others abhor and detests the things they like.[4]

This final sentence should be read not as a quip designed to win regard, but rather as the mark of the true *kijin*, conscious that her work cannot fail to be appreciated and profoundly understood by those who, like her, have an extraordinary mind.

Some scholars are inclined to restrict the definition of *zuihitsu*, properly speaking, to a handful of works in all of Japanese literature, others to no more than three. I am essentially in agreement with these very narrow definitions;

3   Ibid., pp. 26–7.

4   Ibid., p. 267.

the extraordinary is no longer such if there is a superabundance of it. Nevertheless, the masterpiece in this style, after the *Pillow Book,* is *Essays in Idleness* (*Tsurezuregusa*), by Kenkō (c. 1283–c. 1352).

It may seem unlikely that people today would find themselves drawn to the writings of a fourteenth-century Japanese monk, other than out of general cultural curiosity or, worse, in search of the exotic in its aesthetic guise. However, a number of factors make Urabe Kaneyoshi, called Kenkō in his artistic and religious life, the greatest writer of his day, fascinating to present-day readers. Crises of central power, intrusion by the spiritual realm into affairs of state, covert struggles between elements which only a short time before had been held together by shared ideals of social welfare that appeared to be mutual and real, and lack of interest on the part of peripheral administrative bodies in problems and needs, with the subsequent disastrous growth of a competitive form of regionalism: all this had the effect of plunging Japan into an endless series of fratricidal conflicts. Against the background of these turbulent events, and in the midst of the greatest imaginable political turmoil, which seemed at any moment likely to sweep away for ever the fragile society of early fourteenth-century Japan, the subtly ironic figure of Kenkō – isolated, but not for that reason any the less aware of, and sensitive to, what was happening around him – comes to symbolize a moral response that is valid not only for his remote times and on his distant continent but also for the West in the twenty-first century.

The precise dates of Kenkō are not known, but he seems to have lived sometime between 1290 and 1360. Although he was universally counted among the greatest poets of his day, the literary fortunes of this aristocrat, born into a venerable family, who became a monk in order to find the tranquillity in which to read, study and write, are linked above all with the collection of brief thoughts that became one of the key works of Japanese literature. The dispassionate tone of this *hōshi,* or master of Buddhist law, in his observations on things past and present, the doings of the powerful and of ordinary people, shot through with an even, subtle vein of gentle but sometimes penetrating irony, is timeless. Kenkō's delicate, concise observations were written, as tradition would have it, on the spur of the moment. The product of these notes, collected and developed later, is a series of rapid impressions of daily life which, even when they deal with persons of high rank, have a quality of immediacy because of their deliberately informal tone. In their analysis of men and events, they reveal a search for life's deepest meanings behind the masks and facades that hide them. Longings, grand and petty ambitions, passions – but also beauty and knowledge – are stripped of the veil of outward power, pomp, magnificence and prestige behind which human beings tend to conceal the true nature of things, in order to measure them against the undisputed scale of actual human values.

This type of writing in the Zen manner is only superficially the result of 'allowing the brush to run freely'. Kenkō enhanced the *zuihitsu* literary style by drawing creatively on the rich resources of the religious philosophy of Zen, a branch of Buddhism that certainly influenced him though he did not belong to it as a religious order. The apparent spontaneity of the sentences, and the ideas and feelings behind this, is the fruit of patient work, polishing and finishing at one and the same time the medium of expression and the writer's own personality. It appears to be the outcome of a particular attitude to life, rather than of the process of refining a stylistic technique. There is an apparent detachment from events which, while it may lead the writer to declare, 'The pleasantest of all diversions is to sit alone under the lamp, a book spread out before you, and to make friends with people of a distant past you have never met,'[5] in reality leads to a view of the contingent that is penetrating and objective.

Such an approach to life, which is involved and detached at the same time, was first achieved in the relationship with the self, and thus has the power to contemplate even the mystery of death without extremes of emotion, but with a feeling of freshness and wonder. Reflecting on the case of a peasant who, having agreed to sell an ox that dies the night before he is due to hand it over, loses a great deal of money, Kenkō makes an imagined narrator say:

> 'The owner of the ox certainly suffered a loss, but at the same time he secured a great profit, too. [...] Unpredictably the ox died; unpredictably too the owner survived. [...] People fail to enjoy life because they do not fear death. No, it is not that they have no fear of death, rather, they forget how close it is. But if a man said he was indifferent to such external distinctions as life and death, he could certainly be said to have grasped the true principles.'[6]

This passage is like a distillation of human wisdom, all the more perfect because it is offered casually, as if what is being discussed is the most obvious and natural thing in the world, and frequently uses a fact that in itself is insignificant. But this ordinariness is transformed into a valuable tool that shows us the road to achieving mastery over our condition as human beings; it thus acquires exemplary value and raises life's everyday aspects to the level of archetypes.

It used to be said that this subtle irony sounded familiar to Euro-

5 Kenkō, *Essays in Idleness*, trans. D. Keene, Columbia University Press, New York, 1967, p. 12.

6 Ibid, pp. 78–9.

peans in the mid-twentieth century, and of the many possible parallels the most meaningful is precisely that of the attitude towards death. An example of this can be seen in the speech made by the Italian poet Eugenio Montale when he was awarded the Nobel Prize for Literature in 1975, and made a reference to his own prewritten obituary. Or, even more aptly, in what he said to a journalist: 'You must believe me, my dear, I never enjoyed myself as much as in that week following the award of the prize. The flowers, the telegrams, I felt I was taking part, while still alive, in my own funeral. What a pity I'm not really dead; can you picture the delicious headline, "Poet dies on the day he receives the Nobel prize"?'[7]

7   *L'espresso*, 2 Nov. 1975.

Left:
Yanagi Sōri
Butterfly Stool, moulded
rosewood and metal, 1956

Right:
Isamu Noguchi
Akari light sculptures,
mulberry paper, bamboo and
wire, 1950s

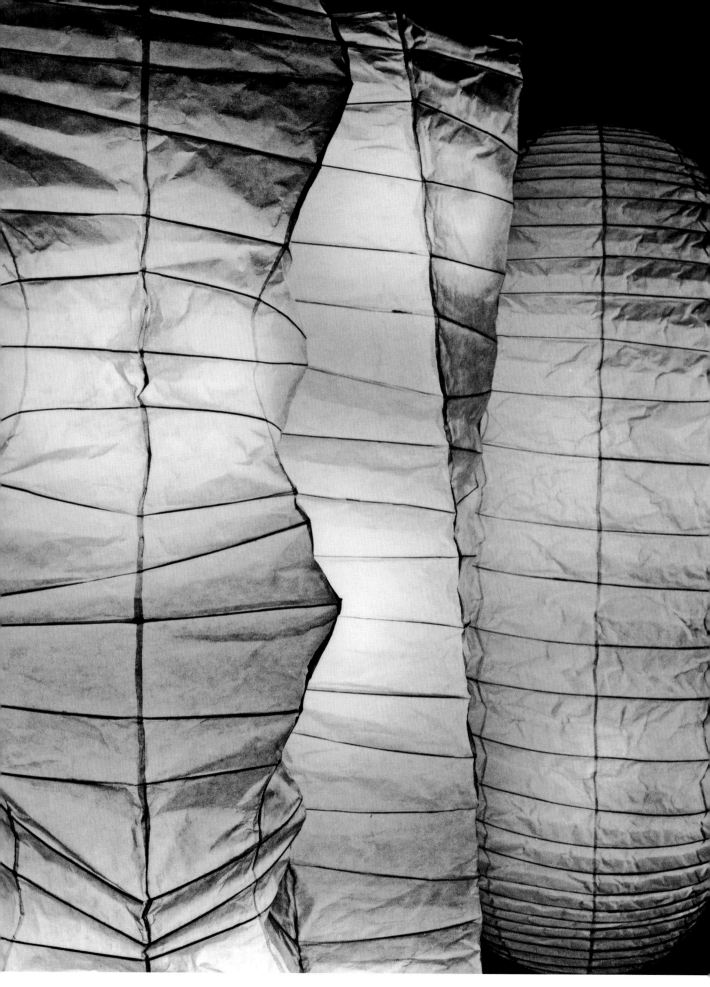

Left:
Suzu stoneware storage jar, early
14th century

Right:
Yanagi Sōri
Teapot, porcelain and bamboo, 1956

Left:
Fisherman's coat (*donza*), hand-woven cotton, late 19th century

Right:
Farmer's coat (*noragi*), hand-woven cotton, late 19th century

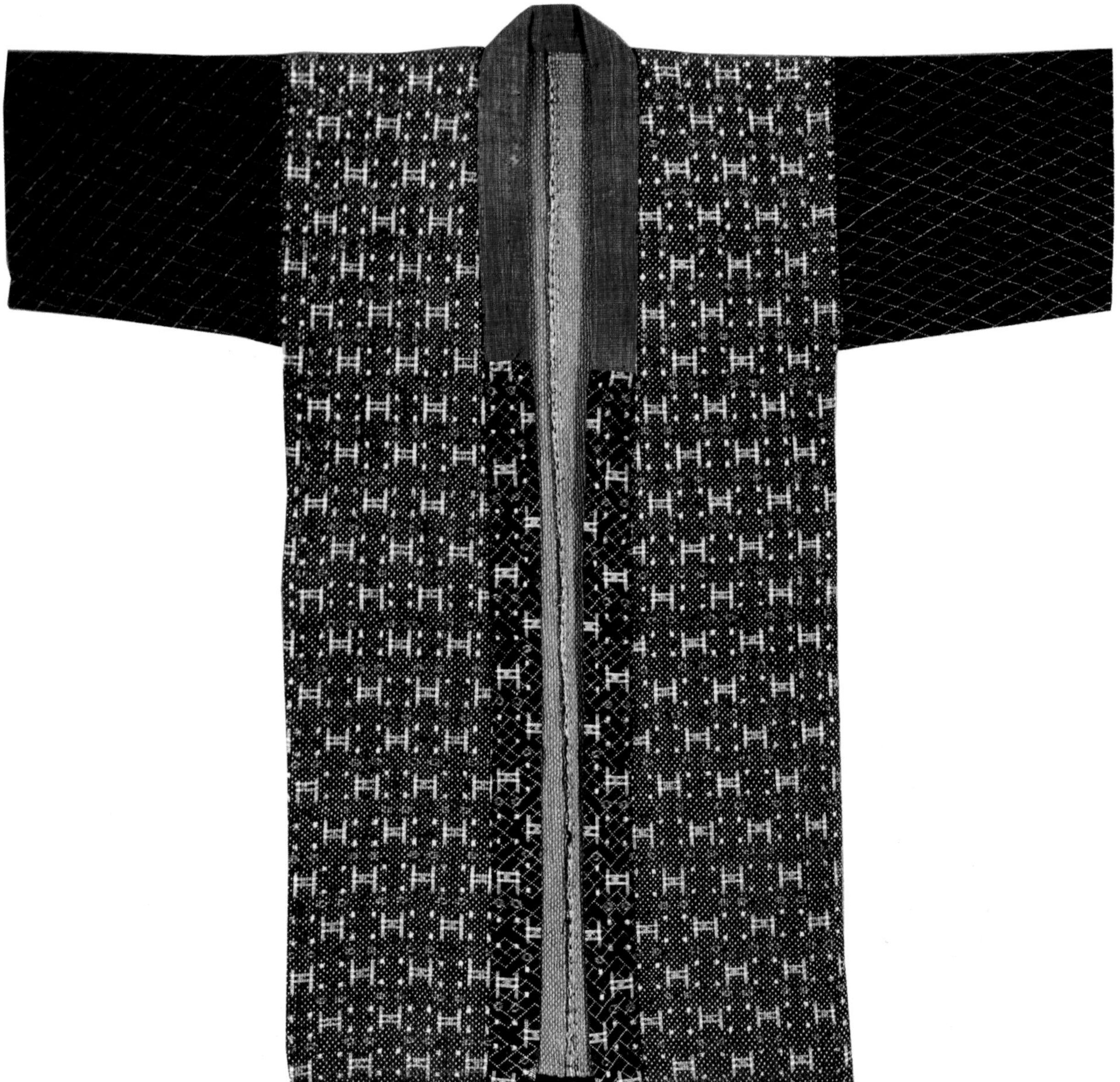

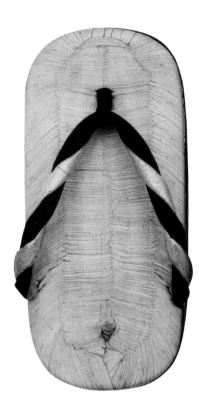
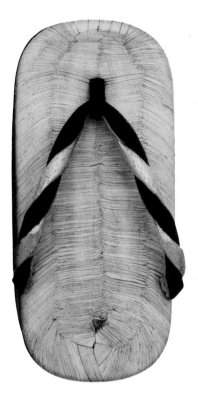

Left:
Stepping-stones in front of the
Kōgetsu-tei teahouse at the
Arisawa Villa, Matsue, photograph
by Iwamiya Takeji

Right:
Sandals (*zōri*), covered with woven
rush, photograph by Iwamiya Takeji

Kono Takashi
Japan, poster, 1955

JAPAN

TAKASHI KONO

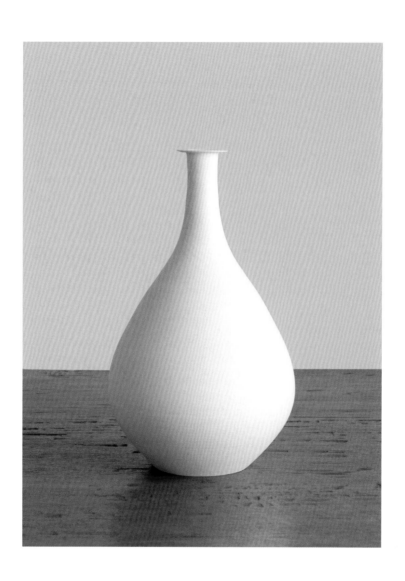

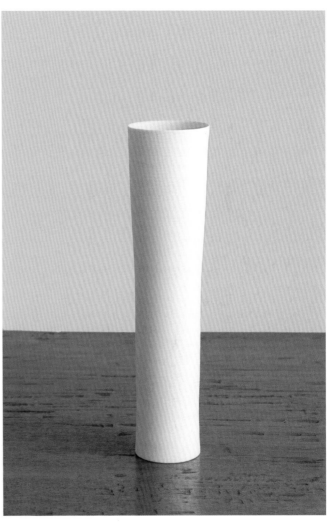

Previous pages:
Kuroda Taizō
White porcelain vessels

Isamu Noguchi
Coffee table, black ash and
glass, 1944

The Secret Message of Nō

A late summer evening in Tokyo, and I am the guest of Umewaka Rokurō, a 'living national treasure', following his performance in *Aoi no ue* (*Lady Aoi*). And – a piece of wonderful good fortune – I have seen one of my favourite works interpreted by a great artist, and have been granted the privilege of photographing the production to remind me of it when I am far from Japan. I was in the presence of an actor still affected by the 'bewitchment' that the ritual element of his performance, which he had entered into with priestly intensity, had induced in him. So it was a set of apparent coincidences that enabled me to overcome conceptual and symbolic barriers, and allowed me to penetrate deeply into that great art, and the wealth of human understanding it contains. Nō is first and foremost a discipline to which the actors subject themselves from a very tender age, and from which even the audience is barely able to escape, inexorably drawn in by the metaphorical power emanating from the action of the drama, which unleashes on the stage the most terrible beasts and the most seductive charms of the unconscious. The ritual gestures, the pared-down quality of the dramaturgy, the rich costumes, the evocative power of the music and the delivery of the words, all endow nō with great symbolic value. It is not an entertainment, then, but a road leading to a deeper understanding of human capacities and possibilities. So it is, says the philosopher John Dewey, with the artist, whose maturity increases with the 'resistances' encountered in bringing into being the expressive act.[1] But nō is an art form which, in order to express its hidden message, demands a high degree of engagement from both parties: actors and audience.

Understanding and appreciation of nō cannot be separated from constantly monitoring one's own part in it. It is not enough to know the complex symbolism of its gestures or the different colours of the costumes; these are only preliminary tools. Spectators must be aware that they are watching a story that may be applicable to themselves. They must be willing to surrender to it completely, to allow the emotions to enter their very souls and awaken there feelings that have been dormant. The human values of nō cannot, therefore, be appreciated if one is not prepared to relinquish one's convictions and open oneself up to a different conception of reality. In a space that is archetypal in its architecture and décor, and thus able to engender an intense response and total participation, events that involve human beings in their purest essence are portrayed. It is only because of a law governing casting that some, the actors, find themselves officiators, while others, the audience, play the part of witnesses. The actor must not simply be an expert, able to take on the greatest possible number of roles; he must, above all,

1   From which my book, *L'incanto sottile del dramma nō. La principessa Aoi* (Scheiwiller, Milano, 1975) originated.

be a man totally absorbed in his 'craft', conscious of the educational function of his art and committed to involving people in it. Unlike his colleagues in the kabuki theatre, he cannot expect wide popular success – the audience for nō is very limited – but may hope to establish an intimate relationship with his public.

The number of people in Japan who took lessons in recitation, singing and dance from famous actors of the classical schools was quite high, even before the old traditional arts became 'fashionable', as they are today. Such lessons are costly, and have no practical purpose in that those who take them will never appear on the stage, but certainly help to develop a public that is informed, and therefore very demanding. It cannot be denied that they bring with them dangers of excessive specialization, one of the most serious being the risk of losing aesthetic pleasure. It is not unusual to see members of the audience sitting through an entire performance with their noses buried in the text, checking the actors' intonations, and thus seeing nothing of what is happening on the stage. But it is a fact that these courses of study, these lessons, even if they are often pursued mechanically for the sake of social prestige, nevertheless instil traditional cultural values and encourage the understanding of a sophisticated and highly communicative art. Nō is a theatrical genre that goes beyond Western traditional forms, though in terms of the educational power it exerts it could be compared with Greek tragedy. It is a form of theatre that involves, and even makes demands on, the audience and can therefore fulfil, and to a certain extent has already fulfilled, a very important function in the West.

The sequence of highly symbolic images in this form of theatre requires that the audience be familiar with the plot, otherwise the action would be utterly incomprehensible, given the difficulty of the text and the way it is spoken. The sound of the voice heightens the impressions and emotions evoked by the musical accompaniment and the visual images. What is fundamental, however, is their role as genuine visions, non-real, but pure forms of truth that reach deep into one's consciousness. Their sequence is enriched by the philosophic and religious content of the text, and they take on a power that provokes emulation. Through the skilful use of architectural space, costumes, masks and, above all, gesture, the action seems to expand and to acquire a dimension that exceeds the normal boundaries of space and time. The performance takes on a sacral tone, and, in order to penetrate its meaning, Western spectators have to divest themselves of a series of preconceptions derived from their own theatrical tradition.

In the West, text is the fixed point, the pivot of every production, around which all other theatrical elements revolve and act as variants. No such separation exists in nō. The plot must be familiar, as with religious rites or Greek tragedy, and the delivery of the lines becomes a musical accompaniment that produces an emotional effect very similar to that of the sung parts of the Mass. The voice, amplified by the mask, helps to magnify the character, and to make still more other-worldly a figure already imbued with mystery by an elaborate, symbolic hairstyle and costume. As with every rigidly ritualistic form, including nō, décor, direction and choreography do not change within a single work. Costumes, masks and movements have been codified for centuries by the five schools that produce this form of theatre. To alter them would provoke the negative feelings that devout Catholics would experience if they saw solemn Masses celebrated by priests in everyday clothes. It would mean that the emotions evoked by the concepts of *mysterium* (mystery), *maiestas* (majesty) and *tremendum* (divine dread), defined by Rudolf Otto as attributes of the sacred,[2] were sacrificed in the name of greater (and more sterile) rational understanding.

Nō would lose much of its value if it came to lack the profound allusions (which only appear to be complex and incomprehensible) that are a feature of the action as it takes place on the stage. The actor recites lines written in a centuries-old language, delivering the words in a manner that is so stylized and uninflected that it is utterly incomprehensible, even to an educated Japanese person; familiarity with the text thus becomes an indispensable tool for understanding the performance. Unless it has been closely studied beforehand, the text per se is less important than the image in allowing the spectator to be drawn into the drama, experiencing every incident as a mythical exemplification of reality, transcending the limits of the phenomenal world, and eliminating the unconscious fluctuation of conditioned thoughts that make everyday life mechanical and alienating.

Such images, which can be interpreted metaphorically, do not provide definitive solutions to human dilemmas, but stimulate individual creativity. This is the direction taken by some of the most interesting movements in current theatre research, dedicated to re-establishing the role of drama in contemporary life by using new forms of expression. For example, Jerzy Grotowski's theatre workshop rediscovered that the most basic symbols and the 'poorest' resources – those devoid of incidental visual or decorative associations – were the most suitable for evoking the realm of deep emotion. They create a 'poverty' that is full of suggestion; objects take on magical power, a kind of mana, such as is present in the ritual objects of indigenous peoples. In nō, 'poverty' goes alongside the essential quality of the gestures, the costumes and the set. Nothing is merely decorative. The wonderful clothes and the sophistication of the masks and stage properties all

2 Rudolf Otto, *The Idea of the Holy*, Oxford University Press, New York, 1958.

have a precise meaning, and the mysterious force that emanates from them arises both from a love of objects passed down through generations and from the unchanging colours, materials and forms that belong to each role. Spectacular effects, in which kabuki, for example, abounds, would be liable to distract spectators from the effort of applying to themselves whatever is evoked by the dramatic action.

Grotowski argues that what we have to look for in nō, and in theatre in general, is a way of helping us 'cross our frontiers, exceed our limitations, fill our emptiness – fulfil ourselves. This is not a condition but a process in which what is dark in us slowly becomes transparent.'[3] Myth plays a fundamental part in this search because, as demonstrated by medieval (and many Oriental) religious performances, it aroused in the spectator's mind '… a renewed awareness of his personal truth in the truth of the myth, and through fright and a sense of the sacred he came to catharsis'.[4] It is a process that is hard to replicate today, because in the modern world people tend to satisfy their need for a relationship with the mythical dimension by affiliating to a collective truth, or a mass model of it. It is a need justified by intellectual or practical necessity, but difficult to sustain through genuine inner involvement. Life thus becomes ever more mechanical and alienating. Individuals are forced to create for themselves masks behind which to conceal their inability to give meaning to their actions. And it becomes ever more difficult to find in art the stimuli needed in order to penetrate the masks they put on every day, according to circumstances. And yet, even today, we can reveal a person's true face if we apply ourselves to the task, one in which the theatre of the East, and nō in particular, can play a vital role.

Psychoanalysis itself and the lines of thought to which it gives rise – surely a distinctly Western development – are only a beginner's attempt compared to what is an immemorial art in the East.[5]

This assertion might seem provocative, the latest in a series of declarations of the 'spiritual supremacy' of the East. But the thought was expressed by Carl Jung in an essay written in 1928. Perhaps its apparently radical and controversial meaning has to be looked for outside the words themselves. Jung certainly had no intention of condemning the Western psychoanalytical method as ineffective in comparison with the improvements on it achieved by Oriental societies. The feeling is that he was trying to suggest to his readers the need for greater efforts in this direction, albeit with special caveats. As an attentive scholar of Eastern philosophies and religions, he could not avoid the fact that the psychoanalytic method, strictly speaking,

3   Jerzy Grotowski, *Towards a Poor Theatre*, Odin Teatrets Forlag, Denmark, 1968, p. 21.

4   Ibid., pp. 22–3.

5   Carl Gustav Jung, 'The Spiritual Problem of Modern Man', in *Modern Man in Search of a Soul*, Routledge, London, 1985, pp. 249–50.

has never existed in societies in the East; given their cultural presuppositions, there has never been a need for it. This would lead to the conclusion that, in using these words, Jung was referring to a number of Eastern ways of life and cultural codes that could in themselves be considered substitutes for psychoanalysis.

For Jung, the psychoanalytic method is the 'specific discovery of the West': our society's most effective tool in helping humanity confront psychic disassociation, the most corrosive ill of the modern age. Both the sickness and the remedy are fruits of Western civilization, and their roots lie deep in the Greek and Judaeo-Christian world views. Analytic therapy is directed towards rebuilding a cohesive strength capable of maintaining the integrity of the person in his or her infinite component parts. Our cultural tradition, with its myths of the supremacy of the individual, the primacy of the Logos, of the single being over his environment, and of reason over feeling and emotion, tends to create separations within an essentially unitary phenomenon. In the struggle to achieve individuation, human beings constantly run the risk of dividing their souls from their bodies; like the material world in general, the body is given subordinate value and in most cases is ultimately seen as an obstacle, an unavoidable encumbrance. It is probably here that Jung sees the essential difference between East and West: in Asia, where the problem of the split between body and soul has never been posed as starkly as it has in the West, it is the culture itself, with all its codes, that serves constantly to bring human beings back to a state of wholeness. Westerners have had to turn to psychoanalysis in an attempt to do the same. Jung himself provides the key to clarifying, from this perspective, the meaning of the thought explored here:

> The body lays claim to equal recognition; like the psyche, it also exerts a fascination. If we are still caught by the old idea of an antithesis between mind and matter, the present state of affairs means an unbearable contradiction; it may even divide us against ourselves. But if we can reconcile ourselves with the mysterious truth that the spirit is the living body seen from within, and the body the outer manifestation of the living spirit – the two being really one – then we can understand why it is that the attempt to transcend the present level of consciousness must give its due to the body. We shall also see that belief in the body cannot tolerate an outlook that denies the body in the name of the spirit.[6]

In contrast, the Asiatic way of thought presupposes the principle of the inescapable unity of the human being, and this is the organic basis of the nō

6   Ibid., pp. 253–4.

drama. It can be argued that of all Japanese forms of aesthetic expression it is this theatrical genre that most fully embodies that unity. Jung's thoughts on the need to reintegrate body and soul are fundamental to an understanding of nō. In trying to reach such an understanding it is necessary to go back to the origins of the human drama: the place where every civilization has located its archetypal, mythic images from which, through the centuries, succeeding generations have drawn the stimulus for their social and cultural development. The very structure of their myths of origin reveals the profound gulf between the Japanese world of archetypes and that of the West. The split between the spiritual and the material, attacked by Jung as the principal factor in the crisis of values besetting the modern world, cannot be attributed solely to the Christian view of life; elements of this split can be traced back to the ancient Greek and Jewish cultures that converged to create European civilization. The difference between the Japanese and Western cultural traditions lies essentially in the relationship between human beings and the universe.

The destiny of Western man, the purpose of his earthly existence, is to struggle with nature and to shape it to his ends; to try to bring it ever closer (without ever entirely succeeding) to the world of ideas that from Plato onwards has been the basis of Greek spirituality. In her *Intimations of Christianity among the Ancient Greeks*, Simone Weil has noted in this clash between an ideal world and contingent reality several points of contact with Christian tradition. It is also a conflict that helped to lead us towards the split between spirit and matter that was the motive force of medieval civilization but which today has degenerated into a fevered and unsustainable, dichotomous conception of reality. And it is this state of primary separation, present in Western civilization's mythic space, that on the one hand makes civilization more fully articulated and more complex, but on the other makes reintegration of the separated parts very difficult. Man's debut in life's drama is marked by his clear separation from the world of the indistinct, the uncreated, and by his entry into that of the objective. Such a beginning projects him on to a stage where he will perform (or submit to) the series of events that make up his struggle for self-realization within the space of time allotted to him. This time is clearly demarcated, between the tolling of the two bells of birth and of death; when it is up, everything must have been completed. The structure of the stage in Western theatre clearly reflects this idea. There is an unbridgeable gap between what is manifest and what is not, between what is on stage and what is behind the scenes.

In Oriental theatre with its metaphysical tendencies, as compared with Western theatre with its psychological tendencies, forms assume their meaning and significance on all possible levels. Or if you like, their pulsating results are not inferred merely on one level but on all mental levels at once.[7]

In fact, as Artaud very acutely observes, this can happen because Oriental theatre, and nō in particular, does not enlarge man's metaphysical dimension. If this were so, there would once again be a division between the worlds of what is manifest and what is not, with the consequent separation between word, Logos (text), and emotion expressed aesthetically through the body (gesture), which Artaud himself so strongly disapproves of in Western theatre. This phenomenon never occurs in nō, and yet it remains true that nō creates resonances on every level of the mind. But, I should like to add, not only of the mind. The body, too, seen as an entity with all its physical and emotional potentialities, is transformed in various ways. In fact, the action of the drama, which is designed to free the individual from his or her state of impasse, seeks to operate on all levels, not just of the mind but of the whole person.

A tree, a rock, a waterfall become charged with meanings, in the sense that there may be perceived in them the divine nature of which man himself is made, not only in his mind but also in his body. Nō theatre makes great use of them as catalysts for forces that are not manifested, but which materialize on the stage through the magical, evocative power that they exert in the world of the non-manifest. A sense of the numinous, an essential vehicle for such relationships, thus pervades every part of the land of Japan, which thereby becomes sacred and the setting for a dialogue with the divine. Life is then lived as a sacred enactment, of which nō is the art form par excellence. In this way are created the archetypal images which, more than any other aesthetic language, play on the soul's emotional resonances and raise the everyday moment to the threshold of the sublime.

Nō drama is pervaded by this sense of the co-involvement of the material and the cosmic, derived from Shintō, which goes far beyond mere pantheism and represents the culmination of a long process of social and aesthetic development, an achievement that along the way has been enriched by contributions from many traditions: influences from India, Tibet, China and the world of the steppes can be traced in its various aspects.

7   Antonin Artaud, *The Theatre and Its Double*, Grove Press, London, 1994, p. 54.

Tears of the Mask

There are fundamental differences between the masks audiences are accustomed to in Western theatre and those used in nō drama. In the West their purpose is to conceal, to hide behind another element (the mask itself) something that is not meant to be seen. They serve to present characteristics, qualities and values that 'fix' a particular state and make it objective and lasting. In both cases, however, the mask is a 'fixed' one; that is, it is designed to assume a given expression and to retain it. The idea that it is an 'identity to be put on' is shared by indigenous peoples, for whom the mask has great religious significance. Its role is to bring human beings into contact with divine essences, which come and move among them through the medium of the mask itself.

The first concept, that of the mask that 'masks' something which is not meant to be seen, would certainly appear to be ruled out in the case of the nō masks (*nōmen*). Their function is, if anything, to evoke, to suggest, even to the point of violently expressing (in the case, for example, of the *hannya*, the *ja*, the *kanawa* or the *shinja*) specific conditions, both human and divine. And it would seem that, despite appearances, the theory of the mask as an identity other than that of the person who wears it, and of which he partakes through the act of putting it on, is also to be rejected, even though it is more attractive than the idea that it is something that conceals. In both cases the masks are necessarily 'fixed', as are those of indigenous peoples. They are genuine receptacles for clearly defined qualities and have value, as such and in so far as they have the ability to embody visually the mana that has been attributed to them. They would thus lose all their meaning if even the smallest degree of expressive movement were to allow the same mask to display a variety of nuances and expressions.

The nō mask, which originally had magical and religious characteristics, has been developed and refined until it has attained great power and expressiveness precisely because it embodies an ancient tradition. The mask 'fixes' in its own features a very specific psychological identity. It leaves no room for ambiguity; it expresses a specific emotion, and no other. 'The mask's action is oriented principally towards the outside,' notes Elias Canetti; the mask creates a character, it is intangible, it creates a distance between itself and the observer, and represents the limits within which human beings can establish a relationship with reality. Its formal rigidity becomes distance; the fact that the mask does not change is precisely what creates distance, as Canetti suggests again:

Everything behind the mask is mysterious. When the mask is taken seriously, as in the cases we are discussing here, no one must know what lies behind it. A mask expresses much, but hides even more. Above all it *separates*. Charged with a menace which must not be precisely known – one element of which, indeed, is the fact that it *cannot* be known – it comes close to the spectator, but, in spite of this proximity, remains clearly separated from him. It threatens him with the secret dammed up behind it.[1]

The mask, with the secret it carries within itself, is threatening but at the same time alluring. According to Canetti, it operates as a barrier that divides, but also as a symbol, a trace, a specific sign. Its pronounced typological characteristics make it stand out from the figures of the indistinct world of the everyday, raising it to the level of the archetype of a clearly defined psychological state. The fixity underlined by Canetti is corroborated in the features of the *hannya*, who displays both a longing to possess the object of her own unbridled passion (a possession whose ends are destructive), and horror at the inhumanity into which she has cast herself, the feeling of anguish and emptiness that seizes her like a kind of vertigo. She is the embodiment of the monster dormant in every human being: the insatiable longing for possession that is never satisfied. The person who allows himself or herself to be ruled by it will never find rest or refuge in feelings of love. The inability to love is precisely what prevents them escaping from their own subjective limits and, imprisoned within themselves, they are identified with the mask. But if they distance themselves too far from the world and its sorrows they ultimately also separate themselves from its joys, and remain as if literally 'petrified' in an inhuman state. Rudolf Kassner has created a powerful image through which to represent the terrible condition of the loss of the soul, using the grotesque figures on the cathedral of Notre Dame in Paris as an analogy for certain types of men:

> in fact, the gargoyles are staring into the abyss: where they look, the abyss opens up. And everything they are trying to seize in their greedy, terrible gaze is swallowed up in this void. In it the gargoyles have lost not only men and women, and Paris, but all the cities and lands and seas and starry skies: as a man who harbors great resentment, or is full of envy, loses, in this envy and resentment, one thing after another, both the days of the flowers and the silent nights.[2]

And this is indeed the terrifying state of the entity that assumes the form of a *hannya*, both as Kassner would see her (that is, as a projection of the

1   Elias Canetti, *Crowds and Power*, Farrar, Straus & Giroux, New York, 1984.

2   Rudolf Kassner, *Gli elementi dell'umana grandezza*, Bompiani, Milan, 1942, p. 56.

monster in whose form a man, having lost his own humanity, finds himself imprisoned) and as Canetti would see her, through the semiotic function of the mask.

The element that the two concepts share is fixity: the condition, both of the monster and the mask, is totally circumscribed within the constraints of its own inescapable limits. It is a typical schema of the Western mentality, but one for which it is hard to find a parallel in the context of Japanese culture, or Eastern culture in general. It presupposes an objective conception of the real, based on antitheses, and operates by distinguishing between unambiguous opposites: beautiful and ugly, harmonious and conflicting, good and bad, positive and negative. While such things are conceivable in the West (or were considered so until the relativist revolution, the development of analytical psychology and the crisis of modern art), they would be unthinkable in Japan. Beauty, and therefore also reality, can never be objective but is dependent on circumstances, on states of mind. It is, rather, the intermediate areas – between beauty and ugliness, fairness and meanness, justice and injustice, light and darkness – that play a primary role: areas that are undefined yet laden with suggestion. Human beings carry within themselves their unconscious baggage, which is beyond their control and constitutes, in a word, the 'shadow'. But this shadow is the place in which the dynamics of individual and social development are played out.

In nō, it is a structural element of every play; it is the fulcrum on which the action turns. The shadow (whatever has not yet revealed itself to consciousness) conceals itself within the symbolic reality of the mask. The task of the nō drama, its hidden message, is to make us see, through the 'subtle enchantment' of its aesthetic language, how it is possible to transform into positive energy our resistances to our own self-realization, to transform the darkness into a fountainhead of light. The crucial tool in this process is the mask. Unlike the other known types of mask – each of which personifies a specific quality that is to some extent magical, and is yet unchangeable, fixed – *nōmen* are able to change their expressions. They are the end point of a long process of development that is both religious (involving ancient shamanistic practices) and aesthetic (with iconographic features originating in India, China and central Asia). For the most part these masks, with their ancient cultural heritage, represent psychological types. But against a background of individual characters – the jealous woman, the nubile young girl, the passionate warrior, the soul in torment – the mask can display different states of mind – grief or smiles, joy or horror, distress or great determination – depending on the angle at which the actor places it by the movement of his head. Even the mask that represents the most terrifying states of mind, for example, the *hannya* whose role is to personify the fearsome spirit of jealousy, is not bound to a fixed expression; it can be varied, and may expose the rupture of a psychological state that has otherwise become rigidified beyond redemption.

It is thus a characteristic of nō masks that they can change their expression to order. In this respect they fulfil the same function as nō itself and the art of the period in which they reached their peak of stylistic perfection. This function is precisely to bring to the surface passions, desires and tensions hidden in the psyche. This is not achieved by presenting spectators with a mask that expresses definitively the state of mind that is to be represented; this must emerge gradually on its features – just as in ordinary life. In essence, the mask must allow for the expression of a wide range of feelings, as on the human face itself. Not only this, but the intensity of these feelings must be variable, to the point where they disappear and give the mask itself a 'neutral' expression that represents a kind of psychic repose. In this way, spectators may perceive on it, in a distillation of the mask-maker's art and the actor's skill, the mental impulses they feel within themselves during the course of their lives, enabling them to confront these, and accept their contradictions and thus transcend their tragic aspect. This process of liberation through the aesthetic reorganization of dissociated parts requires that in some cases the same mask is able to express states in conflict with one another: serenity and anxiety, sadness and gaiety, malice and joy, tears and smiles, jealous rage and gentle sweetness.

It would seem impossible to achieve effects of this kind – using masks without moving parts and with extremely simplified physical features – if there were not the *nōmen* to testify to the perfection attained in this area by the 'culture of feelings', a definition that could be applied to Japan itself. And it is the visual simplicity of these carved masks that gives them their expressiveness. The psychic mobility of the nō mask is achieved through a skilful synthesis of psycho-logical insight and the sculptor's art, and the man who carves it has to be knowl-edgeable about the human psyche and able to apply his skill to reveal its impulses. Each mask represents a basic type, but one that has a wide variety of possible nuances. At the same time these variations must not overlap one another, but must define and separate themselves through contrast according to the actor's movements at the various points of the action being represented. Consequently, the mask must be both simple and intensely expressive; it must potentially be able to contain the synthesis of laughter and weeping, joy and pain, vexation and serenity, in such a way that one state does not superimpose itself on the other and cause emotional confusion. In a certain sense the mask must be able to become utterly 'neutral', in other words, devoid of emotional connotations, when it is in a state of repose. This is done by ensuring that it maintains a specific angle *vis-à-vis* the observer, keeping in equilibrium all the points of refracted light on its surface. In this way the dark areas are balanced by those that are lit, and the mask expresses a sense of the stability of the character it represents.

The degree of artistry and skill the actor must attain in using a mask to evoke emotions is nothing short of prodigious. Exploiting the way light is refracted on it, he can make it assume different moods, so that it appears to weep, laugh or rejoice depending on the angle at which he places it in relation to the light source, and thus to the interaction between the refractive angles he is able to obtain. An actor on the stage is almost blind, because the small holes that correspond with the mask's eyes are not aligned exactly with his own, and even the combination of these with the openings that mark the nostrils does not allow him to see anything more than vague shadows. Bearing in mind that, in addition to this, a difference of a fraction of a centimetre is sufficient for the mask to go from mirth to sadness, or vice versa, we can understand the perfect control of movement that great actors must achieve, and how it is almost impossible to do so without having worked on the stage for decades.

An example of how nō masks are structured is better than any lengthy explanation, and the following description is of the *ko-omote* (small face). One of the best known it is, as its name indicates, very slightly smaller than the others, and the characters it represents are usually girls in the flower of their youth. At first glance, as with all masks that represent young women, the eye is drawn to two areas in particular: the mouth and the eyes, areas almost invisibly connected by the line of the nose. The aim of the person who created the *ko-omote* 'type' was to make a mask that would exude the freshness and purity of a young girl. There is a perceptible feeling of gaiety suffused with naivety, suggesting that life has not yet left on her pure and limpid features the marks of passion, sorrow and inner turmoil. This is the mask's basic condition, but a vast range of states of mind may emanate from it, each giving the previous one a specific tone. The focal points on which the expressiveness of the face depends, the eyes and mouth, are sur-rounded by empty space – a state that is akin to that of the famous silence of the mind in Zen. When the mask is in a state of rest, that is, when the light is not falling obliquely and creating contrasts of light and shade, the refracted light is diffused. Looking at it is like looking at a painting by Sesshū in which there appear, now here, now there, filtered through clouds and mist, hints of a landscape; scarcely perceived suggestions of a more complete visual ensemble, whose reality can be intuited but cannot be grasped in its entirety. Just as we are unable to grasp once and for all the meaning of the constant flux of human life, or penetrate the mystery of a face (the mirror of the soul) and believe we have fully understood its character, the *nōmen*, products of an art that springs from Zen, are a perfect means of expressing evocations, what is alluded to, what is undefined.

The eyes and mouth of the *ko-omote* become the vehicles that enable the viewer to penetrate the mystery of the soul that manifests itself through them. The rest of the face performs the same function as the mist in a *suiboku* landscape: it compels the eye towards a point that emerges and is the intermediary for the message that has to come to the surface. There is nothing in the *ko-omote* that might attract the attention and draw it away from those two crucial areas. The eyebrows, in the manner of the ladies of Heian-kyō, appear to have been removed and painted on again, very high up, just below the hairline. The arch of the brows is itself invisible, and blends into the plane of the forehead, making it very large (the eyes are set exactly in the centre of the face). A similar process takes place with the mouth, so there is no obstacle around these two 'focal points' to prevent refracted light flowing freely over the whole mask. The shape of the mouth is of special importance to the process of communicating feelings. Its corners have a characteristic slight upward curve, which Nogami calls 'reservoirs of smiles'.[3]

Depending on how the actor positions the mask its expression changes completely. A slight forward tilt projects the shadow of the lower part of the nose on to the upper lip, making the distance between them look shorter. The same happens to the upper lip in relation to the lower one; indeed, the effect is even clearer since the black-painted teeth (again following Heian practice) and the black hole of the mouth tend to disappear, creating the impression that the whole area of the mouth, including the corners, is shrinking. Something similar can be observed with the eyes where the upper lid, projecting over the eye and lower lid, creates a shadow round the eye. In essence, the areas in shadow have the effect of limiting the diffusion of the light; the mask becomes 'clouded over' – *kumorasu* in Japanese. The converse happens, however, when the mask is tilted upwards. In this case, the shadow disappears from under the mouth and, refracted against the teeth, it creates different depths of field. Light falls on the section between the lips and nostrils and, most importantly, the corners of the mouth (the 'reservoirs of smiles') are no longer shrunk by the shadow; their effect spreads freely with no obstacle in its way. The entire face brightens (*terasu*) in the way that a light breeze gradually drives away clouds that have built up, bringing back a clear blue sky. It is

3   Toyoichirō Nogami, *Il dramma noh*, IsMEO, Rome, 1940, p. 19.

as if the eyes and mouth were spreading springtime joy and delight over it – the youthfulness of the girl represented by the *ko-omote*. Prominent and isolated, they take on a particular quality, almost surfacing on the face as if by magic. It is precisely the way they are placed that endows the mask with the aura of mysterious beauty, that exerts its magical allure precisely because the subtle enchantment the *koomoto* exudes is so indefinable.

The power of the mask thus lies in its elusiveness, its ability to change its expressive tone and so present changes in mood. It helps us to avoid thinking that a truth or quality is achieved once and for all, and to remember how Zeami (c. 1364 to c. 1443), the father of nō, taught actors, 'the flower *(hana)* is something that is constantly changing'. The flower, the quintessence of drama, becomes such only if the participant spectators succeed in seeing, and the actor in making them see, its freshness and rarity. This amounts to saying that a flower is preserved only as long as it is renewed, just as in nature. The subtle enchantment of these masks lies in their representing a didactic form of art, teaching us, as they do, to face changes in our states of mind; not avoiding them but, on the contrary, accepting the fact of their existence as a way of understanding our own inner contradictions.

The process by which spectators are led to accept, even to seek out and discover, their own contradictions, not condemning them as sinful or evil but understanding them as integral parts of human nature itself, sometimes reaches forms of expression that have great dramatic intensity. There is a series of nō dramas, most of which belong to the fourth group[4] – that of madness and possession – in which the development of the psychological action takes on tones of intense conflict. The first and second phases of the drama, separated by the section devoted to performances of *kyōgen*, are usually clearly distinguishable. In the first, the psychological issue is forced to emerge until it reaches its climax. The second part has the function of heightening the passion, the tension that has become apparent, in order to expose its most extreme aspects until catharsis is achieved through this process of analysing and harmoniously reorganizing the psyche by aesthetic means. In this type of nō drama, the unfolding of the action is usually underlined by a change not only in the costume of the protagonist, the *shite*, but also of his mask.

The *nōmen*, with their ability to embody in their own form different aspects of human experience, take on a religious and magical as well as an artistic value. They are true symbols, in the sense in which Ernst Cassirer uses the word when he states, 'Without symbolism, man's life would be like that of the prisoners in the cave in Plato's famous metaphor. Man's life would be confined within the limits of his biological needs and practical interests. There would be no

4 Nō plays fall into five categories, according to their subjects and treatment, though the classification of some plays varies from one school to another. There are god plays, warrior plays, beautiful woman plays, madness and possession plays, and demon plays.

access to the "ideal world" that is opened to him on different sides by religion, art, philosophy and science.'[5]

This form of art, like the whole aesthetic of nō, takes on the role, as Donald Keene says, of emphasizing 'the eternal lines of the story'.[6] It is precisely this archetypal quality that turns nō masks into mythic images capable of enriching the range of life's meanings. The function of this theatrical genre, with its aesthetic languages, is thus intensely didactic. By emphasizing the timeless features of human experience, it offers each of us the opportunity to see ourselves mirrored in it; of attaining, if we wish, a harmonization of our inner tensions on an aesthetic and religious level, and reaching a higher plane of human existence.

5   Ernst Cassirer, *An Essay on Man*, Yale University Press, New Haven, 1944.

6   Donald Keene, *Nō: The Classical Theatre of Japan*, Kodansha, Tokyo and Palo Alto, 1966, p. 21.

The actor Kanze Tetsunojō in
the nō play *Sumidagawa*,
photograph by Morita Toshirō

Overleaf, left:
Mask of the nō character
ko-omote, the young, virginal
beauty, photograph by Morita
Toshirō

Overleaf, right:
Tanaka Ikkō, *Sankei Kanze
no (XX)*, performing arts
poster, 1966

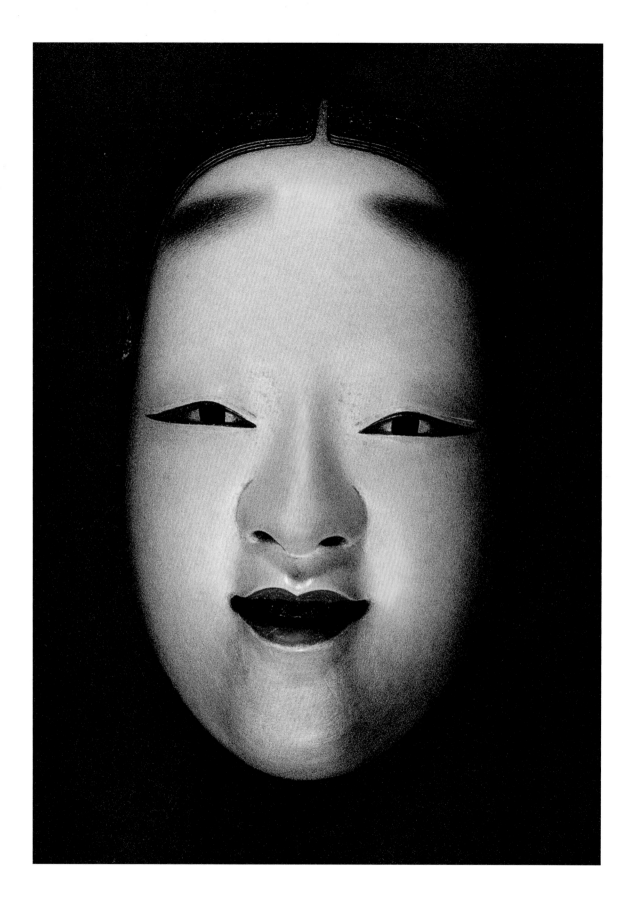

Previous pages:
Nō costumes, photographs by
Morita Toshirō

The actor Tsumura Reijirō in
the nō play *Dōjōji*, photograph
by Morita Toshirō

The Colours of Darkness

> I wonder if my readers know the colour of that 'darkness seen by candle-light'. It was different in quality from darkness on the road at night. It was a repletion, a pregnancy of tiny particles like fine ashes, each particle luminous as a rainbow.[1]

The colours of darkness. Who in the West could ever conceive of a 'colour' of darkness? Such an idea is enough to engender a feeling of dislocation, of being incapable of even beginning to comprehend such a concept. And a look at a sophisticated study of tonal and chromatic variations within darkness, *In Praise of Shadows* (*In'ei raisan*, 1933), by Tanizaki (1886–1965), from which the above quotation is taken, and which reflects a highly developed aesthetic vision of life, gives the impression of being in a world whose rules elude the Western mind. It is governed by unfamiliar laws that are not clear or unambiguous; they are hazy, with blurred edges, creating novel and impermanent images of reality.

For Japanese writers and artists life contains an area where the indistinct reality of the penumbra is the norm. Where colours appear subdued and their brilliance comes from some inner quality, not a dazzling surface. Where darkness is full of heat and colour. Where the dark, warm, malleable world of matter contrasts with the luminous, cold, abstract world of the idea. It is a world that enriches the relationship between human beings and objects, where no kind of light is necessary to see and to know, but where knowledge is attained through glints and glimmering reflections, and shadows that do not extinguish the inner light of objects: a pine branch framed in a window at dusk; a woman's face, the mystery of which we try in vain to penetrate; a bank of mist that blocks our view (in real life or representation), to force us to expand our imagination; or a whispering breeze whose tremulous breath evokes the echo of distant memories.

In *The Grass Pillow* (*Kusamakura*, 1906), an enchanting handbook of aesthetics in fictional form, Natsume Sōseki (1867–1916) writes, 'Light and darkness are but opposite sides of the same thing, so wherever the sunlight falls it must of necessity cast a shadow. [...] In the depths of joy dwells sorrow, and the greater the happiness the greater the pain. Try to tear joy and sorrow apart, and you lose your hold on life. Try to cast them to one side, and the world crumbles.'[2] Indefiniteness is a primary characteristic of the world of Japanese art: avoidance of absolute prevailing ideas and images and, above all, a *horror plaeni* (a fear of filled spaces). Through the play of empty spaces, achieved through effects of haziness and mists, secondary images may come to the fore, depending on the observers' inter-

1 Tanizaki Jun'ichirō, *In Praise of Shadows*, Cape, London, 1991, p. 52.

2 Natsume Sōseki, *Kusamakura* (lit. 'The Grass Pillow'), trans. by E. McClellen as *The Three Cornered World*, Arrow Books, London, 1984, pp. 13–14.

pretative approach and the resonances they are able to evoke within their own souls. In literature, too, from poetry to the novel, there is this kind of interpretative relationship between the reader and the text. In the *haiku*, the short poetic form of seventeen syllables, the process described in relation to painting appears in its quintessence. The first two lines, the 'first level', introduce an image that is self-sufficient and apparently predominant, but whose value and meaning are substantially changed, if not reversed, by the last concept introduced, as in the famous example by Matsuo Bashō (1644–94):

> The ancient pond –
> A frog jumps in,
> The sound of the water.

The third line, the new 'key to the reading', does not cancel the idea embodied in the previous lines but merges with it, creating a delicate, sometimes imperceptible counterpoint. What then determines the interpretation is the relative intensity of the connection that is made (in the composition, but also in the reading) between the first and second parts; in other words, the connection with empty space, the pause that both separates and fuses the two elements in a new perceptual synthesis. In the works of the greatest novelists, from Murasaki (978?–1016?) to Saikaku (1642–93) and from Sōseki to Kawabata (1899–1972), this effect is obtained not through the use of the idea-word, but through the relationship between whole chapters or episodes in which feelings and emotions are heightened or, alternatively, muted, and which always depend on situations where the action is incomplete or unresolved and remains open to various interpretations and inferences.

The reasons for the popularity of Japanese culture in the West are to be sought in this realm of the imperfect, the unresolved, the asymmetrical. Japan's 'westernness', its modernity *avant la lettre* (in addition, obviously, to its staggering present-day modernity), makes it more familiar than other Asian societies, and allows us to absorb more easily the more alien elements of its culture. But beneath this familiarity it is possible to detect messages that are unfamiliar and beguiling, that charm and disconcert, and at the same time offer a new, refreshing model of art and beauty: allusive, rather than descriptive, emotional rather than rational, averse to symmetry, preferring shadow to broad daylight, and determined to avoid perfectionism, which is pursued only through a total, absolute and minute attention to the imperfect.

It is precisely this kind of aesthetic model – flexible, open, attentive to every change and variation, full of symbolic references and allusions, and not given to concretizing description – that encouraged the rapid advance of Japanese art into the avant-garde. As, indeed, took place in sectors other than the aesthetic. Werner Heisenberg (1901–76), for example, claimed that 'the great scientific contribution in theoretical physics that has come from Japan since the last war may be an indication for a certain relationship between the philosophical ideas in the tradition of the Far East and the philosophical substance of quantum theory'.[3] And he goes on to suggest that it may be easier to adapt our thinking to the concept of reality formed by quantum theory when we are not obliged to make it 'pass through the dogmas of the simplistic, materialistic way of thinking that still prevailed in Europe in the early years of the century'; a thought that may be appropriately applied to the field of the visual arts, and to freedom from the fetters of academicism and realism.

But can it be claimed that the arts of contemporary Japan share in this aesthetic model? Is it not more a matter of trends that are detached from these, in which aspects that are in a formal sense 'national' should perhaps be considered stylistic features of Occidentalism? Yet it remains true that the period immediately after the Second World War witnessed a rejection of native cultural values – the fundamental cause, it was said, of Japan's defeat – in favour of the often unreserved and frenetic adoption of the American model. For the most part, this came from the need for renewal, for stimulus and freshness, as vividly described by Kamekura Yūsaku (1915–97), the 'Mr Big' of Japanese graphic design, in his account of his own experience. Nevertheless, apart from the most formal aspects of this development or, rather, among them, there can be detected the persistence of leitmotifs that can be referred to the Japanese aesthetic, as well as to a philosophical and religious worldview. The photographs made by Eikō Hosoe (b. 1933), for and with the famous novelist Mishima Yukio (1925–70), are well known; the rediscovery of Mishima after long and shameful neglect on the part of publishers brought the images to light. They are disquieting photographs, with a flavour of decadence, and show how Mishima liked to be thought of and portrayed – not purely in terms of his confrontation with the avant-garde but as an upholder of the need to rediscover and appreciate traditional values, albeit in an apparently revolutionary guise. To the point of the ultimate statement: self-immolation carried out as a work of art, according to ancient rigorous codes.

Despite all appearances to the contrary, tradition is present even in the case of the 'sexy robots' – fantastical vehicles for the erotic, expressed in cold impersonal steel – created by Sorayama Hajime (b. 1947). The amazing juxta-

3   Werner Heisenberg, *Physics and Philosophy*, Harper & Brothers, New York, 1958, p. 202.

position of metal and flesh, mechanization and voluptuousness, is nothing other than the transposition into a bold, futuristic key of an aesthetic trend that is characteristic of Japanese art. The contrast between strictly geometrical and purely naturalistic forms of decoration is both striking and fascinating, in both architecture and painting. The two styles are traditionally antithetical in Europe, but in Japan they often appear in combination. Abstract geometrical forms – triangles or circles – can be found alongside landscape or floral motifs in the designs of brocades. Not to mention examples like the famous wall, featuring large white and sky-blue squares, that is inserted into the naturalistic context – wood, straw and paper – of the Shōkintei tea pavilion in the park of the imperial villa at Katsura, near Kyoto. It is a tradition that can also be seen in the art of Sorayama, and many others like him, which, whatever forms the artists use, can seem revolutionary in comparison with the styles of the past.

Also interesting in this respect are the embossed white-on-white prints of Nagai Kazumasa (b. 1929), whose rigorous geometry recalls objects made by kinetic artists such as Enrico Castellani, Paolo Scheggi, Getulio Alviani or Agostino Bonalumi. But, even here, pure abstraction is always broken by an element taken from nature: an insect or a small plant. This aspect – geometry within naturalism – is one of the keys to discovering and interpreting avant-garde art in Japan, and the roots that bind it (and will continue to do so) to the cultural and aesthetic values of the country's own tradition.

Sengai Gibon
Frog and Snail, ink on paper,
c. 1800

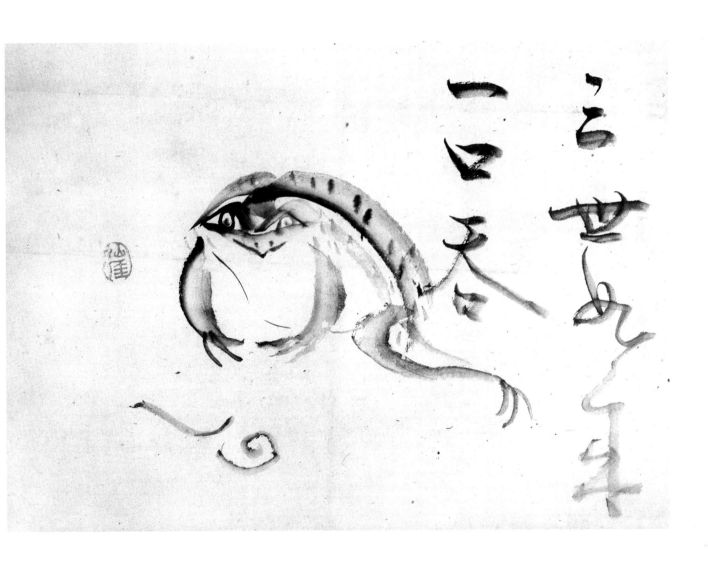

Andō Tadao
Church of the Light, Osaka,
1989, photograph by Richard
Pare

Inner shrine, Jingu temple, Ise
(first iteration built c. 690),
photograph by Ishimoto Yasuhiro

Overleaf:
Tange Kenzo
St Mary's Cathedral, Tokyo, 1963,
photograph by Murai Osamu

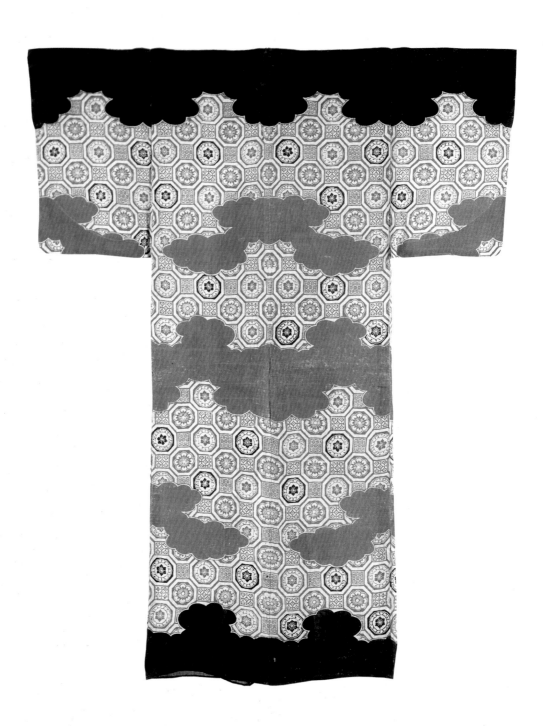

Left:
Funerary robe (*kazuki*),
ramie, 17th century

Right:
Futon cover,
machine-woven cotton,
c. 1920

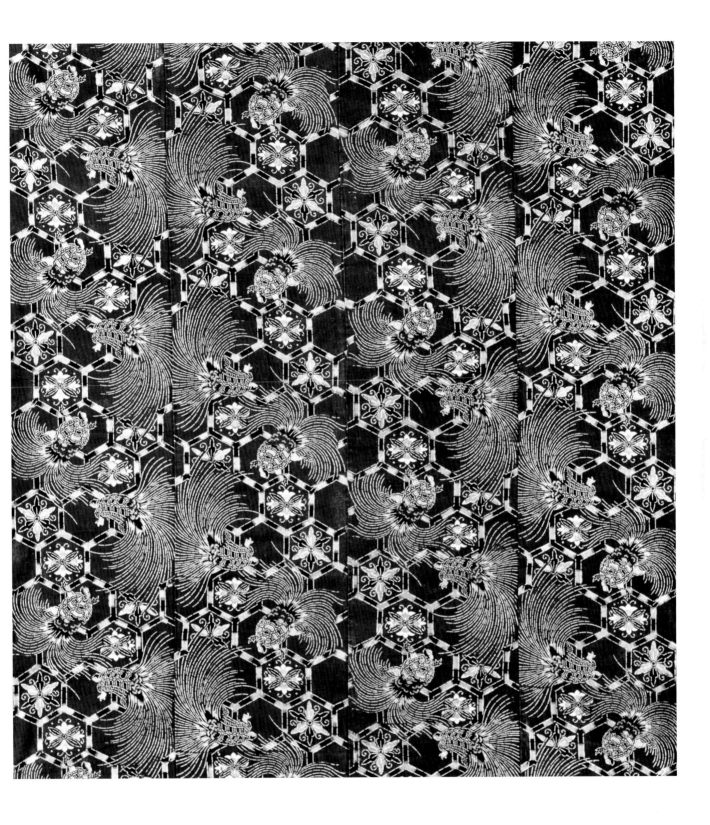

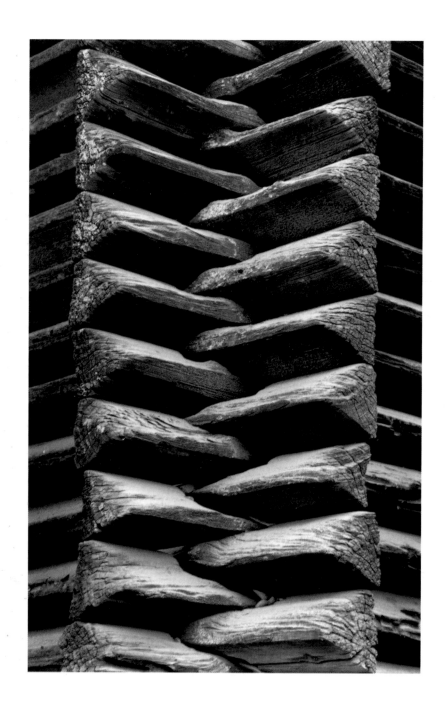

Left:
Corner of a log storehouse
(*azekura*) at Nigatsudō, Nara,
photograph by Iwamiya Takeji

Right:
Section of bamboo fence at
Katsura Imperial Villa, Kyoto,
photograph by Iwamiya Takeji

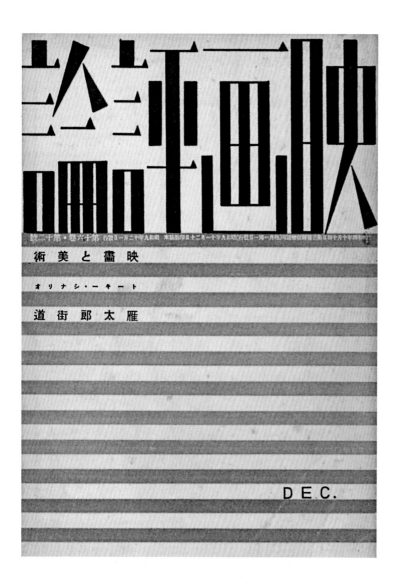

Left:
Kono Takashi
Cover design for *Cinematic
Review* (*Eiga hyōron*), 1934

Right:
Kono Takashi
Magazine advertisement for
the movie *Happy New Year*
(*Kinga Shin'nen*), 1932

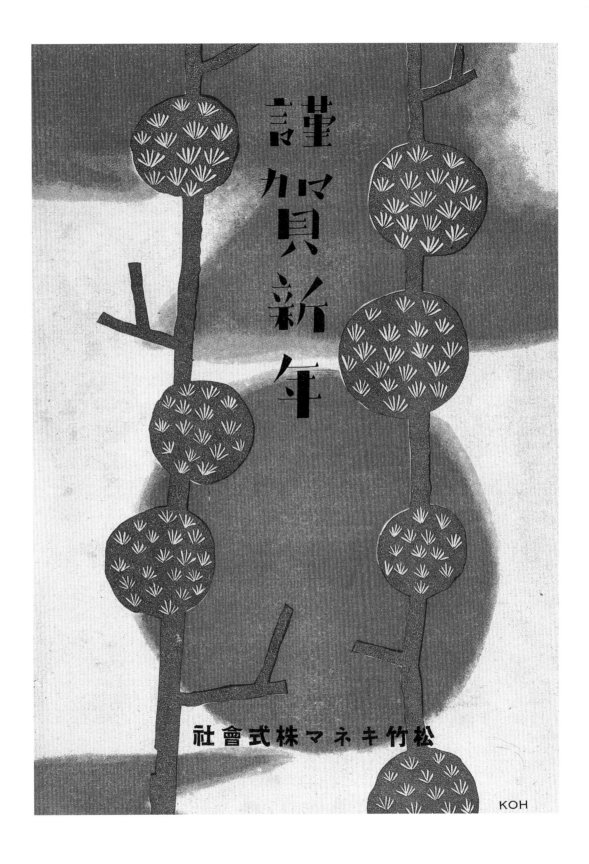

Taniguchi Yoshirō
Okura Hotel, Tokyo, 1962,
photograph by Minakawa
Satoshi

The Old Shoin, Katsura
Imperial Villa, Kyoto, 17th
century, photograph by
Matsumura Yoshiharu

Interlude: Small but Great

'You may be right to admire Japanese culture, but what about bonsai? Isn't that a horrible way to treat plants? Of all the different kinds of sadistic practices, I don't think there's one that shows more clearly the profound cruelty of Orientals!' How many times have I heard this kind of remark, which actually reveals a kind of love–hate attitude towards what people imagine are mysterious Asian forms of sadism? I wonder whether they ask themselves such searching questions about what (to give only one example) the Picolit vine has to suffer every year to produce its precious, unattractive bunches of grapes!

It may seem strange but bonsai, the dwarf trees of China and Japan (not, as some people believe, the whole of Asia), the fashion for which has been spreading in the West for some years, are a product of the marriage between a deep love of nature and the search for immortality. Their historical origins are lost in the mists of time and, contrary to popular belief, lie not in Japan but in China. There were gardens in Shang China (from the seventeenth to the eleventh centuries BC) and from at least the second century AD trees were grown in pots. But why miniature trees? The phenomenon appears to be connected with the magical and religious aspects of Taoism. The eight Taoists who, according to tradition, attained immortality are said to have lived on an island that rises like a mountain in the middle of the ocean, after spending most of their earthly existence in mountains and woods where they looked for herbs that would provide the elixir of eternal life. According to Taoist thought, miniaturizing rocks and plants could allow the forces contained in them to be concentrated and manipulated.

This is certainly true from the aesthetic point of view, as can be seen in a bonsai that has grown into a perfect shape. An example is a pine tree, perhaps two hundred years old, whose rough bark is criss-crossed with deep fissures. It is contorted, and clings to a rock that has determined the way it has developed; a stump, though now dried up, signifies a victory over wind, snow and lightning despite the loss of the branches that once grew from it. All these features communicate the sense that this is not a mere plant, still less an object, but an animate being; indeed, a prince among such beings, a distillation of the qualities of the soul.

Although the technical and philosophical origins of bonsai are in China, it is Japanese animism and close relationship with nature that have made its cultivation an art, almost a religion. In Japan bonsai is a symbol of the beauty of nature; a beauty that is understood not in the classic Western sense of formal harmony, but, on the contrary, as the expression of natural forces, their conflicts and the marks they have left. The scars these conflicts leave in the living wood, and even in stone, are considered signs of beauty because they are evidence of experience, lived and suffered. It is a very different beauty, however, from that which is dearer to the Western tradition, whose goal is to preserve the semblance of the untouched and immature. Over millennia the Japanese have learnt to love the beauty of an old plum tree in the natural environment, hollowed out by time and by wind and weather, whose rough shape is able to put out new shoots and flowers in the spring. A sacred rope is put round it, a stele is erected and propitiatory offerings are made to the spirit that must surely inhabit it, given the tree's extreme age and the perfection of its imperfection.

Youth may be beautiful because it appears inviolate, but age is sublime because it carries the marks and dignity of experience, the lines of sorrow that has been faced and overcome, the lineaments of joys savoured to the full; in short, it is a distillation of human existence. And bonsai is the symbol of the nobility and great age of plants; or, even better, of man's capacity to discover and appreciate these qualities.

A popular nō drama, *The Potted Trees* (*Hachi no ki*), underlines the importance accorded to bonsai since ancient times. A disgraced samurai and his aged spouse are living in poverty in a wretched hovel hidden away in mountains. They are reduced to existing on a handful of millet, and the wealth and lands the warrior once commanded vanished long ago. But he has kept three dwarf trees: a plum, a cherry and a pine. Hundreds of years old, they are symbols of ancient glory and family tradition. One night there is a great blizzard and the samurai sacrifices the bonsai to provide an unknown pilgrim-monk with a little warmth. In fact, the monk is his old overlord, the regent of Japan, in disguise, whom he has not recognized. As the fire devours the little trees (the chorus sings during this part of the drama), with each spurt of flame the old samurai's heart is also burned. But, at the same time, his past valour and greatness are rekindled in his noble soul and, in words and gestures, he pledges again – to himself, his wife and his guest – undying loyalty to the highest values of chivalry, albeit at an incalculable price. He declares to the pilgrim-stranger his eternal devotion to his lord, and swears he will always be ready, despite his age, his dilapidated equipment and the wrongs he has suffered, to answer a call to arms without a moment's delay. The regent returns to the capital and summons his vassals from all over the land. The samurai, who has come as he had promised, finds to his own amazement, and that of everyone else, that his lands and honours are restored to him, with the addition of three fiefdoms, one for each of the bonsai he sacrificed.

Katsushika Hokusai
The Talisman, colour
woodblock print, 1822

2

The Feeling of Nature

The Harmony of Things

The relationship between human beings and nature is one of the cornerstones of Japan's cultural and artistic traditions, and understanding it is therefore vital in analysing the distinguishing features of 'Japan style'. It is in the ways it places itself in relation to the natural world, and the world of the divine that is inextricably linked with this, that Japan has developed its undeniable originality. In the realm of art in the broadest sense, encompassing literature and painting, graphic design and music, theatre and architecture, sculpture and the tea ceremony, the approach to nature has given rise to a wide and entirely original range of forms of expression and modes of behaviour.

In the vast array of concepts that Japanese culture has developed to express ways of relating to nature, one that is especially useful is that of the deeply personal 'perception of things', which is the driving force that defines Japanese culture through the relationship with nature, a force nourished and enriched through being actively exercised. It refers to a concept in the national aesthetic, the *mono no aware*, which has been a fundamental element in Japanese history and civilization but which, over the centuries, has undergone profound changes in meaning as ideas about lifestyles and forms of dress have altered.

The word *aware* is found in the earliest texts, used at first as an exclamation of surprise or delight, wonder or astonishment, but later as an adjective meaning pleasant or interesting. And as early as the eighth century a feeling of *aware* was very often evoked by poets on hearing natural sounds like the melancholy calls of birds and other creatures, or the pattering of rain in springtime.

In the eleventh century, the time of *The Tale of Genji*, the word expressed a subtle sadness, and enhanced a sentence not so much by adding to its meaning as by giving it a particular colour or fragrance; in other words, by intensifying it. Therefore, at the apex of its fortunes, the concept of *mono no aware* was used to infuse literary pieces of unusual beauty with the sense of profound emotions, while in the eighteenth century it acquired the value of 'sensitivity to things', such as a falling blossom or an unshed tear.

For these reasons, I believe that the expression 'intimate harmony' is a satisfactory equivalent to the term *aware* as it was variously understood over the centuries. Furthermore, with its forms of expression in the spheres of both figurative and gestural art, it seems to lend itself well to being used to reflect the deep feeling for nature that has always been cultivated in the Japanese soul. But the premisses governing the relationship between human beings and the created universe are essentially different in Japan and the West; and this profound difference between the Japanese conception of nature and our own can be seen in the very structure of our respective myths of origin.

The split between mind and matter, one of the leading causes of the crisis of values that afflicts the modern West, can be ascribed not only to the Christian vision of life that is usually identified as its primary source. Elements can be traced back to the ancient Jewish and Hellenic worlds, the two strands that converged to form European civilization. And the difference between the two cultural traditions, those of the West and of Japan, presents itself essentially in terms of the relationship between human beings and the universe. In the world of the Old Testament, the boundaries of nature are very clearly established; there is a creator, and there is a creation which is passive and undergoes the act of creation. The created is matter, devoid of a soul, inert. Man redeems himself from the state of subjection in which he too would be submerged if, and in so far as, he is able to recognize himself as a dualistic being and distinguish between his body, which is material, a perishable phenomenon that has been created, and his soul, the invisible element breathed into him by the creator's own breath. Man therefore cannot confuse the creator, unique and uncreated, with what is generated by his creative acts, even in their loftiest aspects – for example, the sun. The appearance of man on life's stage thus occurs with his clear separation from the world of the indistinct, the uncreated, and with his entry into the world of the objective. To struggle against nature, and to shape it, becomes the destiny of Western man; the goal of his earthly experience is to strive, without ever entirely succeeding, to make the world of nature resemble ever more closely the world of the principles that transcend it.

An approach of this kind is fundamentally different from Japanese cultural tradition, which sees itself as based from its beginnings on a state of unity between the material and the spiritual, making it almost impossible to distinguish between them. This close connection is attributed not so much to the Buddhist vision of life (an outside influence on Japanese culture) as to the native religion of Japan: Shintō. This is, so to speak, an autochthonous form of worship, the basic role of which is to create and maintain a harmonious relationship between the forces of nature and members of society, by means of purification rituals. The myths that make up its organic texture represent for the Japanese an inexhaustible fund of archetypal images to which they can turn, consciously or unconsciously, in shaping their own lives. The primary source for the study of these myths of origin, Japan's equivalent of the Old Testament, is the *Records of Ancient Matters* (*Kojiki*, 712 AD). Despite many signs of Chinese influence (it dates from the period when writing was introduced in Japan, and characters were imported from China and used to transcribe Japanese language), this work is universally acknowledged as a characteristic product of the national mentality. Despite the fact that it begins with a cosmological model comparable with the Hebraic sacred text and Hesiod's *Theogony*, its account of the process of creation is different. In the *Kojiki* there is no creator god, eternal and unchanging, who creates an impermanent, changeable world that is objective and conceptualized in terms of opposites: light and darkness, day and night, land and sea. In the Japanese tradition the divine is born with the universe of phenomena with which it remains infused:

> when heaven and earth were first divided, the three deities became the first of all creation. The Male and Female here began, and the two spirits were the ancestors of all creation.[1]

The gods, as ancestors, share the nature of the things they create; they are, in the same way, created beings. The first couple, who were also created, in turn created all the individual parts of the universe, and did so by giving birth to them. They created the gods that people the world and the rocks, trees and mountains, which are themselves deities, and founded the human race. The mythic image of the original couple, with their divine nature, who took their place in a world full of deities, is at the origin of the feeling for nature that the Japanese have cultivated for centuries, both directly and through the mediation of art. A majestic tree, a rock, a waterfall of a distinctive shape, a space, an environment or a panorama - all become charged with meaning, since there can be seen in them the divine quality of which man himself is made up, not only in his spirit but also in his body, and they become defined as sacred. The sense of the numinous, the essence of such relationships, thus pervades every part of the land of Japan, which itself becomes sacred and a place of dialogue with the divine. From this concept of the divine essence of specific places there developed in turn the iconographic, environmental, even touristic tradition linked with the particular personalities and fortunes of such locations, from which sprang the genre of *meisho-e*, depictions of famous places.

In the earliest Shintō traditions gods inhabit the universe, and mountains, rivers and beaches have a divine nature, as have rocks of an unusual shape, or especially ancient and gnarled trees on which the depredations of time and weather have left their mark. In short, those beings (and also natural environments like certain landscapes) have a divine nature that possess a degree of individuality so strong as to make them exceptional. These 'special' places are fenced, in order to contain the divine presence; a twisted rope, *kumihimo*, is placed round

1   Donald L. Philippi (ed.), *Kojiki*, Tokyo University Press and Princeton University Press, Tokyo, 1968, p. 37.

them to prevent the god departing, as in an archetypal incident in Japan's myths of origin. A rope of this kind was used to seal for ever the cave from which the sun goddess Amaterasu Ōmikami, the chief deity in the Japanese Shintō pantheon, was dragged after she had been offended by her brother, Susano-o no Mikoto, the storm god. The rope came to symbolize the divine presence. With it, human beings endow with divine value whatever is exceptional, not for its harmony of form but for its travail in coming into being.

In some cases they even transfer to natural phenomena their own social institutions, as in the case of the two separate rocks symbolically united in marriage. The rope circumscribes the divine space and 'binds' the god, ensuring that he remains present, and at the same time unites the rocks in marriage. The archetypal figures created in this way rely, more than on any other aesthetic language, on the emotional resonances created in the soul, and raise the everyday moment (in this case, contemplation of nature) to the threshold of the sublime.

The arrival of Buddhism with its broad and complex religious and philosophical framework, instead of obliterating the practices dictated by another religion, Shintō, strengthened and enriched the themes of relationship with nature, deepening and internalizing them. A comparison of works from the protohistorical era (which in Japan lasted until the sixth century AD) with others that followed the absorption of Buddhism in the same period provides the first overwhelming evidence of the capacity for rapid assimilation that is typical of Japanese culture, and which in the past two centuries has especially fascinated and sometimes even intimidated the West.

A typical feature of Japanese civilization in the protohistorical era are the terracotta figurines, *haniwa*, that were placed round the tombs of the sovereign or members of the imperial family. The earliest examples are plain cylinders – later ones were modelled in the form of human beings, animals or buildings – and were placed on top of the palings surrounding the imperial tombs. Their purpose was to recreate around the deceased the social environment he or she had enjoyed in life. A famous example shows a pair of singers, symbols of the festive, musical ambience of the court. They are formed of cylinders, made to be placed on the posts beside the tomb and decorated with simple features designed to show their roles. The arms of each figure are raised in a dramatic gesture, and on its flat face the mouth, open in the act of singing, is indicated in the simplest possible way. But it is precisely the expressionless face, vertically bisected by the nose which points like an arrow towards the open mouth, that communicates the sense of drama, of a culture waiting for a miracle that will make it rise again. The lack of expression comes from the sense of emptiness, emphasized by holes representing the eye sockets and the mouth that open on the flat surface of the face with a dark void behind them. They seem to exist solely in terms of the social function they are meant to perform, with no inner power beyond themselves. It is as if such pieces of sculpture – singers, dignitaries or warriors – are demonstrating functions that are indeed important, but because they possess no inner world they are in need of a spiritual flame to bring their souls to life. Their faces are blank, like flat screens not yet animated by images. Their orifices suggest an underlying emptiness, one that is not a deliberate absence but a lack – a lack of active interior life.

It was Buddhism and Chinese culture (which brought Buddhism to Japan) that slaked the thirst for introspection. The 'noble truth' of suffering as an unavoidable condition of existence was confronted by the Buddha, and resolved with the development of the system that leads to the extinction of its causes. It is the path that human beings must follow in their inner beings, in order to understand the personal impulses and laws that bind them until the moment of their final liberation and release: nirvana. In sixth- and seventh-century Japan the influence of dharma, the law of Buddhism, and with it of Chinese civilization, which was its vehicle, had a considerable cultural effect, as if water had fallen on ground that was parched and scorched by the sun, and within the space of a few years Japan bloomed like the desert after rain.

A supreme example of this cultural shift, almost contemporaneous with the *haniwa*, is the Miroku Bosatsu in the monastery of Chūgu-ji, near Nara. One of the world's most outstanding sculptural works, it is carved out of camphor wood and has become blackened over the centuries by the incense burned by the faithful in their devotions. It represents Maitreya, the future Buddha, the messiah who, in Buddhist tradition, must come again in order to relieve the world's suffering. Another theory has it that it is the figure of the young Siddhartha, in the act of meditating that will lead him to abandon his father's palace and the life of a prince in order to gain 'blessed serenity, born of peace' and attain the condition of Buddha, the saintly, the perfectly awakened. Or its iconography may be more general, as expressed through the concept of the thoughtful bodhisattva. His body rises like a lotus flower from the waters of a pool, with no sharp angle that would prevent light falling gently over its surface. The folds of his garment round his pelvis and legs, which are arranged in a version of the *lalita asana* or 'posture of royal ease', are also smooth and rounded, softer than those required by the aesthetic rules of the Northern Wei in China, from whom the art of the period drew its inspiration.

The face is suffused by a gentle, radiant smile, which appears to extend along the nose, which is straight and slender (but not rigid) and has no sharp angles, until it reaches the eyes, which are half-closed and seem to be looking within. The delicate arch of the eyebrows, which contains and protects the gaze and smile, is less distinct than in other contemporary examples, such as the Kyoto Kōryū-ji, that show a stronger Korean influence. The brow seems to have no edges and light flows unobstructed from the eye to the forehead. This smile, this gaze – in other words, this heart – carry the light all the way to the mind, from which will spring the wheel of doctrine that will be set in motion by him who is also called blessed and infinitely compassionate.

The development of introspection, the discovery of human passions and the laws regulating their expression (together with the means of containing and sublimating them), and the very exploration of the world of feelings that Buddhism provoked in the Japanese eventually spilled over into the realm of nature. Like human beings, nature has a soul; it trembles and rejoices with the seasons; it shares its conditions with man, but not in the romantic sense of reflecting man's emotions. It has a vitality and spirituality of its own and some of its elements are deified, just as some human figures are mythicized. And there are rocks and plants that have attributes that emphasize that the divine is within them. The relationship with Buddhism led to a great flowering of culture, but also to the intensification of the relationship with nature, which became more deeply embedded within that culture.

The Japanese had no form of writing until they adopted the Chinese system. They also gradually developed a kind of phonetic spelling to express the parts of the language that were not provided for by written Chinese. In this connection, and to give an idea of the intensity of the relationship between human beings and nature in Japanese culture, and its organic development in people of all ages and classes, it is worth lingering for a moment over this form of writing. Before it was reorganized according to current rational and abstract criteria, the syllables that make it up were arranged in the form of a poem which every child committed to memory at an early age, memorizing Japanese spelling at the same time. The spelling poem, called *iroha* from its first three syllables, reads as follows:

iro ha nihoedo   *ui no okuyuama*
chirinuru wo   *kefu koete*
wa ga yo tare zo   *asaki yume miji*
tsune naramu   *wehi mo sezu*

Though the colour is bright,	As today I cross the deep
The blossoms scatter;	Mountains of *ui*,
Who in this world of ours	I shall have no shallow dreams,
Will last for ever?	Nor shall I be drunk[2]

This way of reciting the alphabet produced complex effects. First and foremost, it encouraged learning not through abstract concepts but through images that were expressed lyrically, and were thus better suited to a child's mind. Second, it trained children in the understanding and appreciation of poetry and, more importantly, it introduced profound religious and philosophical concepts from the Buddhist tradition. It did so by using images from nature: to be ephemeral is intrinsic to flowers, to the glory of their colourful petals. Their condition is in every way comparable to that of human beings, bound one and all to the process of constant change in the manifest world. But this manifest world is illusory; even though it may seem solid and rugged like a mountain, we should not remain bound to it but should relinquish the intoxication of our vain illusions ('nor shall I be drunk') and cross its boundaries. The poem (which is also a primer to the relationship with nature) was probably written in the ninth century by a great speculative thinker of the East Asia: Kōbō Daishi (774 – 835), a monk who travelled to China and perhaps India, and studied Sanskrit. This innovation had extraordinary effects; in the preface to his celebrated *Collection of Ancient and Modern Japanese Poems* (*Kokin Wakashū*, 905), Ki no Tsurayuki (868?– 945), a poet and nobleman at the imperial court, sings the praises of Japanese aesthetics:

> Japanese poetry has its seeds in the human heart and burgeons into many different kinds of leaves of words. We who live in this world are constantly affected by different experiences, and we express our thoughts in words, in terms of what we have seen and heard. When we hear the warbler that sings among the blossoms or the voice of the frog that lives in the water, we may ask ourselves, 'Which of all the creatures of this world does not sing?' Poetry moves without effort heaven and earth, stirs the invisible gods and demons to pity, makes sweet the ties between men and women, brings comfort to the fierce heart of the warrior.[3]

The complete fusion of more speculative Sino-Indian Buddhist ideas and the Shintō concept of nature took place in the early eleventh century, with the writing of a classic of world literature: *The Tale of Genji* by the court lady

2 Quoted in Donald Keene, *Seeds in the Heart: Japanese Literature from Earliest Times to the Late Sixteenth Century*, Henry Holt & Co., New York, 1993, p. 220.

3 Ibid., p. 246.

known as Murasaki Shikibu. The vast range of the themes developed in it, the depth of the emotions explored, the rich repertoire of situations described and the images that spring from them, make this novel one that everyone ought to read and reread. It is like a bible from which we may gain insight into men and women and their passions, and the countless forms of beauty that flow from human beings.

Left:
Miroku Bosatsu, Chūgu
temple, Nara, camphor wood,
7th century

Right:
Ryōsen-an at Daitoku temple,
Kyoto, 1961, photograph by
Rene Burri

Bamboo Forest, 1930s,
photograph by
Umesaka Ōri

Previous pages:
Katsushika Hokusai
*Shichirigahama in Sagami
Province*, colour woodblock
print, c. 1830–2

Kazahinomi no miya-mi bridge,
Jingu shrine, Ise (first iteration
built c. 690), photograph by
Ishimoto Yasuhiro

Wedded rocks at Futamigaura,
1946, photograph by Horace
Bristol

Haniwa figures, clay, 6th
century

An Intimate Perception of Reality

It is true that Japan is indebted to many other nations, including Korea, China, India, Tibet and those of the West, for the sources of its culture, but it is equally true that in one respect it is indebted to nobody: its very particular relationship with nature. It is this that has enabled Japan to absorb the cultures of other countries, including their religious faiths, in their entirety and to transform them for its own use. In the Japanese tradition, the components of the universe contain in themselves the very nature of the gods that inhabit it; its spiritual and material aspects are therefore not separate, and as there is no dichotomy between human beings and the natural world cultural concepts take a different form in Japan. This unique relationship with nature reached a crucial turning point when the policy of isolation from continental Asia, introduced in 894, meant that cultural treasures absorbed through relations with China and Korea were intensively revised in the light of native traditions. *The Tale of Genji* (*Genji monogatari*) by Murasaki Shikibu, a towering classic of world literature, is one of the fruits of this new movement.

It could be said that Murasaki did for the Japanese language what Dante did for the Italian vernacular, in that she 'showed what it could do'. Japanese was to Chinese as Italian was to Latin and, while Murasaki's work had some great native predecessors, *The Tale of Genji* remains the foundation stone of Japanese fiction, and a constant point of reference throughout the country's literature. Many people, including great writers such as Tanizaki, have tried to render it in modern language, and have been profoundly influenced by it. Murasaki's study of her characters' psychology is incredibly rich and complex – the Western novel had to wait for Proust and *In Search of Lost Time* before it produced so deep an exploration of the human soul.

The plot revolves round the figure of the aristocratic Prince Genji, his love affairs, his achievements in politics, high society, literature, architecture and painting, and the cost of the sufferings, misunderstandings, jealousies, envy and betrayals that the author believes she must make him endure so that he may embody the 'Shining Prince' – the ideal human being in the highly sophisticated cultural circles of the imperial capital at the turn of the first millennium: Heian-kyō, present-day Kyoto.

Around the year 1000, there developed in the city an exclusive culture that was a perfect combination of more speculative Sino-Indian Buddhist ideas and the Shintō concept of nature. Kyoto, founded in 794, and the capital of Japan for over a thousand years, became the epitome of beauty and refinement, and remained so for centuries, even during the worst of economic times. To live there during the Fujiwara period (so called after the family who held power – formally, at least – from 894 to 1185) was to be steeped in civilization and culture, just as to live far from it meant being sunk in barbarism. Life in Kyoto could be described as 'celebratory', in that every act was ritualized, not in the religious sense but in the sense that life itself became a work of art. By the ninth century the Fujiwara had established firm control over the emperors, who withdrew into private life; but they maintained courts and so did their consorts. Kyoto thus became a city with many courts that competed with one another in terms not of wealth but of culture and elegance. Literature is full of passages describing the anguish of people forced to leave the capital, and so lose contact with the network of human relations that was for them true culture and the only reason for living.

Descriptions of palaces and gardens create a picture of an architecture based on wood, with few and very lightweight masonry walls – one that was open, light, almost aerial. Nature with its rhythms and the passing of the seasons could come and go freely; people had no need to try (or be able) to retain within solid walls the advantages of one season during the passage of another. Pavilions, residences, palaces and walkways seem to have been constructed so as to increase the feeling of harmony between human beings and nature. Indeed, buildings and gardens were designed with the aim of enhancing such a relationship, and of creating interior and exterior environments that would allow each season to be appreciated in its own right. Many works written by women around the millennium depict this human world, and they are an inexhaustible source of cultural information. The most complex, but also the richest from the documentary point of view, is *The Tale of Genji* itself. As Genji sees it, everyone is distinguished by a bond with one season of the year in particular:

'And when all these weighty matters are off my hands,' said Genji at last, 'I hope I shall have a little time left for things which I really enjoy – flowers, autumn leaves, the sky, all those day-to-day changes and wonders that a single year brings forth; that is what I look forward to. Forests of flowering trees in spring, the open country in autumn … Which do you prefer? It is of course useless to argue on such a subject, as has so often been done. It is a question of temperament. Each person is born with "his season" and is bound to prefer it. No one, you may be sure, has ever yet succeeded in convincing anyone else on such a subject.'[1]

A similar study of the relationship between the self and the natural world is likely to trace assonances that reveal profound aspects of a person's nature, as described by Murasaki Shikibu:

1   Murasaki Shikibu, *The Tale of Genji*, Modern Library, New York, 1960, p. 380.

By this time the snow was lying very deep, and it was still falling, though now very lightly. So far from obliterating the shapes of pine-tree and bamboo, the heavy covering of snow seemed only to accentuate their varying forms, which stood out with strange distinctness in the evening light. 'We decided the other day,' said Genji to Murasaki, 'that Lady Akikonomu's season is autumn and yours spring. This evening I am more sure than ever that mine is winter. What could be more lovely than a winter night such as this, when the moon shines out of a cloudless sky upon the glittering, fresh-fallen snow? Beauty without colour seems somehow to belong to another world. At any rate, I find such a scene as this infinitely more lovely and moving than any other in the whole year. How little do I agree with the proverb that calls the moon in winter a dismal sight!' So saying he raised the window-blind, and they looked out. The moon was now fully risen, covering the whole garden with its steady, even light. The withered flower-beds showed, in these cold rays, with painful clearness the ravages of wind and frost. And look, the river was half-choked with ice, while the pond, frozen all over, was unutterably strange and lonesome under its coat of snow.[2]

There is assonance and resonance between human beings and nature, but it also appears from *The Tale of Genji* that the art of landscape design was very advanced, always in the way it fostered harmony in man's affective relationship with nature:

At the foot of this slope the lake curved with especial beauty, and in the foreground, just beneath the windows, he planted borders of cinquefoil, of red-plum, cherry, wistaria, kerria, rock-azalea, and other such plants as are at their best in spring-time; for he knew that Murasaki was in especial a lover of the spring; ... Akikonomu's garden was full of such trees as in autumn-time turn to the deepest hue. The stream above the waterfall was cleared out and deepened to a considerable distance; and that the noise of the cascade might carry further, he set great boulders in mid-stream, against which the current crashed and broke.[3]

And, again, Murasaki makes Genji himself remark:

[...] even within the narrow compass of my own walls, I might well have learnt what sights and sounds distinguish each season of the year, having as you see not only provided for the springtime by a profusion of flowering trees, but also planted in my garden many varieties of autumn grass and shrub, brought in, root

2   Ibid., p. 395.

3   Ibid., p. 430.

and all, from the countryside. Why, I have even carried hither whole tribes of insects that were wasting their shrill song in the solitude of lanes and fields. All this I did that I might be able to enjoy these things in the company of my friends, among whom you are one.[4]

The novel's fifty-four chapters were illustrated for the first time a century later in that great work of art, the *Genji monogatari emaki*, a series of perhaps ten horizontal scrolls, which were taken apart in the seventeenth century in order better to preserve them. The fragments that survive cover only twenty chapters, and are put on display every ten years in the two museums that own them: the Gotō Museum in Tokyo, and the Tokugawa Museum in Nagoya which holds the majority. The scenes, of which there were probably between one and three for each chapter, were separated by sections of the text written in an elegant script; calligraphy and illustration are by different hands.

The sense of the seasons passing with the direct, physical participation of human beings in their changes, and an architecture that was expressly devised to underline this communion, ultimately emphasize the ephemeral nature of reality and the mutability of everything that surrounds the characters. This sense of the transitoriness of things, and therefore of the impermanence of the human condition, is certainly of Buddhist origin, but in contrast with other Asian cultures where Buddhism also triumphed in the fields of art and architecture, though using more durable materials, in Japan (and this was due to the country's highly individual approach to nature), the Buddhist sense of transitoriness was heightened and extended as nowhere else. The *Genji* scrolls used a special technique, 'blown-off roof',[5] which further enhances the relationship between human beings, nature and architecture.

The text runs in flowing script on paper whose texture, achieved by including pieces of gold and silver leaf, gold and silver dust, protuberances and depressions, and varying hues and tints, gives visual emphasis to the subject and the psychological situation described in a particular section. That this work is the product of more than one hand can be seen, for example, in the different ways in which the white pigments have oxidized over time, indicating that the colour was prepared by different artists, using different methods. Current scholarship is inclined to attribute the scrolls to women, thus confirming that in that epoch they played a significant part in the visual arts. The faces in the illustrations, which are identical and stereotyped, reveal the characters' psychological impulses solely through the relationship established between the forms of their bodies and the environment and architecture that surround them.

4 Ibid., pp. 380–1.

5 Miyeko Murase, *Iconography of the Tale of Genji*, Weatherhill, New York, 1983, p. 12.

In the surviving section of the fortieth chapter, 'The Law' ('Minori'), now in the Gotō Museum, Genji appears seated opposite Murasaki. She is the woman with whom he has been most closely connected throughout his life, and whom he has brought up and educated since she was a small child, caring for her in a thousand ways and making her his life's chosen companion, his safe refuge in times of private and public turmoil or the sweet accompaniment to his own song of joy at moments of the greatest beauty. The two figures are placed between the transverse lines that create the structure of the interior in which the scene takes place. The space appears to be steeply and dramatically inclined, and across the whole painting the mats on the floor, like the horizontal beams, form a sort of corridor that seems to start from an unknown point in the upper right-hand corner and dip towards another in the lower left. The space of the room is also marked by the vertical lines of the pillars and the bands that decorate the characters' 'screens of state' – lines that make more insistent the clearly perceptible rhythm with which the whole episode comes to a head. Murasaki is dying; ravaged by a mysterious sickness, her body appears to be in the process of becoming dematerialized. The two characters are sitting on the same mat. Genji, below, is bent over under the weight of the grief that makes even heavier his already imposing physical mass; Murasaki, above, is weightless, like a butterfly about to separate itself from the trail of scent that had bound it to the earth. Her sorrow, expressed in the way she is drying her tears with her sleeve, is connected with the thought that Genji will be left alone. And while his words and those of the Empress Akashi, Murasaki's adopted daughter, who can just be seen behind a pillar, reveal their strong attachment to the dying woman, Murasaki's reply reflects the Buddhist consciousness of another world that may alleviate the pain of separation, and of the ineluctable transitoriness of things:

> 'So briefly rests the dew upon the hagi.
> Even now it scatters in the wind.'

> It would have been a sad evening in any event, and the plight of the dew even now being shaken from the tossing branches, thought Genji, must seem to the sick lady very much like her own.[6]

Outside in the garden the season is now almost wintery. Few leaves still cling to the long, creeping branches of shrubs indicated by a few brown lines against the silver, almost moonlit background; the wind bends and shakes

6   Murasaki Shikibu, *The Tale of Genji*, Harmondsworth, Penguin Books, 1981, p. 717.

them, but gently, almost delicately. Nature is pensive, turned in on itself, echoing the feelings of those present and, above all, the suffering of Genji, perfectly framed in the architectural structure of the palace: interior and exterior architectures alike bring out clearly the state of transitoriness and impermanence contained in the scene and the story as a whole.

These literary and pictorial examples give a sense of the efforts made throughout the centuries by aesthetes and those engaged in the arts – architects, painters, playwrights and tea-masters – to pursue the interpenetration of the human and the natural environment. A house should not be a barrier isolating human beings' space from that of nature, from whose invasion they are to be protected (and neither should a park, the exterior image of the perfect geometry of the palace, like a garden in the Italian style). Rather, the traditional Japanese house is a shelter, a place of solace and reflection, into which is brought a distillation of the feelings and emotions that flow from the relationship with nature. This relationship is continued within the house, which thus has an open, organic structure, following the contours of the ground on which it is built: an approach that was established in the West only with Frank Lloyd Wright and his theory of organic architecture.

Genji scrolls (*emaki*), ink and
colour on paper, 12th century:
left, 'Bell Cricket'
('Suzumushi') chapter; right,
'Law' ('Minori') chapter

Left:
Large Veranda and Moon-viewing Platform, Katsura Imperial Villa, Kyoto, 17th century, photograph by Matsumura Yoshiharu

Right:
The eastern entrance to the Large Veranda, Katsura Imperial Villa, Kyoto, 17th century, photograph by Matsumura Yoshiharu

Overleaf:
Kuma Kengo
Great (Bamboo) Wall guesthouse, Beijing, 2002, photograph by Asakawa Satoshi

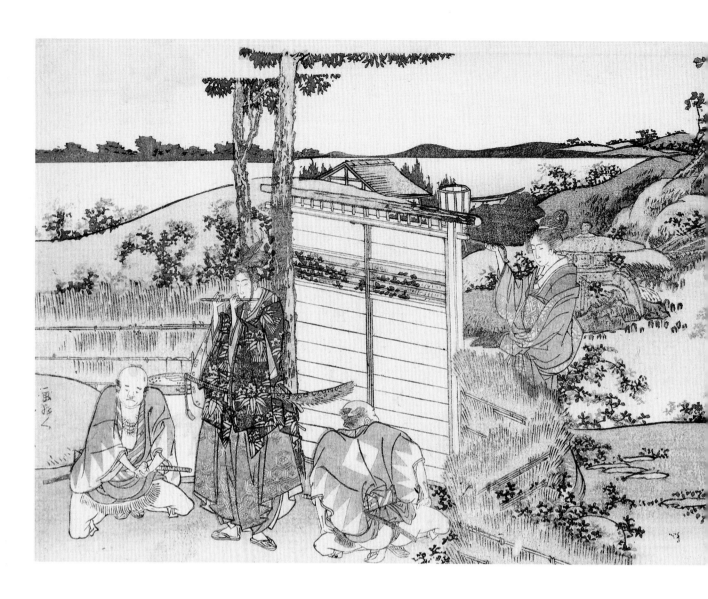

Katsushika Hokusai
Ushiwakamaru and Jōrurihime,
colour woodblock print, c. 1805

Overleaf:
Great Map of Kyoto in Detail,
colour on paper, 1714–21

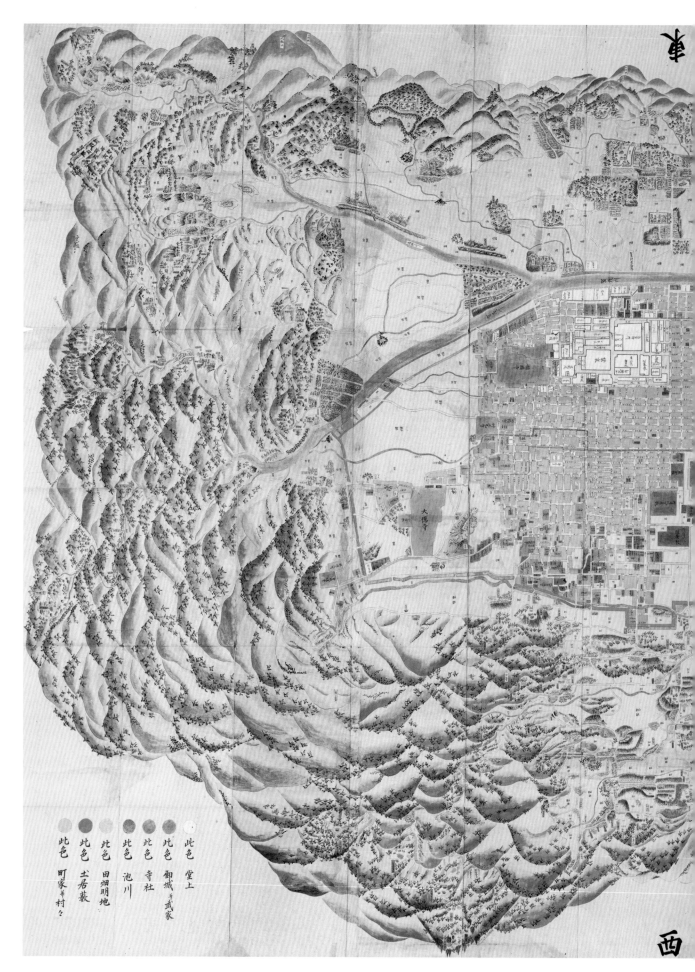

北

西

大德寺

此色　堂上
此色　御城并武家
此色　寺社
此色　池川
此色　田畑明地
此色　土居藪
此色　町家并村々

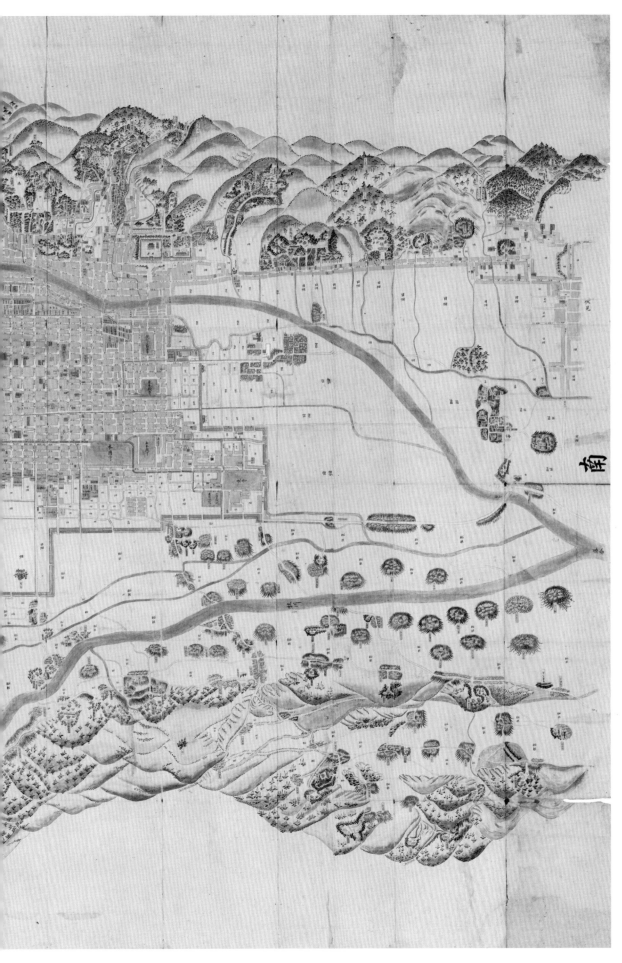

Left:
Ceremonial Ainu robe (*attush*),
hand-woven elmbark fibre,
c. 1850–1900

Right:
Workman's coat (*kawabaori*),
deerskin, 19th century

Previous pages:
Andō Tadao
Water Temple, Awaji Island,
1991, photograph by Richard
Pare

Kuramata Shirō
Miss Blanche chair, acrylic,
aluminium and artificial
flowers, 1988, photograph by
Mori Hiroyuki

The Dragon in Tranquillity

The spread of Zen Buddhism after its introduction to Japan brought an expansion of the spiritual domain, and had a powerful influence on both lifestyles and art forms. Zen (whose name is derived from the Sanskrit word for meditation, *dhyāna*, via the Chinese word *chan*) seeks out and strengthens the relationship with a person's inner world, and pursues it by opposing all forms of dogmatism, whether intellectual or spiritual. In art, great importance is attributed to empty space, a metaphor for the silence that is required if the inner vision is to appear. Buddha-nature cannot manifest itself, nor can the state of being spiritually awake be achieved, if the individual's inner space is cluttered with other things and their mind is teeming with thoughts. In painting, emptiness and mist are often synonymous with this state of openness, of inner listening, the manifestation of Buddha-nature, wakefulness. These qualities may be appreciated by studying specific paintings, for example, *Pines in the Mist* by Hasegawa Tōhaku (1539–1610).

From the misty background of two large six-panel screens measuring 7 by 1.5 metres (23 by 5 feet) there emerge four groups of pine trees, painted in ink in various shades of black and grey. They are mysterious and evocative presences, whose reality manifests itself and at the same time seems to lose its materiality through skilful use of allusion and description, thanks to the very specific role played by mist and emptiness – space that is kept aside. The subject of the painting is the pines themselves, divorced from any surrounding landscape, although in the upper part of the first panel of the second screen (Japanese works are read from right to left) the sketchy, tenuous outline of a mountain can be glimpsed (or just made out). The clouds that shroud everything thus serve to strip every other element of importance, turning the painting into a kind of portrait of the tall trees.

The work's point of departure is a black pine, its trunk bent from years of battling the elements, which springs from the bottom right-hand corner of the first screen. Its powerful personality is underlined by an image, a lighter and more diaphanous reflection, that it seems to create behind itself as if it was reflected in the mist, or even as if this second image was actually its soul or a kind of psychic aura. The movement of these two trees, as if they were stretching leftwards with open arms, towards the empty space in the next two panels is echoed by another tree in the background of the central group. This one, light in both colour and form, seems to be answering their call as it bends towards the right and repeats the movement of a third tree in the first group; this too is in the background, moving in the opposite direction from the black pine and its reflection and thus restoring balance to the overall image.

By contrast, the pines in the three panels on the left are erect and powerful. The foliage of two of them is painted in thick, dark ink, using densely crowded brush strokes over a structure of trunks and branches depicted in lighter, thinner tones. The brush strokes are cut off bluntly at their ends, but the abruptly interrupted strokes are continued using the tip of the brush, creating a series of long, narrow rings in the form of a tight spiral that gives the individual strokes resumed in this way (the separate bunches of needles and the crowns of the trees) a strong upward movement. Here again, in the background other trees emerge from the mist, painted in thinner ink: presences that are more diaphanous but no less real and visible than the two most prominent pines, and which support and enhance their vigour.

The left-hand screen, although made using the same technique and in the same form, expresses a different mood; it is more delicate, and the view is not interrupted even though it contains broad expanses of mist. The feeling of continuity and of greater gentleness is created by an imaginary line that runs from top right to bottom left. It starts from the hint of a mountain in the distance and descends gradually (the ink becoming thicker as it goes), bringing the trees closer to the observer. As with a later double screen by Maruyama Ōkyo (1733–95), entitled *Pines in the Snow*, the clear impression is that the artist intended to give one screen a masculine personality and the other a feminine one.

Pines in the Mist is one of the most famous and important Japanese paintings; it contains the quintessence of the aesthetics of Zen and of the tea ceremony, but it also represents an entirely new, even revolutionary way of conceptualizing the relationship with nature and expressing it in painting. Tōhaku created it as a mature man; at that period of his life his major works were monochrome, and in this he was associated with the great Chinese landscape tradition of the Song dynasty and with that of Sesshū. His predilection for monochrome, his ability to reinterpret the work of his early predecessors, both Chinese and Japanese, and his undeniable genius for reworking all these elements into a highly personal vision of man and nature brought him close to the worlds of Zen and the tea aesthetic. Many of his paintings, screens and sliding panels were executed for detached pavilions in the important and influential Daitoku temple. Another eminent cultural figure of the time, the great tea-master Sen Rikyū (1520–91; see p. 19 above), was very close to Tōhaku, who painted his posthumous portrait in 1593 when he was rehabilitated after Toyotomi Hideyoshi (1537–98) had forced him to commit suicide.

Suzuki, the greatest Zen scholar of the twentieth century, says of this genre of painting:

Very likely, the most characteristic thing in the temperament of the Eastern people is the ability to grasp life from within and not from without. And Zen has just struck it.[1]

This is the realm of the indefinite and of harmony between empty and occupied spaces; spaces that are not in conflict, but enhance one another. This is seen in the famous Ginkaku-ji, the Silver Pavilion in the celebrated residence at Higashiyama of Yoshimasa (1436–90), the eighth Ashikaga shōgun and grandson of Yoshimitsu (1358–1408).

With its garden attributed to Sōami, who lived between 1455 (?) and 1526 and was also the curator of the shōgun's collection of Chinese paintings from 1485, the Silver Pavilion is considered the quintessence of the refined, elegant and highly cultivated aesthetic environment created by Yoshimasa and his court in the imperial capital, Kyoto, during a time of war, social upheaval and terrible economic crisis. The pavilion fits perfectly into its natural setting. The small, simple structure shows Chinese influence in its upper storey, which was designed for worship, but the lower one is in the Japanese style: a place in which to receive friends and drink green tea while contemplating the luxuriance of nature, writing poems or discoursing on precious ceramic *tenmoku*. Approached diagonally, its structure recalls Suzuki's remarks on asymmetry and its aesthetic significance. Looking at the little building's external walls, the eye is attracted, drawn in even, by the empty space that is created at a certain point, a dramatic hiatus that produces a sense of disequilibrium in the structure itself. But it is this very disequilibrium that adds energy and creates new and stimulating aesthetic relationships.

Where you would ordinarily expect a line or a mass or a balancing element, you miss it, and yet this very thing awakens in you an unexpected feeling of pleasure. In spite of shortcomings or deficiencies that no doubt are apparent, you do not feel them so; indeed, this imperfection itself becomes a form of perfection. Evidently, beauty does not necessarily spell perfection of form. This has been one of the favourite tricks of Japanese artists – to embody beauty in a form of imperfection or even of ugliness.[2]

With the coming of Zen a particular type of garden developed, designed to provoke not the contemplation of nature as it surrounds man, but of nature within man himself. It is a device whose effect is analogous to that of mist and empty space in painting.

1   Daisetz T. Suzuki, *Zen and Japanese Culture*, Bollingen Series, New York, 1959, p. 24.

2   Ibid.

The most famous of these asymmetrical gardens in the Zen tradition is the Ryōan-ji in Kyoto. It looks like an expanse of white gravel, finely raked into straight lines, with random groups of grey rocks appearing, round which the same lines form concentric circles. Its iconography has been interpreted in countless ways: rocks rising out of the sea, for example, or high peaks piercing the clouds. All the interpretations are interesting, but none is more convincing than another. However, in all of them the rocks are seen as symbols of whatever can free itself by rising above the contingent and above its own contradictions. The nakedness of the stone is accentuated by small clumps of moss and lichens that seem to have been placed as if to testify to an earthly life in an ambience that is suspended, abstract, almost lunar, as the rocks emerge abruptly from the white surface in which they are set. They have even been compared with islands floating on a sea of dreams.

Very little is known about the origins of this wonderful garden, and even what is known verges on myth. The Ryōan-ji has been dated to both the sixteenth and the seventeenth centuries, and there are many divergent theories as to who created a work whose perfection is almost superhuman. It has often been associated with Sōami, the great painter and aesthete, arbiter of art and style in early sixteenth-century Kyoto. So let us try to imagine its creation, on the borderlines of myth and imagination.

Picture Sōami at the Ryōan temple – his custom whenever he felt it necessary to remove himself from the pressures of the Ashikaga court. This great family, then at the apex of the political hierarchy (while the function of government was in steep decline), brought together a cultural sophistication and a refined lifestyle that are without equal. In his roles as curator of Yoshimasa's art collection, as well as painter and master of the tea ceremony, Sōami was exhausted by the constant requests of his lord, the shōgun. Withdrawal to Ryōan-ji meant a restorative plunge into interiority, the rediscovery of the very meaning of life, of cultural and family tradition, and of the spiritual inheritance passed down to him by his father and master Geiami (1431–85), and by his grandfather, the great poet and painter Nōami (1397–1471).

On this early spring morning of the year 1520 a ceaseless flow of thoughts and emotions was distracting him from his studies. Sitting on the veranda outside the monks' quarters, facing a messy, uncultivated patch of ground, he could not empty his mind of passions he believed were dulled for ever; he was his country's greatest art critic, nobody challenged his authority with the shōgun, the ruler of Japan, nobody excelled him in garden design; and in his monochrome painting he was establishing everywhere a new aesthetic, softer, more evocative, which might have led to a more effective understanding and expression of the inner reality of things, to the truth that lies behind the mists of appearance. It was a reality that had cost him much torment to achieve, and which Mu Qi (1200?–70?), the great thirteenth-century Chinese master from whom he drew inspiration, could make appear and disappear with calm simplicity.

Simplicity! There, at last, was the key. To let a wall of warm, vital energy block the barren and mechanical energy of unchecked thoughts (the scored lines that cross the mind and soul). To lay down a layer of white in order to dissolve the tumult of emotions in the silence of its impersonality. Perhaps that is how, emerging from the infinite white calm, the most profound truths of existence appeared to him: firm and solid, like peaks rising out of an ocean of clouds, like indestructible rocks in a sea of passions quietened by the power of inner calm. Perhaps it came about that on that early spring morning, Sōami opened his eyes like a man born to a new life of the spirit and of nature: the answer to his nagging cares was so simple, natural and close at hand. But the process of attaining it had become a vision, and the vision became art: the garden of the Ryōan-ji or the temple of the 'Dragon in Tranquillity'.

Previous page:
The Sumiyoshi Pine, Katsura
Imperial Villa, Kyoto, 17th
century, photograph by
Matsumura Yoshiharu

Hasegawa Tōhaku
Pines in the Mist (two six-
panel screens), ink on paper,
end of the 16th century

Maruyama Ōkyo
Pines in the Snow (two six-panel screens), ink, colour and gold on paper, late 18th century

Zen garden at Ryōan temple,
Kyoto, 16th century

Nature's Magnificence

Like so many other media through which traditional Japanese culture is expressed, architecture is the vehicle for a more intense relationship with nature and, for this reason, a dwelling cannot be a barrier between human beings and nature, but is a refuge, a kind of screen or filter. Involvement in the seasons, the quivering pulse of nature itself and its changing aspects, becomes more natural, more direct, more channelled and more harmonious. Japanese buildings therefore follow their natural environment, the contours of the terrain; they do not act on it or change it in order to bend it to their own geometrical structure.

Architecture is often part of an ensemble that includes water, trees and the contours of the site, and this applies equally to the overall structure and its internal features. A house changes throughout the year, increasing or modifying what can be seen outside; its external and internal walls slide, opening and closing, so that from one season to another they frame the spaces of the surrounding environment in a different way, or create particular images of it through the use of scenes depicted on the internal walls and changed according to the time of year. In other words, the house is taken into the natural world, and nature is brought inside the house. It was by drawing on ideas like these that Frank Lloyd Wright was able to carry out his 'organicist' revolution in modern architecture. The imperial villa at Katsura, near Kyoto, completed in 1620, is a building whose purity of style exercised an incalculable influence over pioneers of contemporary architecture from Frank Lloyd Wright to Walter Gropius, Bruno Taut, Le Corbusier, Mies van der Rohe and Richard Neutra. The sight of its white sliding panels (*shōji*) probably also influenced the painter Piet Mondrian.

The Western concept of the facade is entirely absent in Katsura, while what is clearly visible is the way the forms of the structure flow and evolve, just as the ground rolls away towards the trees. Every feature – its sober style, its movement following the contours of the site on which it stands, its panels (both wall and window) that open on to the garden – is a way of bringing in the outside environment, like a living painting. When the sliding panels are opened new spaces are created, facing outwards, framing the surrounding landscape in different ways, and offering anyone inside the opportunity to enjoy as intensely as they wish the spectacle of nature: the massed vibrant colours of azaleas in late spring, the red of maples against the dark green of conifers in autumn, the white mantle of snow in winter that muffles sounds and senses, and at the same time makes them sharper. At the point most directly overlooking the lake, a terrace has been built from which to contemplate the autumn full moon, and the link with *The Tale of Genji* (*Genji monogatari*) suddenly becomes apparent. Like Genji, the hereditary prince Toshi-hito (1579–1629), for whom Katsura was built, must have had a vivid perception of snow and the beauty of the forms it highlights, removing details and revealing their essential structure, as first described by Murasaki in her work.

The practice of bringing nature into houses, palaces, residences and the reception rooms of temples (not only by opening the *shōji*, but also by representing nature pictorially on walls, sliding panels, and screens) assumed a special form from the second half of the sixteenth century. It was the time of the great lords, the *daimyō*, who were always in conflict among themselves, competing first militarily and then in the splendour of their way of life. Painting, and the view of nature it portrayed, changed radically to reflect their power and this splendour. The development was the result of a new conception of painting, in which traditional Chinese linear concepts fused with the Japanese use of colour. And it is very likely that the means of expressing a 'Japanese' sense of nature within the parameters of Chinese monochrome linear conventions came from Kanō Motonobu (1476–1559), who initiated the style by assimilating the *yamato-e* techniques of painting from the Tosa, the guardians of national tradition. It is thought, in fact, that he married the daughter of Tosa Mitsunobu (1434–1525), and was thus able to learn secrets jealously guarded in the narrow circles of imperial academic art. His twofold approach seems to have enabled him to create a new style that combined the strong compositional structure of Chinese painting with the rich colours of its traditional Japanese counterpart.

Kanō Eitoku (1543–90) was the originator of a new, striking way of decorating internal partitions, using rich gold backgrounds painted in vivid colours, combined with the heavy use of lines drawn in ink. His sumptuous style was the basis for the Kanō school's dazzling success and found favour with members of the military elite, who began to turn to him whenever an important building was constructed. In their work, Eitoku and the other members of the Kanō family depicted, and made widely familiar, images of their feudal lords, the *daimyō*. As well as painting their portraits, they represented them as stately eagles ready to swoop on their prey, or as tigers and leopards terrorizing the countryside. The *daimyō* identified themselves with these powerful creatures and felt that their own strength and magnificence was enhanced. This glorious conception of the natural world underlined the magnificence of the owners of the castles and palaces of the day, and painters captured (beyond individual behaviour that was often terrifying) a sense of their energy and vitality, expressing it in opulent, vibrant images.

This is an approach to painting that finds its perfect expression in a screen that shows a white eagle perched on a large, black, five-needled pine tree jutting out over a ravine depicted in lapis-lazuli blue. The bird is on the point of swooping on its prey, and the whole scene takes place against a brilliant, luminous background of gold leaf – the kind used to cover statues of the Buddha or *bodhisattvas*. Gold backgrounds increase the symbolic significance of the figures represented, and instead of disappearing, as they would against a more realistic background, the images stand out like jewels mounted in the precious, uniform colour.

The Kanō school was so successful that the quality of its art declined; because its works were in such demand there was a kind of general inflation, and this great style of painting, which had introduced a new way of understanding nature and presenting powerful and evocative images of it, eventually became repetitive and stereotyped. Yet it was from this tradition that a new approach to seeing and painting nature emerged. Purer, and at the same time adhering more closely to the national tradition, it preserves the richness of colour already achieved, and the grandeur of composition, but rejects the 'nerve structure' of outlines in ink and the concept of painting with 'bones', for a softer, curvilinear approach which has an ancient, southern, 'boneless' feel. In a way it is as though the ascendancy of the Kanō school had led to a reinterpretation of the *yamato-e* approach, which the Tosa were keeping alive even if they sometimes lacked creative vitality. In the seventeenth and eighteenth centuries, this tradition was passed on to two important movements in the revival of *yamato-e*. One was led by Tawaraya Sōtatsu (?–1643?) and the Rinpa school; the other was *ukiyo-e*, the art of the floating world.

Rinpa painting grew out of the meeting between a cultivated aesthete, ceramicist, calligrapher and talent-spotter, Hon'ami Kōetsu (1558–1637), founder of a school of fine craftsmanship, an art and design community *avant la lettre*, in the village of Takagamine, north-east of Kyoto, and a young painter and maker and decorator of fans, Tawaraya Sōtatsu. Sōtatsu created a new style in which the use of monochrome ink disappeared almost completely, giving way to a technique of pictorial composition using areas of flat, dense colour that was especially effective on the large surfaces of screens and wall panels. It was well received in the cultured circles of temples and their abbots, as well as in the homes of wealthy merchants, and was applied to scrolls and fans, as well as to large screens. At an earlier stage the images were executed in a single colour, with pure lines, sometimes in gold or silver, that blended with Kōetsu's elegant script, as in the famous *Deer Scroll*, in which the animals seem to be dancing in the air to the sound of the calligraphy, which falls from above like musical notes.

The lines that depict the deer are painted in gold; a female turns away, indifferent to the male's display as he makes himself beautiful and important in the mating dance he performs for her. The poem praises the wind in autumn (for deer, the season of love) and the beauty of the colours at this time of the year. The delicacy of the design, the sophisticated use of colours and the ability to embellish them with the subtle use of gold and *gofun* together created a visually ravishing rendering of nature, as Sōtatsu, having freed himself from dependence on Kōetsu, started to work on his own account while maintaining his connection with his old friend. The result was paintings such as the famous pair of screens, at that time in the Shōun temple at Sakai and now in the Freer Gallery of Art in Washington, traditionally called *Matsushima* (lit. *Islands with Pines*). The bay of Matsushima, like Ama no Hashidate and Miyajima (the three most scenic places of Japan's coast), is one of Japan's most celebrated landscapes: 300 kilometres (186 miles) north of Tokyo, it is studded with small, fantastically shaped islands topped by venerable pines bent and shaped in extraordinary ways by the force of the wind and the elements. Sōtatsu has shown them set in a foaming sea, but one whose waves are carefully dressed, like hair, into locks and partings rendered in white, silver and gold. The effect of the waves – both the more turbulent ones on the left-hand screen and the tamer, less foaming ones on the right – is to stylize and formalize the movement in forms that are solid, flat and two-dimensional, but, at the same time, are never static. The other elements give the same impression: the rocks rising out of the water, the twisted pines, the clouds in the sky. A kind of idealization of nature and its power is created, making the painting iconic and thus highly symbolic.

The cloud edged in dark purple, and contrasting with the other colours, resembles a storm cloud silhouetted against the light and moving rapidly across the sky blown by gusts of wind. *Tarashikomi*, a technique that involves applying one wet colour on another, was popularized by Sōtatsu and can be seen in the purple outlines of the areas of golden mist, perhaps indicating a line of shadow against the brightness of the sun which is shining on the rest of the scene. The central area is darker than the other parts of the landscape, since it is seen from below with the sun behind it. But, in fact, the view of the two screens is a kind of *kunimi*, a 'bird's-eye view'. Sōtatsu, then, has provided a double viewpoint for the observer, who seems at one and the same time to contemplate from two opposite points the scene that is depicted. This device was taken up by later painters, such as Ogata Kōrin (1658–1716) in the screen entitled *White Plum and*

Red Plum, Katsushika Hokusai (1760–1849) in his famous print *Amida Waterfall* and, much later, by Picasso in his Cubist period.

In *Islands with Pines* there is thus a movement towards contemplation of nature, but in the sense of idealizing the natural world, which uses the spareness of economical and utterly revolutionary forms as another way of rendering its vision of an unearthly and highly spiritual beauty. There come to mind the lines of the great poet Bashō who, on seeing the bay of Matsushima, and writing a haiku that would express the emotions it inspired, could but exclaim:

Matsushima ya,	Oh, Matsushima,
Aa, Matsushima ya,	Oh, Matsushima, Ah
Matsushima ya	Oh, Matsushima!

Sōtatsu's teachings were collected and developed by Kōrin, who, although born after the master's death, considered himself his spiritual heir – so much so that he became the central figure of the movement in painting later called Rinpa, or 'school of Rin'. While it was held to descend from Sōtatsu himself, it took its name from Kōrin. In Kōrin's work nature is interpreted by combining a very spare, abstract design with convincing representation that comes from close observation of detail and colour. More specifically, and especially in his mature style, Kōrin succeeded in matching Sōtatsu's use of colour with Kanō's powerful sense of composition. This combination produced paintings whose chromatic richness is accompanied by expressive design and composition, creating pictorial grandeur as well as visual evocativeness.

White Plum and Red Plum, a pair of two-panel screens now in the MOA Museum in Atami, is considered his masterpiece and is a happy example of this. Here the forms of two old, twisted trees on opposite banks of a river, the treatment of their clouds of differently coloured blossoms whose reflection is refracted in the water, and the abstract design of the current rendered in precious, stylized spirals of gold and silver (in contrast with the naturalism of the trees, enhanced by the rich *tarashikomi* work depicting the mosses, lichens and moulds on their trunks), all have a flawless formal perfection.

The trunks of the trees appear to emerge very distinctly from two clouds or banks of stylized mist, which correspond with the banks between which the sinuous current flows. Rendered by a mass of blotches, the trunks have practically no outlines, but are perceived through juxtaposition with the flatly applied gold of the clouds or banks of the river in the background, which is not painted but is covered in squares of gold leaf.

A close look at them shows that the application of wet colour on wet creates a line between inner and outer patches, which produces an outline that is not so much blurred as imprecise. In other places, the artist achieves the same result by dripping colour on to spots of ink. This creates a rough, grainy edge, and gives great vitality to the trees, whose bark (which might otherwise appear flat and stiff) is instead made up of patches of moss and lichens, swellings and depressions, which give them solidity, movement and vitality. In order to give a greater impression of an outline, and to increase the sense of contrast, the artist has used *gofun*, which helps to create an even greater impression of solidity.

In his treatment of the current and waves in relation to the two plum trees Kōrin has employed double perspective, a technique that would be used by Hokusai 150 years later. The trees are viewed frontally while the surface of the water is seen from a typically Western perspective, organized vertically with the foreground below and background above. A few spots create the impression that the bark on the trees, with its different tones, is reflected in the water, while eddies of current break up and fragment the reflection of the trees.

As they lean forward to form an imaginary, invisible bridge, their shapes reflected and repeated in the water, the image of the two trees, idealized and framed against the gold background and separated from the white and gold spirals of the precious river, is like that of tutelary deities protecting human beings on their journey along the river of life – which starts from an unseen point outside the frame and here, in the present moment, draws level with the plum trees and then flows on.

Tokonoma, Middle Shoin,
Katsura Imperial Villa, Kyoto,
17th century, photograph by
Matsumura Yoshiharu

Overleaf:
Tawaraya Sōtatsu,
Matsushima (two six-panel
screens), ink, colour and gold
leaf on paper, 17th century

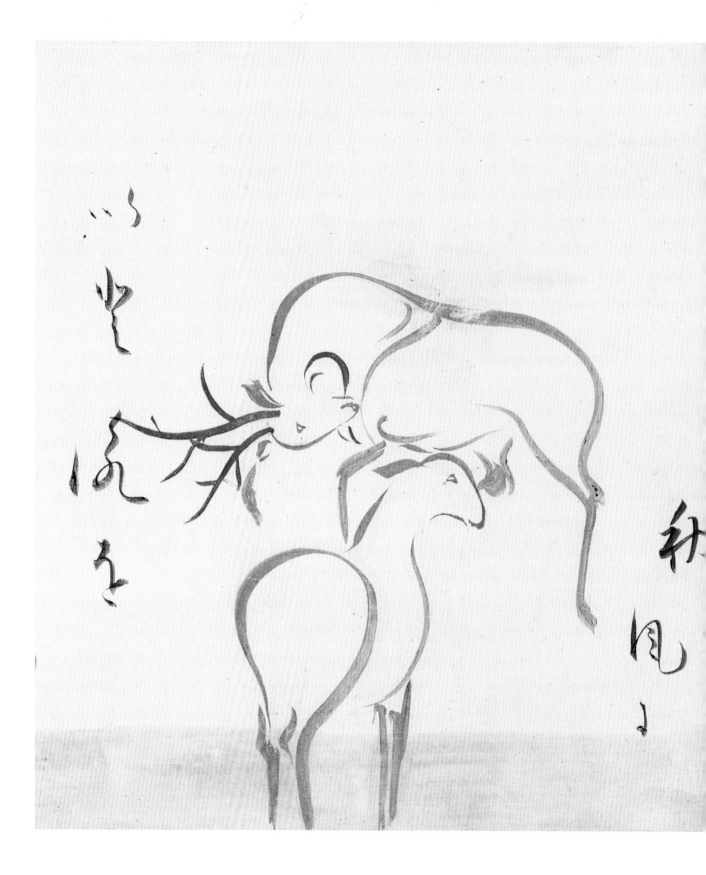

Tawaraya Sōtatsu and Hon'ami
Kōetsu
Deer Scroll, ink, gold and silver on
paper, 17th century

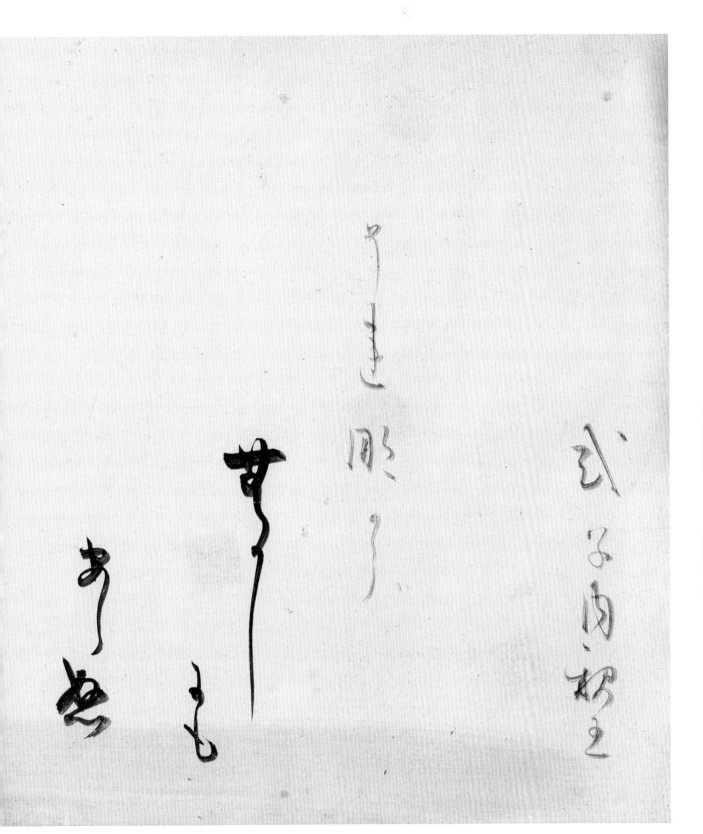

Ogata Kōrin
White Plum and Red Plum
(pair of two-fold screens),
colour and gold on paper,
18th century

Takeuchi Seihō
'Flowers in a Mountain Village',
from *Masterworks of Seihō*,
colour woodblock print, 1940

Nature and Beauty in the Floating World

Awa wa mata　　　　　Once again the foam,
urami mo asaki　　　　a pang of faint regret,
sakura kana　　　　　oh, the cherry blossom!

This short poem, a seventeen-syllable *haiku* which the girl in a famous woodcut by Ishikawa Toyonobu (1711–85) is attaching to a branch of cherry blossom, contains some of the central themes of Japanese aesthetics, especially in its relationship with the natural world.

There are subtle connections, and not only visual ones, between the dainty, graceful figure and the flowering branch of the old tree. It is around the year 1760, and the girl is on the Ueno hill, or else at Asakusa, two well-known spots in Edo, today's Tokyo. It is the third month of the lunar calendar and the cherry trees are in full bloom. A group of friends and relatives are making an excursion to admire the glorious sight. A curtain is hung between four trees, bearing the emblem of the kabuki actor Ichikawa Danzō III (1719–72), an *edokko no kami-sama*, a 'matinee idol' of the day. On the ground there is a platform on which people can sit, dance, play music, eat and, of course, enjoy the view and the just perceptible fragrance of the flowers in the soft, mild April air.

The *jeune fille en fleur*, who has slipped in front of the curtain, is stretching up to reach the highest possible point on which to hang the auspicious *tanzaku*, the small rectangular sheet of paper on which the poem is written. The outer layer of her kimono has a delicate design in patchwork brocade, in which diagonal geometric and naturalistic motifs contrast elegantly with one another. The bow in which the girl's *obi* is tied brushes against the old tree trunk, and her face, bright and suffused with a faint flush of pleasure, stands out, a flower among flowers, in the warm noonday air.

The picture, like the poem, expresses a sense of the ethereal evanescence of youth and beauty, which pass rapidly across the firmament of this life, like the clouds of cherry blossom, whose petals fly away on the breeze like sea spray or drops of foam on waves. In the poem there is also a veiled allusion that gives the 'pang of faint regret' a note of yearning that is more intense than mere awareness of the radiant, but always too brief, flowering. The first word, *awa*, does indeed mean 'foam', but as Pietro Silvio Rivetta has pointed out, its sound is very close to *awan*, the negative form of the verb *au*, 'to meet one another'.[1] It is not a true double meaning, because the words *awa* and *awan* are different, but is a very

1　Pier Silvio Rivetta, 'Bellezza e curiosità della lingua nipponica. IV Il fascino dell'inespresso', *Yamato* I (4) (April 1941).

delicate, subtly hinted reference to a meeting that is not taking place, or did not, or will not do so. Does the 'faint regret' refer to love, then? Perhaps, but not explicitly; it is barely whispered, confided as it is to the foam of the cherry blossom (*sakura*).

In this way poem and image take on a wealth of religious and philosophical, as well as aesthetic, allusions with implicit Buddhist references to the transitoriness of things, expressed in the juxtaposition of the girl's youth and the fleeting, ethereal blossoming of the old cherry tree. There is also a sense of a special relationship with nature, revealed in the girl's act of confiding her feelings, expressed so lyrically, to the tree, to which is ascribed a power that to Westerners would be 'supernatural' or, at least, 'extra-natural'. In other words, she treats the tree – old, gnarled, but nevertheless covered in blossoms – as if it were an old sage, or a benevolent deity to whom she can entrust her poetic invocation with the hope that it will be accepted.

Using techniques of detail and foreshortening (a distant echo of the art of southern China), the artist seems to have captured in an exquisitely structured composition an everyday moment which is nevertheless of great intensity. And yet the picture, full of complex cultural meanings and aesthetic values, is not a great painting; it is a simple woodblock print, a mass-produced, inexpensive object for everyday use, almost 'disposable', which by a stroke of luck has not been worn out with handling but has survived. And if an ordinary, widely available work like this contains so subtle a mixture of human sentiments and feelings for nature, expressed in ways that are delicate, allusive and entirely without the excess with which Western romanticism is prone to inflate things (human effort often obscures nature's spontaneity), we must recognize a profound cultural achievement: a tradition endowed with the maturity that enables harmonies of this sort to echo so coherently throughout a work of such scant commercial value and, on the face of it, such little social importance.

Beautiful women are, of course, one of the most frequent subjects of floating world prints and, as in the one described above, there are many examples in which nature plays a primary role, even acting in counterpoint with the human figures. One of the first artists to emphasize its influence in depicting women was Suzuki Harunobu (1725–70), the great master and pioneer of polychrome engraving, who turned them into something like earthly goddesses: deities in the literal sense, pictorially speaking, since he was the first to place the figure slightly higher up from the observer's point of view, a position traditionally reserved for deities.

Pictures like the one of a girl holding up a lantern at night contain all the allure of Harunobu's depictions of beautiful women, as well as the enchantment of the secret language of nature. The young woman is probably going clandestinely to meet her lover, and is in the garden, walking across a bridge or along a balcony leading to the gate where he is waiting. As she goes, the light from the lantern falls on the blossom of an old plum tree and she turns for a moment, rapt in contemplation. Everything is dark, apart from the froth of blossom, the girl herself, the bridge or balcony and the tree trunk. But the real subject of the scene is the light cast by the lantern. It is the lantern that casts light on this new event in the young woman's life that life itself is offering her. The lantern, which seems to be suspended in the blank, impenetrable blackness, creates a relationship between her fresh young face and the plum blossom, also fresh, but soon to fade. As she goes where the life force calls her, she stops to look at the budding flowers for a moment – a moment the artist has caught for ever in an image that is real and, at the same time, highly symbolic. Light makes a connection between the white of the blossom and the white of the face and the path, which is also the path of life that leads towards the impermanence of the affections, of beauty, youth and existence itself. In this way, the observer becomes more deeply aware that the consuming charm of youth and beauty, and of the affections, lies precisely in their transitoriness and in a person's power to exceed their limits every time, just like the first.

Previous page:
Eishōsai Chōki
*A Beauty at Dawn on New
Year's Day*, colour woodblock
print, 1794–5

Girl in kimono, from *Faces*,
1980s, photograph by Araki
Nobuyoshi

Left:
Suzuki Harunobu
Girl Admiring Plum Tree
Blossoms at Night, colour
woodblock print, 1766

Right:
Ishikawa Toyonobu
Girl Tying Verse to a Cherry
Branch, colour woodblock
print, c. 1760

Previous pages:
Kitagawa Utamaro
Pleasure of the Four Seasons,
Colours and Scents of Flowers,
colour woodblock print, c.
1783

Kobayashi Kokei
The Hot Spring, watercolour
on silk, 1918

Interlude: Eating with the Eyes

In Japan the act of eating – nowhere very edifying to watch – is regarded as an often embarrassing necessity that has to be concealed from sight by taking various precautions, and by observing an etiquette that is radically different from that in the West. First and foremost, it must not be a contest between the person who is eating and their food; no offensive weapons are involved – just two chopsticks with which to pick up what has been carefully prepared in the kitchen. Diners never help themselves to a dish, which would indicate greed, but are served by waiting staff and, within certain limits, by their host. And Japanese are not comfortable with the idea of entertaining in their homes. When they do, the woman of the house does not sit at the table with her guests, but serves the meal and participates in it in a different way to a Western hostess. It is therefore preferable to eat in a restaurant, where women will not be put in a potentially embarrassing position with strangers, and use the services of staff trained to entertain diners, who will themselves certainly feel more at ease.

This is where, over the centuries, the Japanese have created a unique entertainer: the geisha. Precisely because eating must never be a simple matter of ingesting food, her role is to stimulate conversation, accompanying, pacing and separating the different stages of the meal, but also dancing, singing and serving the various dishes as if it were a game. It is her job to intuit diners' moods and intervene with a witty quip, or even offer a special titbit of food which she may bring straight to a diner's lips. She may do this with his chopsticks – or with her own, which she otherwise doesn't use because she doesn't eat. In this way she controls the mood of the occasion, making it more convivial or more relaxed. It is always over such meals that important business deals are concluded – the parties may have spent exhausting months at the negotiating table – or social agreements are made.

Western cuisine, especially in France, is oriented towards creating complex flavours obtained through fusion, contrast and combination, and training is necessary in order to evaluate at leisure the many ingredients, the balance of their proportions and the overall result. Japanese cuisine is not like this. As in aesthetics, so with flavour: the primary aim is to preserve natural characteristics. Every season has its own dishes, from the point of view not only of producing and storing food, but also of colour relationships; in other words, there must be a correspondence between what is served and the colours connected with the time of year. A similar criterion applies to the order in which food is tasted. This is why, apparently from necessity but in fact from a deep need for communion with the rhythms of nature, each season has its own particular dishes, whether in colour or taste, and how the palate comes to appreciate its range of flavours and their nuances.

Freshness is everything, unless it is intentionally sacrificed to heighten other characteristics of the food. Nowhere else in the world do restaurants have tanks quite like the ones in Japan that hold fish, molluscs and crustaceans, to be served practically alive, selected and prepared before the customer's eyes. How dreadful, you may say. But no. The chef makes his simple, intent movements, as if he was officiating at a religious ceremony, and in his hands fish or vegetables become sacrificial victims in an ancestral rite. The preparation of food is beautiful to watch. Whether or not it is intended for himself, the quasi-ritual actions of the chef and his assistants, the respect with which the materials, be they animal or vegetable, are handled, the great care and precision applied to every detail, encourage in the observer an attentive and discriminating sense of involvement with them. To get to the heart of this 'agape', it is necessary to forget the idea of eating food in order to provide and stimulate refined taste sensations; eating becomes a form of communion with nature, through the consumption not only of its physical components, but also, or above all, of its particular messages. In reality, over and above the food, it is the flavour of nature itself that is ingested.

A Japanese proverb says food should be eaten using the two organs made just for that purpose: the mouth and the eyes. Little if any mention is made of the nose, which is so important to Western diners. And anyone who looks for the first time at the courses served during a Japanese meal will be amazed by their beauty, by the juxtaposition of colours, the choice of shapes and the way they are composed; by the care with which each element is cut, arranged and dressed, without losing its visible freshness; and at how these elements are handled in the same way that a flower is placed in a vase according to the strictest and most refined rules of *ikebana*, the art of arranging flowers.

Vegetables do, in fact, come to resemble flowers. When the lid is taken off a bowl containing the very lightest of broths, as clear as a mountain stream, small coloured shapes appear: a little red daisy, a blade of grass, small pebbles at the bottom. This is how the Japanese aesthetic has transformed the cutting of a carrot, a thin strip of leek and some grated tofu. Rules govern how each vegetable, each fish, is cut, scored or folded in such a way as to enhance their beauty and transform their taste. It is a sculptural operation, which takes away the physical reality of the food and spiritualizes it, so to speak, turning it into nourishment for both body and soul.

The Japanese do not eat meat, or, rather, they did not eat it in the past. Their traditional diet is based on vegetables and fish, and even eating poultry was slightly frowned upon – there is a wealth of tales, stories, plays and farces that present bird catchers in an unfavourable light. Their antipathy to meat was certainly intensified by Buddhism, which forbids eating it, but it was the country's geography that, since prehistory, made it almost impossible to include it in their diet. The islands that make up Japan are mountainous and not suitable for raising livestock, while the abundant variety of fish and seafood meant the Japanese saw these as their natural foods. Meat-eating was practically unknown until it was popularized by Westerners. Some of the dishes that are best known in the West, such as sukiyaki and the different kinds of *teriyaki*, are not truly Japanese; and nor, strictly speaking, is tempura, which is a local adaptation of a deep-fried dish adopted from the Portuguese in the sixteenth century.

Of course, when the Japanese take something up it is developed to the furthest limits of perfection. And this applies to meat, that awkward interloper in the country's cuisine. Steak has come to represent beef in its most perfect form because the little that is produced, in Kobe, must surely be the best – or at least the most elaborately raised – in the world. It comes from top-grade bullocks fed on beer and massaged regularly to make their meat especially tender. Blind masseurs (the best there are, as with musicians) have not yet been employed, but as a result of the way the animals are treated, the steaks, with their fine marbling of fat and incomparable flavour, literally melt in the mouth and are probably the most sought after and expensive in the world. Who knows where the idea of giving calves a daily beer came from – perhaps from the Chinese practice of raising turtles on the fumes of wheat wine.

The sudden death in Kyoto in 1975 of the kabuki actor Bandō Mitsugorō VIII (1906–75) caused an enormous sensation. Mitsugorō was not only a matinee idol; he was one of the greatest exponents of Japan's popular theatre and he had been officially registered as a 'national human treasure', an honour bestowed on very few people. The fact is, he died a gourmet's death but not, as one might expect, from high cholesterol, alcoholism, cirrhosis of the liver or indigestion – none of those. Mitsugorō, true to type, died in the most civilized way imaginable: he died from eating *fugu*.

This rather vague word refers to different kinds of globefish that can be scraped out, blown up and dried to make pretty little lanterns, or that can even be eaten. Fillets of *fugu*, from fish caught in the winter (otherwise the flesh does not have the proper texture) are cut into paper-thin slices and eaten raw, dipped in a delicate vegetable sauce, and are perhaps the choicest dish in the whole of Japanese cuisine.

But the true, incomparable gourmet does not look for a fillet of *fugu*, but for the fish's liver. However, the bile contains a powerful poison, tetradontotoxin, which paralyses the respiratory nerves, causing progressive, irreversible asphyxia and leading to a terrible and inevitable death. For this reason, very few restaurants in Japan are authorized to handle the tiny liver; the slightest error and the bile would contaminate the part to be served to the customer, with fatal results. Bandō died after eating, it is said, four livers: a huge quantity, despite their tiny size. But the insistence on the part of some of his Japanese friends that the great actor had put too much faith in destiny arouses suspicions, and thoughts that on that fateful evening something different from what was reported had taken place. But what? It is possible that it was not a question of livers contaminated with bile, but of something less accidental, perhaps very much more deliberate and tragic. Supposing Bandō had died from tasting another, much more disquieting, stimulating (and illegal) delicacy?

With due respect to the claims of its devotees, fillet of *fugu* is not very tasty, but some gourmets understand the art of making it so, even sublimely so. The paper-thin slices are arranged to resemble the petals of a rose. For a customer he knows he can trust, the chef places on each petal an infinitesimal portion of the deadly poisonous bile, which is alleged to give the dish an incomparable flavour. It is up to the diner to recognize the point at which his body has reached the limit of what he can safely absorb, and to stop. But this is difficult to judge and act upon, both because the poison has a progressive action and because the drop of bile gives the bland, transparent slice of fish a heavenly flavour. And how can anyone resist entering Paradise once they have crossed its threshold?

Was the famous Bandō Mitsugorō VIII perhaps caught in this subtle, sublime and exquisite dilemma?

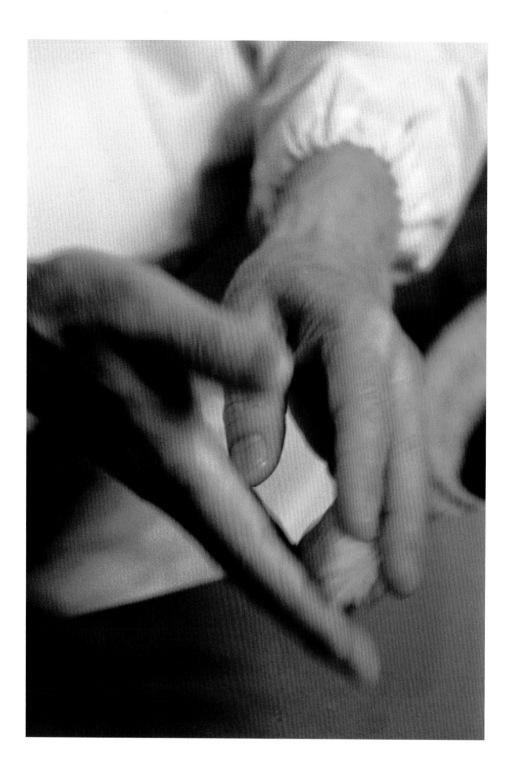

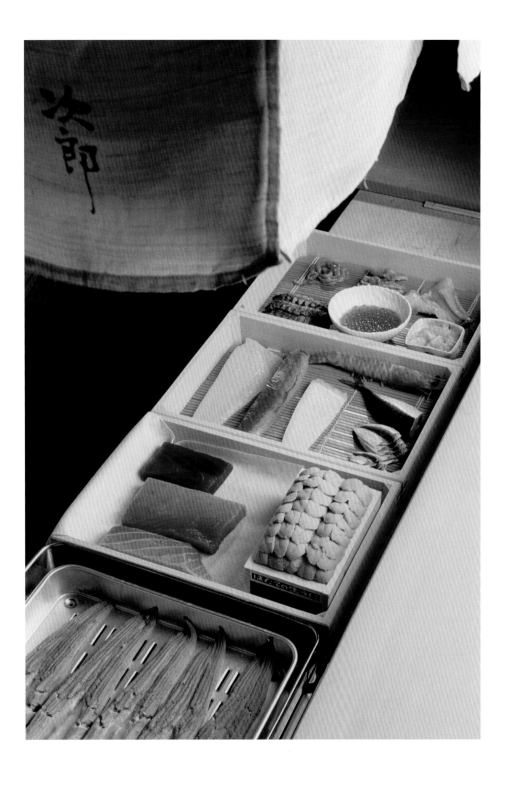

3

Masters of Art

Zeami: The Flower in the Demon

The birth of Japanese lyrical drama, to borrow the felicitous phrase applied to nō by Noël Péri, can be dated to as early as 1374, when Kan'ami (1334–84), the head of a troupe of *sarugaku* actors, and his son Zeami performed before Japan's most powerful political figure, the shōgun Yoshimitsu.[1] The great Ashikaga prince, then barely seventeen years old, immediately recognized the actors' great artistic talent, and received them in his court at Muromachi, a quarter of Kyoto, where he provided them with the conditions and support they needed in order to expand and develop this form of theatre.

Yoshimitsu's regency marked the beginning of a period of splendour comparable in creative richness and intensity with the Italian Renaissance. But whereas in fifteenth- and sixteenth-century Italy the search for new canons and criteria was oriented towards creating an objective universe governed by eternal and immutable laws, of which man, with his capacity to organize and set clear, unambiguous boundaries on the world of phenomena, was the measure and the centre, in Muromachi Japan there was created a civilization that could be defined by symbol and allusion. The objective of its cultural codes was not to produce a firm definition of man and the world around him; rather, it was to provoke a constant search for relationships of harmony with the world, by creating nuanced and allusive expressions of reality. In this period, appropriate vehicles of expression were developed to portray a form of reality that was understood symbolically, and which was neither stable nor immutable. In architecture, asymmetry ruled; with its constant rupture of formal equilibrium it forced the individual to find in his or her inner world the connections that govern life's ideal rhythms. It is the realm of the everyday moment transformed into a work of art. There is an avoidance of all that is 'closed', because what is closed is finite, contained within itself, and can at the very most represent an idea, never the pulse of life with its hidden rhythms and intimate resonances.

Like a Renaissance nobleman, Yoshimitsu had a villa built which became a centre of vibrant cultural life, and of which the famous Kinkaku-ji, Golden Pavilion, an architectural gem, survives. Artists, Zen monks, courtiers, writers and craftsmen gathered round the great patron. The renewal of Japan's relations with China made it possible to absorb cultural and aesthetic idioms in which to express the Zen philosophy of life. But there were still fundamental differences, which arose, above all, from the peculiarly Japanese approach to nature. In China, the principal tendency is to produce objects whose form is distinct from the material from which they are made; the conceptual rather than the material aspect of the work of art is foregrounded, hence it is universalized as an ideal form. In Japan, by

1   Noël Péri, *Le Nô*, Maison Franco-Japonaise, Tokyo, 1944.

contrast, intimate, personal communion with nature, derived from Shintō, gives priority to the intrinsic material properties of the object. In China clay is transformed into fine porcelain, into a translucent, chilly receptacle for light; in Japan it reveals, under the rustic glaze, the coarseness of the raw material. Ceramics show that they are products of the earth, shaped by human beings, not a natural element become an idea. The taste for the physical is savoured to the full, and in this communion human beings find aesthetic and physical fulfilment. Love of the particular, the simple and the natural tends to eliminate any idealization of form, in favour of appreciating what life offers, just as it is with all the conflicts that reveal its dynamic progress. This produces an art whose rhythms appear surprising and unexpected to people in the West, and whose equilibrium is based on criteria whose parameters, while satisfying us, tend to elude us at the point where they 'embody beauty in a form of imperfection or even of ugliness'.

In the 'lyric drama' spectators are often faced with situations that seem to be intended to provoke not only repulsion, but even horror. Yet what is experienced is a feeling of a quite different kind. Traditionally, the most demanding roles in Japanese theatre are those representing characters who embody the negative side of life: inner or bodily ugliness, violence, cruelty, madness. Playing them demands great stagecraft of the actor, and the highest degree of professional maturity. If it is hard to hold an audience in thrall with the image of a delicate young girl or a bold warrior, it is all the more difficult to do so with that of a woman possessed by demons, or a decrepit, blind old man. But it is precisely there that the subtle spell of nō lies.

In the sophisticated atmosphere of Yoshimitsu's court, Zeami became the chief exponent of Japanese humanism, the epicentre of which was Kyoto. Taken, with his father Kan'ami, under the protection of the great shōgun, he very soon became his favourite and participated in the intense aesthetic activity that was taking place around him. After Kan'ami's death in 1384, Zeami found himself at the head of the company that, in the course of time, became the most famous and powerful 'family school': the Kanze. Zeami's personality, judging from what little is known of it (mainly from his writings), shows great aesthetic and emotional sensitivity. And it is what is known about the exile to which he was condemned, at the age of seventy, through the envy of his grandson and successor, On'ami, that reveals his great human stature.

As a theatrical figure Zeami is one of the most rounded and complete in the history of world theatre. As well as being a very great actor, he wrote a number of treatises on the art of nō, which were rediscovered in the early twentieth century and reveal him to be the greatest theoretician on the subject; indeed, to be the creator of the poetics of the genre. In addition, critics have traditionally tended to attribute to him a good number of the 250 plays in the surviving repertory. Regardless of the fact that in recent years Japanese scholars have begun to revise this canon, reducing it in number, Zeami was nevertheless a figure of the very first rank, who combined practical stagecraft and an aptitude for literary composition with his theoretical work.

Zeami's theatre and his life show the constant need for unity of thought and gesture to which Artaud referred. In fact, his treatises are far more than pure theory; they reflect the craftsman's constant concern with the emotions to be aroused in the audience. Feelings that must never be the final outcome of a particular performance, a given moment on the stage, but a gradual process, in which the spectator's interest is constantly kept alive, to discover the human message contained in the drama. In a sense, it could be said that the aesthetics of asymmetry is the basis of Zeami's art of nō: asymmetry understood as the absence of formal balance among the parts, within a lucid and unambiguous idea.

Such a concept is without doubt at odds with Western ideas of beauty and perfection. The sense of the beautiful in Japanese art seems to be expressed in forms that are not clearly defined, works whose character is 'fluid'; which is to say that they lend themselves to several interpretations, they reveal a world that is not yet complete but is caught at one moment of its creation. They are works that highlight the human aspect, the effort expended in transforming matter into a higher form of life. In the image of a tree the observer should not look for a harmonious arrangement of trunk and branches, designed to give the impression of a 'great organizer' in charge of creation, or for an idea of arboreal perfection to which the tree corresponds as closely as possible. What will be emphasized is the contorted shape, the crevices, the scars left by branches that have long since fallen: evidence of life, of constant change. This is confirmed by Suzuki when he argues that the Japanese aesthetic tends to embody beauty in a form of imperfection, even ugliness.

Zeami's great experience on the stage gave him a fine sensitivity to the infinite nuances of the human psyche, and his poetics, in both his plays and his treatises, tend to linger over certain aspects of life that are incidental rather than ideal.

An old man's way of following the rhythm consists of tapping his foot and extending and withdrawing his hand, slightly behind the beat marked by the drum, the singing and the tambours, in such a way that all his attitudes and postures are slightly deferred in relation to the rhythm. This experimental method, more than anything else, is the norm in old age. It is sufficient to bear in mind this particular treatment, and otherwise to perform it in the usual way, as brilliantly as possible. It is quite clear that in his heart, an old man wishes to behave youthfully in everything he does. However, despite his efforts, his limbs are heavy, he is hard of hearing, and therefore, although the intention is there, the action no longer matches it. Knowledge of this principle results in a faithful imitation. In one's own performance, then, in keeping with an old man's wishes, one will need to present a youthful posture. Is this not perhaps to render the state of mind and the bearing of an old man who is envious of youth? For all that the old man adopts a youthful posture, the principle of his helplessness lies, despite his efforts, in this delay in relation to the rhythm. And in this youthful posture adopted by the old man lies the principle of the uncustomary. As if a flower were to blossom on an old tree.[2]

Over and above its aesthetic value, this passage, taken from *On the Transmission of the Flower of Interpretation* (*Fūshi kaden*), also known as *Kadensho*, reveals the writer's subtle analytical skill and his deep knowledge of the human heart. When Zeami speaks of a flower opening on an old tree, he arouses a sense of wonder at the miraculous occurrence of rejuvenation in what had seemed no longer capable of generating new life. But at the same time, the beauty of old age is revealed precisely in something that is far from harmonious: getting the rhythm of the dance wrong so that movement lags behind the musical tempo. In this way, what could have seemed discordant, uncertain, unsteady and lacking in fluidity – in short, ugly – becomes of the greatest interest; it reveals an inner rhythm of its own and ultimately exerts a powerful appeal over the audience. Ugliness has become beautiful.

The power of this subtle magic lies precisely in extracting beauty, an aesthetic concept, from what might seem, to all appearances, devoid of grace, vivacity, energy – the figure of an old man weighed down by his years, or an ancient beggar-woman whose body, ravaged by life's vicissitudes, shows nothing of its beauty.

2   Zeami, *Il segreto del teatro nō*, ed. R. Sieffert, Milano, Adelphi, 1966, pp. 132–3.

Zeami
Tennyomai (left), a celestial
maiden dancing, and *Rōtai*
(right), an old man, sketches,
14th century

老躰

開心遠目

見

三躰之人歌

Hokusai: The Old Man Mad about Painting

One of Hokusai's pupils, Iitsu II (?–1891), left an undated drawing of the master in one of the last homes the painter occupied. It depicts a room in the house where Hokusai and his now elderly daughter Ōei are living. She is sitting very close to a brazier, apparently leaning on a long, slender pipe, and looking towards her father, who is on the other side of the room. Between them, on the wall, hangs a notice signed 'Miura Hachiemon' (Hokusai) saying that orders for textbooks or painted fans are not accepted. In fact, Hokusai, with his wrinkled face (which his pupil has, perhaps out of respect, partially concealed behind a pillar), is on the floor under a futon, but in front of him is a sheet of paper on which to paint vertical pictures, and in his hand he is holding a brush with which he is painting. Beside him is a stone on which to dilute blocks of ink and some small bowls for the different colours, and his daughter's gaze is clearly focused on the painting rather than on her father. It is obvious that Hokusai was extremely weak, but it is also clear that every ounce of his remaining energy is concentrated in the wrist and hand that emerge from under the futon to guide the brush on the paper. What was the artist painting in Iitsu's portrait?

In the winter of 1848–9 Hokusai's health suddenly deteriorated and it was difficult for him to walk, so much so that he was forced to decline an invitation to Obuse, in the Japanese Alps, from his pupil and patron, Takai Kōzan. According to Iijima Kyoshin, his first biographer, the master produced his last paintings in the early spring of 1849 – in other words, around the beginning of February – and in mid-spring he fell ill and could no longer stand up. Perhaps it was while he was in this state that Iitsu II depicted him in his drawing. Hokusai was aware of his condition, and could even joke about it if, as seems to be the case, he wrote to a friend:

> Enma [the god of the underworld] is preparing to retire from business due to old age. So he has had a nice little house built in the country and has asked me to join him there to paint him a *kakemono*. This is why I have to leave, and when I go, I'll take my paintings with me. I'll rent a small flat in Netherworld Street, where I shall be happy to welcome you when you're passing through.[1]

Meanwhile the end was approaching and, following an ancient tradition, Hokusai wrote his valedictory poem. Even here, and though facing inevitable death, his indomitable, ironic spirit can be detected in his words:

1   Edmond de Goncourt, *Hokousaï*, Bibliothèque Charpentier, Paris, 1896, pp. 207–8.

Even if as a ghost
I shall walk for pleasure
through the summer meadows.[2]

Death came on 10 May 1849 (the eighteenth day of the fourth lunar month), and Hokusai, with his ceaseless concern for perfection in painting, is said to have exclaimed, 'If Heaven would only allow me ten more years'; then after a pause, realizing his wish could not be granted, he went on, 'If Heaven could only have allowed me five more years, I could have become a true artist!'[3]

Painting, his divine obsession, was for Hokusai the indispensable condition of his entire existence, the guiding principle of all his fundamental decisions. His life demonstrates countless signs of this absolute dedication, starting with the name he chose to take as an artist – 'the Studio of the Pole Star', Hokushinsai, which was shortened to Hokusai – and his other nickname, 'The old man mad about painting', which, from 1834, accompanied his signature like a kind of vow or talisman. To capture the essence of things and people, and to communicate their spirit in pictorial form, was his unshakable ambition, as he wrote in what many have called his spiritual testament in the colophon to one of his most famous books of illustrations, the *One Hundred Views of Mount Fuji* (*Fugaku hyakkei*):

From the age of six I have had a passion for copying the form of things and since the age of fifty I have published many drawings, yet of all I drew in the last seventy years there is nothing worth taking into account. At seventy-three I partly understood the structure of animals, birds, insects and fishes, and the life of grasses and plants. And so, at eighty-six I shall progress further; at ninety I shall even further penetrate their secret meaning, and by one hundred I shall perhaps truly have reached the level of the marvellous and divine. When I am one hundred and ten, each dot, each line will possess a life of its own. If I can express a wish, I ask whoever among you will live a long life to check whether what I say is true. Declared by Manji, the old man mad about painting.[4]

Hokusai could sometimes give the impression of living a chaotic, disorganized life, but he was nevertheless extremely rigorous as far as the quality and perfection of his work was concerned, although less in the technical sense than in that of its spirit, and was always preoccupied with the task of infusing life into everything he drew. Michel Revon tells how a pupil who was taking lessons in the master's studio once confided to Ōei that he could not manage to control his brush,

2   The poem is inscribed on the left-hand side of the master's gravestone in the Sensō-ji temple in Asakusa.

3   Michel Revon, *Étude sur Hoksaï*, Lecène, Oudin et Cie, Paris, 1896, p. 111.

4   Hokusai, *Fugaku hyakkei* (*One Hundred Views of Mount Fuji*), in the colophon to vols. I and II.

and that he feared he would never become a painter. To encourage him, Ōei is said to have told him that the same thing happened to her father, the great Hokusai: 'From childhood he has not ceased to search and he is still searching now, at over eighty years of age. The other day he crossed his arms, weeping in despair and saying that the brush would not obey his will, and that he would never succeed in endowing even a cat with life. It is the story of every artist, but is not the beginning of progress precisely when we realize that we are still not competent?' Hokusai, who had listened to the exchange, exclaimed: 'It's true! It's true!'[5]

Before reaching the simplicity and power of expression that made his art universal, Hokusai had to undertake a long journey which, as he said in 1834 in the colophon to *One Hundred Views of Mount Fuji*, he saw as never ending, since that is the symbolic meaning of 110 years in a country where the average life expectancy was then less than thirty.

Hokusai would have been a great artist of the floating world even if he had not been responsible for the revolution in depicting landscape and aspects of nature and the human figure that later characterized his vast output. The transformation he brought about in art is closely allied with his constant and unswerving effort to surpass any point he had reached, an effort that is also reflected in his private life, with his changes of name (over 120 including all the variants) and residence (over ninety), and his use of many different seals. The thousands of works in his *oeuvre* include paintings, prints, illustrated books and manuals of instruction for aspiring painters or artisans. He began in the *ukiyo-e* tradition of images of the Floating World, the movement in culture and art that emerged in the Edo period (1615–1868) and was centred on the world of kabuki actors and the courtesans of the Yoshiwara pleasure district of Tokyo. But he subsequently developed a pictorial approach and a style that were entirely his own, although strongly influenced by tradition as well as by the art of China and the West. The splendid culmination of this came when he was over seventy, with the series of landscapes entitled *Thirty-six Views of Mount Fuji* (*Fugaku sanjūrokkei*, 1830–2) and the three volumes of the *One Hundred Views of Mount Fuji*, which depicted Japan's sacred mountain, the series of famous waterfalls and bridges, and the prints of the great poets of China and Japan side by side. It can also be seen in his stupendous paintings of flowers that are observed and portrayed in such a way that they express distinct personalities and emotions that are the equal of those of human beings.

Although Hokusai was equally prolific as a painter and a graphic artist, he owed his fame principally to his prints, some of the best known of which

5 Revon, pp. 125–6.

– the *Great Wave* is an example – have come to represent the epitome of Japanese art. While he was perhaps unique, rather than unusual, among *ukiyo-e* artists, he was as great a painter as he was a print-maker. The wealth of genres and styles he developed over a period of more than seventy years is an impressive achievement for a single artist. His works range from prints depicting scenes from the theatre, made early in his career, to delicate, exquisite greeting cards, *surimono*, made for private circulation; from woodblock prints using shading and perspective to the large landscape series executed in the 1830s; from inexpensive multivolume 'yellow books' to illustrated Chinese classics, luxurious anthologies of poetry and manuals of instruction; from paintings of 'feminine beauty' to scenes of everyday life, and from lightning sketches in the *Manga*, to detailed drawings of complex architectural structures.

Even in late old age Hokusai's output did not decline, and his last years were among his most productive. His habit, when he felt he had fully mastered a style, was to move on to another one, so if his *oeuvre* is surveyed in all its complexity the works seem to be by several different hands. When he made such a change he gave up his artist's pseudonym and the seals associated with it, and often allowed a pupil to use them.

Many stories told about Hokusai would qualify him for inclusion in the category of *kijin*: eccentric artists or, more correctly, 'extraordinary men'. According to Iijima,[6] on the thirteenth day of the fourth month of 1804 he carried out the first of many 'performances'. On a sheet of paper measuring about 200 square metres (2,153 square feet), he began to make marks with a reed broom, which he dunked in a tub filled with ink. When the painting was hung up on a scaffold there appeared, to the amazement of onlookers, an enormous portrait of Daruma, the patriarch of Zen. Shortly afterwards, this gigantic picture was balanced by one depicting a flight of sparrows, executed on a grain of rice.

At about the age of forty Hokusai's interest in literary subjects, which probably began when he was in his teens working as a delivery boy for a travelling library, led him to change his subject matter somewhat and he partially gave up the *ukiyo-e* genre of portraiture in favour of book illustration; in a short time he became the leading illustrator of storybooks. His most prestigious work in this genre was for the translation by Takizawa Bakin (1767–1848), a famous man of letters, of the great Chinese classic *Shuihuzhuan* (*All men are brothers*), which appeared in 1805. Hokusai abandoned the project after illustrating the sixty-first volume, published in 1838, and passed it on to his pupil Taito II, who completed it with the ninety-first volume.

6 Iijima Kyoshin, *Katsushika Hokusai den*, Hōsūkaku, Tokyo, 1893, vol. I, pp. 18 below and 19 above.

He retained his passion for literature throughout his life, and developed it even when he was totally absorbed in revolutionizing landscape painting. A famous print in the series *Mirror of Chinese and Japanese Verses* (*Shiika shashinkyō*), published by Moriya Jihei in about 1833–4, depicts Li Bai (c. 700–62), the great poet of China's Tang dynasty. He is looking at a waterfall on Lu mountain, in Kiangsi. Li Bai had taken refuge in the region after a revolt against the emperor, and dedicated a poem to the falls, which he greatly loved. The print is a masterpiece in its depiction of the interpenetration of nature and the human spirit. Li Bai, leaning on his tall walking stick, contemplates the waterfall from a promontory overlooking the cascade. This erupts from outside the edge of the image, falling into an abyss whose bottomless depths cannot be seen; in Prussian blue, with white stripes indicating the foaming water, it divides the print into two distinct parts. The poet, drunk on wine and beauty, is immersed in the scene into which, in a kind of pantheistic ecstasy, he would plummet physically were it not for two little attendants who restrain him. The space he occupies, in the lower left of the print, is balanced by a rock in the upper right from which a twisted pine tree (an allegorical image of the poet) leans out over the waterfall, as if embracing its force with its extended branch. It, like Li Bai, draws the essence of its existence from its precarious but splendid balance, bound as it is to the fate of the superb cascade as it ceaselessly, endlessly falls.

Throughout his career Hokusai maintained that painting is an indispensable good for mankind, and that everyone should therefore try their hand at it. Painters, then, should constantly refine their technique and their way of portraying people, nature, objects and movement. From the age of fifty onwards he produced nineteen manuals, some of them in several volumes. Architects and craftsmen are always in need of technical guidance and instruction, and pictures of structural and decorative elements; and painters must have a clear idea of the forms and construction methods of man–made structures if they are to represent them correctly. Hokusai's manuals are therefore varied, and designed for disparate purposes. Of first importance are those intended for artists, both amateur and professional, which contain instructions on the art of painting, with advice on drawing as well as the use of colour. He also produced books of pictures for craftsmen like makers of pipes and combs, for which he sketched figures to be engraved on the objects the men made, illustrated with the necessary technical details. And then there were manuals such as one for learning how to dance by oneself (*Odori hitori geiko*), using as a model a famous actor of the day, Ichikawa Danjūrō VII (1791–1859), who also wrote the pref–

ace; and volumes on many other subjects including designs for printed and woven textiles.

The monumental collection of the *Manga*, the first volume of which was published in 1814, is a case unto itself. It consists of illustrations whose function is to offer painters and craftsmen a detailed guide to the widest possible variety of subjects, as well as passing on the master's style to his pupils. In the vast range of topics it covers, the *Manga* ultimately represent a compendium of the life, society and traditions of Japan. They have been acclaimed as such in the West since the time of Félix Braquemond (1833–1914), who prided himself on being the first to popularize them. It is a work whose size and variety make it uncategorizable. Figures of wrestlers or warriors alternate with those of grotesque or comic characters, but also with flowers and birds, landscape sketches, technical drawings (including models of firearms, showing details of their firing mechanism) and the roofs of temples and palaces, all in dizzying profusion like a volcano of images in full, inexhaustible flow. The painter Degas was familiar with the images and drew heavily on them for inspiration, for example in one of his favourite subjects – ballet dancers exercising at the barre. He said: 'Hokusai is not only one artist among others in the Floating World; he is an island, a continent, a world in himself.'[7]

But, if Hokusai articulated his sense of his own limits in respect of the art of painting, this did not apply to his relations with other artists, especially those who were fashionable, whom he fiercely criticized. The shape of the nose is an important characteristic of human faces and in a letter dated the seventeenth of the first month of 1837, written to his publishers from the village of Uraga, to which he appears to have fled in order to avoid his creditors, he described it in great detail. He also recommended that his drawings be engraved by Egawa Tomekichi, a woodblock engraver who was very faithful to the style of the originals, so as to 'make an old man happy who has only a short time to live'. The request was followed by a drawing that shows him walking with the aid of two sticks in the form of brushes. In another letter he asked the engraver, 'not to add the lower eyelid when I do not draw it. As for the noses, these two noses are mine [he inserts two sketches], and those that you usually engrave are Utagawa [a competitor print designer's school] noses, which I do not like at all, and they break the rules of drawing. And it's the fashion to draw eyes like this – [another sketch] – but I like these eyes no more than the noses.'[8]

It is possible that after the age of eighty Hokusai began to suspect, though without admitting it to himself and still less to others, that he might not, after all, be able to reach the age of 110 years which would enable him to become

7   'Hokusai n'est pas seulement un artiste parmi d'autres dans le monde flottant, c'est une île, un continent, un monde, à lui tout seul.' (A. Terrasse, 'Degas à travers ses mots', *Gazette des Beaux Arts*, série 6, 86, 1975, p. 42.)

8   Iijima, pp. 55–8.

a great painter, unless he took special steps. By the early 1840s, when he was in his eighties, he was definitely old and probably in poor health. He had suffered a stroke some years previously and had recovered by taking potions, described in one of his texts, that he had invented himself. In 1839 a fire had broken out in the Honjo district where he lived, and destroyed his house; he escaped miraculously after grabbing his brushes – his most precious belongings – but lost paintings and drawings that had been in his possession for a long time. The visits he made to Obuse in the Shinano mountains as Kōzan's guest certainly rejuvenated him, but they were not enough. Something more efficacious was needed to protect him from the reverses of fate.

Hokusai began to draw Chinese lions, and produced over two hundred images of them between 1842 and 1844. The lions are mythical creatures, symbols of strength and perseverance, and are considered benign beings, bringers of energy and growth. Legend has it that they subject their cubs to the harshest ordeals, including jumping off cliffs, and raise the survivors with great severity. Hokusai drew them in the early morning, just after getting up, because he believed they would bring good luck: they were talismans against disease, death and the problems of everyday life. Some of the drawings, dated with the month and day when they were made, were later collected by a patron under the title *Nisshinjōma* (*Daily exorcisms*). Masterpieces of bravura, speed of execution and humour, they reflect different states of mind probably related to the artist's personal circumstances. There is a lion which, abacus in his hand, is doing his accounts, but the text is full of untranslatable puns from which it emerges that he is counting not money but lions. There is a depressed, melancholy lion in a torrential downpour, and a lion of the lion dance; there are lion acrobats, and a terrified dog barking at a man dressed as a lion.

In the year before his death Hokusai published his pictorial master-work: the *Illustrated Manual on Colouring* (*Ehon saishikitsū*). A two-volume work on how to use colour in painting, it was intended, as the master himself said, for children and beginners. Typical of his approach as a painter and his way of life, it was meant to be an inexpensive work, popular but serious, which many people would be able to buy and use. How can one live without painting, Hokusai must have thought. Yet it is far from easy to follow and, even more than his earlier manuals, it is a testimony to the master's greatness as a painter and technical virtuoso, rather than to his stature as a teacher, a field in which he was hardly active despite the more than 200 pupils who are attributed to him. His manuals, like his art, were above all a measurement of himself and of the boundaries – in his eyes, unreachable – of great painting.

Among the paintings dated 'ninety years' there is one that, more than any other, is emblematic of Hokusai's life, his art, his 'struggle against the demon' and his iron determination to go beyond the limits he had reached. It bears an inscription and signature that indicate the month of the tiger, the first month of the lunar year – that is, February in the year of the rooster, 1849. It is signed 'old Manji, an old man mad about painting, at the age of ninety years', followed by a seal indicating 'one hundred' that Hokusai had recently adopted. This means the painting was made about three months before he died as, despite age and illness, he continued to harness his last energies in the struggle to make a painting that was still greater, still purer. It would be nice to imagine that this is the work that, old, dying and at the limit of his powers, he insisted on painting, sitting on the floor under his futon, as portrayed by Iitsu II in his drawing. It is a painting that is a kind of self-portrait, and depicts an old tiger.

It is mid-winter and a blizzard is raging. The tiger is old and sick; its limbs seem elongated as if its muscles are no longer holding them firmly together. Yet it is moving over the ground, which is invisible under a white blanket of snow; indeed, it is running between the bamboo stalks, bent under the snow's weight and the force of the wind, the sole reference to a real world, while everything else has disappeared in the greyish whiteness of the storm, which melts earth and sky into a single substance. With a smile that is also a sneer, the old tiger painfully, but joyfully, ironically, preceded only by its intense, penetrating gaze, makes a great leap upwards, towards the infinite.

Left:
Katsushika Hokusai
Li Bai (the Chinese poet),
colour woodblock print,
c. 1833–4

Right:
Katsushika Hokusai
Minamoto no Tōru (the Japanese poet), colour woodblock
print, c. 1833–4

Previous pages:
Katsushika Hokusai
Beneath the Wave off Kanagawa
('The Great Wave'), colour wood-
block print, c. 1830–2

Katsushika Hokusai
Old Tiger in the Snow, colours, ink
and *gofun* on silk, 1849

白鳳

さ尾

Previous pages:
Katsushika Hokusai
From the *Illustrated Manual on Colouring*, monochrome woodblock print, 1848

Katsushika Hokusai
'Dance of the Servant', from *Manga*, colour woodblock print, 1815

KAWABATA: THE POWER OF THE ETHEREAL

When Mr. Kawabata was at creative work, the original root of his life, which you might call 'soul' or 'spirit', had left his body beforehand to wander around and return to the body again bringing back what you might term the honey of creation … however, it had turned out to be very difficult, and he had to have much toil and pain for calling his soul back to the body … It has been told that Mr. Kawabata commited suicide. However, I think he had an urgent necessity of writing and tried the fastest possible measure to calling the soul back to his body. The measure he tried [sleeping pills and alcohol] had been too dangerous so that his heart had stopped its beat before his soul reached to Mr. Kawabata's body. This is how I feel about his death. His soul which did not return to the body must be somewhere in the universe.[1]

This striking image was presented to several hundred world experts by Serizawa Kōjirō, president of the Japanese PEN Club, at the opening of the First International Conference of Japanese Studies, in Kyoto in 1972. Even if it paints a slightly soft-edged picture of reality, it seems particularly appropriate to the life and work of Yasunari Kawabata, the winner of the 1968 Nobel Prize for Literature and, at the time of the conference, the only Japanese man of letters, among all the country's great writers, to have been judged worthy of the award. What truth is there in this vision of Kawabata's death? It may be fantastical, but it is also in keeping with the writer's art, with his subtle, almost dematerialized way of describing everyday events beyond the limits of the world as we perceive it in order to enlarge their visible forms so that they acquire metaphorical tones and transparencies. Eros and Thanatos constantly intermingle in his fiction, but in contrast with the novels of Tanizaki Jun'ichirō, in which sensuality may appear to exist beyond the bounds of earthly life, in Kawabata's works they seem to be veiled in a light mist that covers the impulses of the spirit like a shroud, filtering out all their dramatic colour.

The image of Kawabata's spirit, his *ki*, wandering through the universe like a comet, is in keeping with both his love of travel and his weightless, disembodied style of writing. It is a delicate, almost fairy-tale image, like the world of his novels. A world in which readers seem to live with bated breath, as if time had stopped and had created for them a dimension in which everyday events expand, going beyond the ordinary dimensions of reality. The same can be said of an eroticism which, as in *House of the Sleeping Beauties* (*Nemureru bijo*, 1960–1),

1   Serizawa Kōjirō, *Nihon bunka kenkyū kokusai kaigi-gijiroku*, International Conference of Japanese Studies–Report, Nihon PEN Club, Tokyo, 1973, vol. I, pp. 65–6.

has an unreal and suspended elegance but (sister to death as it is) is not, for all that, any the less hard and pitiless; here the action appears rarefied and free from coarse concretizing forms.

So, beyond the crude, objective facts of death (Kawataba took his life by gassing himself), Serizawa Kōjirō, who succeeded him as president of the PEN Club, seems, in his speech at the conference that Kawabata himself promoted, to have wished to establish the idea that he died as a result of a crisis in his life as a writer. Serizawa interpreted his suicide as a kind of fable, turning it into an event in keeping with the famous author's own fiction. What had driven the great writer to this act? What meaning could there be in him taking his life at the age of seventy-two, when he had recently attained the pinnacle of success with the award of the Nobel Prize? Kawabata left no note when, having taken off his kimono and replaced it with the scruffy Western clothes that suited him so badly, he left his fine traditional Japanese house in Kamakura, home to Tokyo artists and writers, for the even more exclusive neighbourhood of Zushi where, in a studio in an anonymous European-style building, he took his life.

Kawabata's hypersensitivity and his temperament – reserved, but hungering for love – meant he could create unforgettable female characters. So it is with the charming little girl in *The Izu Dancer* (*Izu no odoriko*), published in 1926, and, in a different way, with the passionate geisha Komako, in *Snow Country* (*Yukiguni*), the book that in 1936 marked him out as one of the great novelists of contemporary Japan. This is sometimes considered his greatest work, since in it his major themes are already fully developed: female figures, some strong, some fragile; a man who is weak and passive in comparison with both types of woman; a setting that seems to inhabit a mythic dimension almost outside time and space, emphasized by its isolation (it is reached by train at the end of a long, black tunnel) and an evocative landscape. Set beside Komako, the real protagonist, her lover Shimamura with his uncertainties, and conflicting fears and desires, seems to act simply as an amplifying device. The female characters are predominant even when they are apparently weak and delicate, like the young sisters Chieko and Naeko in Kawabata's 1962 novel *Koto*. The freshness of their emotions stands out against the enchanted setting of the old capital, Kyoto, with its venerable buildings, ancient traditions and superb landscapes, and makes them richer in meaning and more incisive than the novel's male characters. For Kawabata, women are possessors of the life force; it is they who expose themselves to the blows dealt by passion and are frequently crushed by them, but who also, as a result, have a rich existence, a life worth living. In comparison with them, their male counterparts almost always seem to play second fiddle, as background figures designed to enhance the heroines' personalities and emotional depth. In a way the contrast between man and woman comes out more clearly in *Beauty and Sadness* (*Utsukushisa to kanashimi to*, 1963) than in any of Kawabata's other novels. It is emphasized by a further comparison between two kinds of femininity in counterpoint: the gentle, submissive, appealing Otoko and her strong, wilful follower Keiko, who is tied to her by subtle bonds of affection and loyalty.

At a certain point, the source of images of the feminine seemed to dry up and Kawabata was driven to look for new creative directions and stimuli. It is as if he forced himself to invert his typical structure, using the idea of femininity or youth to bring his male protagonist into sharper relief, but found no freedom in doing so. On the contrary, his new man was always still the loser and by no means triumphant. In some of his last novels, such as *The Master of Go* (*Meijin*, 1942, 1954) and *House of the Sleeping Beauties*, the central theme also changed, in the first case using the long, exhausting stages of a game of go, and in the second the feelings of an old, impotent man as he lies next to deeply sedated, naked young girls.

In *The Master of Go* Kawabata appears to be comparing two worlds, that of the great master and custodian of an ancient tradition, now approaching his end, and that of his young pupil who has less regard for the game's ceremony and etiquette but is filled with a new vitality. The two worlds seem to represent the old and the new Japan, and perhaps also its old and new literatures. In *House of the Sleeping Beauties* the ever more urgent need for the stimulus provided by the freshness of youth in renewing creativity becomes a symbol of inner crisis, and of the need to renew aesthetic ideals. In this attempt to conquer new ground, Kawabata tries to change his style. Actions are repeated in the minutest detail in hundreds of different situations, and the analysis of feelings becomes obsessive, a relentless, exhaustive exploration of emotions. Ahead lie defeat and end. Of a world whose social values are giving way to younger and unbiddable ones. Of one's own aesthetic universe? Of life itself? It is as if his hero, now an old man like Kawabata himself, was facing his final crossroads, a crisis of indolence, of passivity in the face of emotion, of yearning for love and fear of loving, and was forced to be a helpless witness of his own defeat, of the end of everything, of death. Is it possible that the novelist was projecting an image of what he thought had become his own situation?

When Kawabata took his life there were those who believed that the example of Mishima Yukio (1925–70), who had committed suicide in a dramatic public act of *seppuku* less than two years previously, was in some sense the cause. It is possible that the younger writer had appealed to him in some way, and it seems that in his last days Kawabata was distressed by the thought of Mishima calling him to join him, and, in recurrent nightmares, reproving him for not having the courage to commit suicide for the sake of a high ideal. But he was not Mishima, and had no ambitions to be a public figure despite the fact that in the past year he had made an inept attempt to enter politics, with disastrous support from a Liberal-Democratic Party candidate, in the Tokyo local elections. At the same time, Mishima represented strength, self-confidence, success, intelligence, youth and creativity, even in death. Kawabata was beset by a sense of the passing of beauty, which comes with old age, and the fear of intellectual, in addition to physical, decline. Like Mishima, and before him another writer, Akutagawa Ryūnosuke (1892–1927), he may have wished to end his life before that fear became a certainty.

Others, however, attribute Kawabata's suicide to his winning the Nobel Prize and the agonizing 'writer's block' the award induced in him. He received it in a year that was highly significant for his country: 1968 was the hundredth anniversary of the restoration of the Meiji emperor, which had led to the dazzling transformation of Japan from a feudal society, closed to the outside world, into a modern industrialized nation. As the first Japanese writer to become a Nobel laureate, Kawabata represented to the people of Japan the recovery of national prestige after their defeat in the Second World War, something that was still painful to them in the 1960s and, in some respects, remains so today. But the glory brought by the prize, and his subsequent success, which exposed him to the luxuries and demands of literary consumerism, were probably fatal to the diffident, reserved writer. In 1964 he had begun to publish what would be his last novel, *The Dandelion* (*Tampopo*), in instalments in the literary magazine *Shinchō*. When he was awarded the prize in October 1968 he stopped publishing and never started again.

Kawabata was an artist of great subtlety and a talented critic. His style, which is difficult even for Japanese readers because of its fine psychological nuances, belongs to the country's oldest literary traditions. His art springs from his skill in describing events in a way that takes them beyond the world of the everyday; a way of representing reality that endows the most trivial happenings with a mythical quality. A character's simplest acts, most ordinary feelings, take on the savour of rare sensations often shrouded in a veil of melancholy – the sweet, yearning melancholy, perhaps, that goes with the awareness that every thing, every tender feeling, must pass; or melancholy that comes from Kawabata's sad childhood as an orphan deprived of the warmth he longed for. His delicate yet intense sensuality is always combined with an awareness of the transitoriness of things, of endings and, in the final analysis, of death itself. It is a sensuality that, rarefied and immaterial as it is, seems able to transcend the very limits of earthly existence.

In a short essay, 'The Existence and Discovery of Beauty' ('Bi no sonzai to hakken', 1969), Kawabata suggested that a source of his poetic vein was the aesthetic world of feelings described in Murasaki's *The Tale of Genji* (*Genji monogatari*) over 900 years earlier, and thus its code, literary as well as aesthetic, which was also a way of living and which had exerted its influence throughout the centuries. The sense of the importance of small things, the ritual quality of everyday actions, the inner harmony with nature that typify Japanese literature and ways of living, and of which Kawabata was the great interpreter of the twentieth century, were formulated in the era and imperial society of which *Genji* is the supreme literary example. This classical tradition is sometimes a subtle presence, as in 'Chrysanthemum in the Rock' ('Iwa ni kiku', 1952), in which Kawabata seems to refer to the legend of the beautiful ninth-century poet Komachi, who kept her lover waiting in her garden for a hundred nights before she would yield to him – but he died, thirsty and exhausted, on the very last day. In Kawabata's story, which is also a study of the aesthetics of simplicity and polish, modesty and elegance, bareness and refinement, the situation is reversed, and at its centre is the soul of a woman endlessly, unswervingly awaiting one who will not appear.

Through these female figures, Kawabata enters the forest of the emotions that attract and frighten him at the same time, and there is thus created in his novels and stories a marvellous dichotomy between the feminine and masculine characters. The former experience life's passions and enter into them through choice, guided by feeling and almost always with suffering; the latter provide the opportunities for these passions, but do not have the courage to participate in them with the same intensity as the women. But it is precisely this ever-present dichotomy in his fiction that enables Kawabata to observe and describe events with the slow, limpid, ethereal vision that makes him unique. His art of the fable reaches its peak in *Koto*. There is nothing in the setting he describes, in his characters, in his visions of glorious nature with its compositions of colour that change with the seasons, that might transcend the everyday moments of life to attain the fabulous or the epic, the legendary. His sublime but intimate and profound poetic lies simply in his ability to delve into the human soul and bring to light its most tenuous, delicate feelings. Despite it being a cultural characteristic, this language of his has a universal quality and is also present in his short stories, such as 'First Snow on Fuji' ('Fuji no hatsuyuki', 1958), or the very brief 'Palm-of-the-Hand Stories' ('Tanagokoro no shōsetsu', 1924, 1926, 1930, 1948), in which there is the same elegance of language as there is in his longer works, an expression of heightened sensibilities, presented in an ethereal, disembodied way.

As with Kawabata's other novels, the little world described in *Koto* is full of everyday sentiments, but they are not treated with the hauteur towards simple things that is typically shown by some writers; rather, they are tasted as if they were rare sensations. Limited as they may appear, they reflect the whole of human experience, not just one part of it. It is as if, looking at a great painting and attracted by a detail in it, we focus our attention on that detail and discover, through a magical process of magnification, that it carries the message of the composition as a whole. Kawabata derives his knowledge of this aspect of life's essence (which involves not only human beings but the whole of nature with its tremors and harshness) from the long-standing aesthetic tradition of *mono no aware* – intimate participation in the life of things – which finds its highest expression in *The Tale of Genji*. In *Koto* it is everyday life that raises human nature to the level of archetype. Even habitual actions acquire an aura of fable, suffused as they are with an atmosphere almost of ritual. But it is a light-hearted ritual, in some passages carefree, almost feminine, as if Kawabata's soul had to some extent absorbed the freshness and grace of the pretty girls with whom he liked to surround himself in life. And the setting exudes a magical spell; in bringing to life the world of the dexterous young brocade-weavers in Kyoto, he sets the human action in a world that is no longer of our time. Yet it is precisely this apparent contradiction, the blending of everyday life and other-worldly atmosphere, that achieves the effect of raising the one into an archetypal image of existence and bringing the other back from the world of the dead in which it was about to be engulfed. It is a message of eternal youth, of the constant renewal of human experience, beyond the spatial and temporal limits of earthly contingency.

In essence, it is an indirect confirmation of the words of Serizawa, which acquire even greater emblematic value if they are read in association with Kawabata's story 'Lyric Poem' ('Jōjōka', 1932):

2   Kawabata, 'Lyric Poem', trans. F. Mathy, *Monumenta Nipponica*, 26 (3–4) (1971), pp. 287–305.

Even souls do not detach themselves from the body within an hour, like so many fireballs, but leave the body of the dead little by little, like a trail of perfume, and gather in one place in Heaven, where they re-form themselves in exact copies of the bodies left on earth. And so the human form in the world beyond is identical with its form in this world.[2]

We do not know whether, on the afternoon of Sunday 16 April 1972, when Kawabata chose to leave his earthly life, he found the inner image he had intuited and written about exactly forty years earlier.

Kawabata, 1970, photograph by Mario de Biasi

Mishima: When Will You Kill Yourself, Master?

Who really was Mishima, the writer who more than any other made twentieth-century Japanese literature internationally famous; who was several times shortlisted for the Nobel Prize; who, by the time of his death at the age of forty-five, had written over a hundred books, not to mention articles and novels translated to universal acclaim all over the world; who founded a small private army; and who killed himself in a dramatic and very public ritual disembowelment while at the peak of his powers and celebrity? Today, more than thirty years after that horrific gesture, as the ideological currents that sometimes lionized and sometimes denigrated him are vanishing like dreams at dawn, his art is increasingly placing his work on a level with the classics, while the key to interpreting his life seems ever more hidden and indecipherable.

It was early morning when the boy presented himself at the great writer's door. An unknown young man, without an introduction, he did not ring the bell but waited for something to happen. This is what may happen to novices, who sometimes stand in the cobbled entrance hallway of a Zen temple for days on end before being allowed to enter. In the same way, an otherwise unapproachable celebrity could be persuaded to allow someone into his or her presence after making them wait for a length of time that, in the Far East, is anything but humiliating; on the contrary, waiting is a sign of devotion, and the longer it lasts the worthier it is of respect and honour. This wait in the morning was followed by more hours of standing during the afternoon and evening. Mishima was aware of the presence of the young man, so hopeful and deferential. He asked for him to be let in and welcomed him, saying he was very busy. He would allow him a single question. The student, exhausted by his long and tense wait as well as by the emotional impact of the now unexpected meeting, asked: 'When will you kill yourself, Master?'

The answer came a year later, at noon on 25 November 1970, a day made beautifully clear by a northerly wind which, at that time of year often cleanses Tokyo's air, so heavily polluted by the waste products of consumerism. Mishima, having delivered to his publisher the final pages of his four-volume epic *The Sea of Fertility* (*Hōjō no umi*, 1965–70), entered the headquarters of Japan's Eastern Army. With him were four members of the *Tate no kai* (Society of the Shield), his elegantly attired symbolic private militia. Commander Mashita, like many soldiers in a defeated and dismembered army, was sympathetic to what he presumed was the great writer's militarism. He received him without delay, but was immediately overpowered by the group which barricaded itself inside his office. Mishima stepped on to the balcony and began to harangue the soldiers below him with the intention of stirring up a revolt against the constitution imposed on the country by the United States after the Second World War, and forcing some changes to be made to it. The soldiers, unable to hear him because of the deafening noise of the helicopters from television networks that had rushed to the scene, did not grasp the dramatic nature of the situation and laughed at him. Mishima went back into the commander's office, knelt on the carpet, stripped himself to the waist in front of his bound hostage and, after shouting three times 'Tennō Heika banzai' ('Ten thousand years of life to His Majesty the Emperor'), followed the strict protocol of the ritual by plunging his dagger into the bottom left-hand side of his stomach; then, pushing hard with both hands, he dragged it diagonally to the top right-hand side, tearing himself apart. Mishima committed suicide not in the manner of so many other writers in the course of the twentieth century, but like a samurai who knows that all is lost and he is in danger of being captured by the enemy – by committing *seppuku*, better known in the West as *hara-kiri*.

His gesture, as gruesome as it was sensational, became the subject of hasty interpretations: he had been a writer at the pinnacle of his career and his success, but feared an impending creative block; he had been immature and narcissistic, devoted to the cult of his physical appearance and his own ego; a homosexual who, in the throes of an impossible passion, had resorted to making a *shinjū*, or double love suicide; a nostalgic imperialist who advocated a return to a militaristic and expansionistic feudal system, and simply had a fit of madness; an artist full of anguish at not being able to express, with the means at his disposal, the absolute within himself; a lunatic, or a fanatical neo-fascist whose dangerous ideas had to be kept out of the public eye.

It was a fact that in my home country, in Italy, he was hardly published any more. Almost laughably, a publishing house that prided itself on its political commitment, and had long appreciated and published Mishima's novels, wished to have no more to do with him. It hastily disposed of *Death in Midsummer* (*Manatsu no shi*, 1952), which was already typeset and ready to print, by selling the rights to another publisher, Longanesi, who was not as badly afflicted by ideological hysteria. As it happened, the buyer struck an excellent deal as the book, complete with an introduction by Alberto Moravia, sold extremely well. But the ideological crisis must have spread to Longanesi because it kept *Forbidden Colours* (*Kinjiki*, 1953), which had already been translated, under lock and key for twelve years until a third publisher, Editoriale Nuova, bought the rights and published it.

These were times of considerable ideological prudishness, and in 1980 when I organized several events to commemorate the tenth anniversary of

Mishima's death they fell on stony ground in Europe – a desert, it could be said, of indifference. A few months later, however, Mishima was propelled into fashion once again: a major French publisher, Gallimard, launched his tetralogy (translated from the version in American-English) with added publicity provided by an essay by Marguerite Yourcenar, *Mishima ou la vision du vide* (*Mishima: A Vision of the Void*), a piece which, frankly, did not seem particularly convinced or convincing. Ironically, although there were no changes in its editorial or political position, the Italian publisher who had disposed of *Death in Midsummer* began to reissue the titles it had locked away, and even published others; to its credit, it is still doing so. Mishima must have succeeded in changing his own position, posthumously! I have always maintained that it would be impossible to apply any kind of label to him; and that definitions such as fascist, imperialist or paranoid mythomaniac, among many others, do no more, even if they are positive, than reveal an inability to understand his complex and multifaceted reality, the art that is so inextricably bound up with his way of life.

As far as the impossibility of defining Mishima is concerned, I shall not hide a certain reluctance to deal with his homosexuality, whether real or presumed. This is not because I believe the subject is shocking, but for the same reasons that I would have if I were dealing with his heterosexuality; and because it has been used and abused in order to praise or discredit his life or work. Some have even used his homosexuality to remove the 'right winger' label that had been applied to him. Mishima cannot be made to fit into any political pigeonhole, and trying to do so runs the risk of removing one label only to attach another. There is no doubt, in fact, that his homosexuality, even if used for this 'positive' purpose, is a label just like any other. Personally, even leaving aside my lack of enthusiasm for labels generally, I am not sure that Mishima can be described as homosexual any more than he can be called heterosexual, a husband and father. I am inclined to think that if he did indeed have sexual relationships with men it was to satisfy his unquenchable thirst for self-knowledge, his need to understand the depths and complexities of his being and the infinite number of unexplored areas within himself. And the same can be said of his first heterosexual experience, which he confided immediately to an American friend, who later became his biographer and had no qualms about putting it in print!

It is also important not to underestimate the aspect of homosexuality that is associated with 'heroes' and 'warriors'– the aspect akin to the sense of brotherhood, in the physical sense also, that existed between men of arms in earlier civilizations such as ancient Greece, and in the samurai tradition as so effectively portrayed by director Ōshima Nagisa (b. 1932) in his elegant and obsessive film *Gohattō*. Invoking Mishima's homosexuality from this point of view, as some have done, would not remove him from the pantheon of right-wing culture. For reasons of both form and substance, I am also unable to agree with the theory that interprets Mishima's suicide, and that of his disciple Morita, as a double love suicide, a *shinjū*. This practice became more common, notably in the seventeenth century, when the dizzying expansion of the urban classes, of the merchant middle classes and of popular culture (the latter finding its chief expression in the idiom of the so-called Floating World) gave rise to deep conflicts between the existing and solidly rooted sense of duty on the one hand and on the other the world of passion for so long devoid of cultural expression and repressed by the conventions of a society steeped in neo-Confucian traditions. At the time, the conflict between new yearnings and old duties often led to difficulties that could not be resolved; almost inevitably, if they were to do with affairs of the heart they ended in tragedy – frequently in elopement and a suicide pact – or on the gallows.

The *shinjū* was the last resort when circumstances were desperate, when it was impossible to control passion and overcome the social constraints that thwarted its development. If passion had existed between Mishima and Morita, who could have prevented its consummation? A double love suicide is thus totally excluded. Even from a formal point of view this could not have been a *shinjū*. The intention had been that everyone in Mishima's group except the youngest would commit *seppuku*, each in turn administering the fatal sword stroke to a fellow member until the youngest who had been chosen to carry out acts of piety on behalf of the dead was left alive. However, this is not what happened. Morita failed in his first attempt to give Mishima the *coup de grâce* and everything collapsed in chaos. It is unnecessary to go into the details of what actually happened, but it is none the less clear that this was intended to be a collective suicide and not a *shinjū*.

If it is impossible to say *what* Mishima was, is it at least possible to say *who* he was?

According to his father's plans, Hiraoka Kimitake (Mishima's birth name) was not destined to become a writer; rather, he was to follow family tradition and become a high-ranking civil servant. So accepted was this that when he wrote his first short story, *The Forest in Full Bloom* (*Hanazakari no mori*), in 1941 his teachers, who wanted to see it published in a leading magazine, made him adopt a pseudonym so as not to hurt his father's feelings. This is how Hiraoka Kimitake became Mishima Yukio.

Mishima's early years were far from happy, spent as they were in the narrow confines of his paternal grandmother's sickroom with its strong smell of medicines. He was forced to live with her after she had taken him from his mother in 1925 as a newborn baby, and to stay with her even after his parents had set up on their own. This sorry state of affairs, which lasted until he was twelve years old, had a deep impact on the boy's psychological and physical life – Mishima was slightly built, and, although he would have been happy to make the ultimate sacrifice for his country, he was declared unfit for military service. There is no doubt that his extremely sheltered life in a sickly and almost exclusively female environment, and his near-total isolation from other children, contributed to an upbringing that followed the conventions of a girl's education rather than a boy's. At the same time, however, it was from his grandmother, an aristocrat of the old school and the frustrated wife of a pleasure-loving, happy-go-lucky middle-class man, that he absorbed the values of the samurai ethos.

Mishima's arrival at his parents' home at the difficult moment of the onset of puberty had an overwhelming effect on him: he fell in love with his mother. After their long separation her response was to reciprocate fully. In later years she took to calling him 'my love', and her feelings led her to engage in a secret battle to rescue him from the civil-service career his father had planned for him. His relationships with the opposite sex, already strained, were made harder still by the illness and death of his younger sister, who died of typhoid in 1945. Mishima spent day after day at her bedside, caring for her, and was deeply disturbed by this family tragedy.

Exposed to samurai tradition, but brought up in a female environment; destined for a bureaucratic career, but endowed with a writer's aspirations; admitted to Gakushūin, a prestigious school for aristocrats, but mocked for his middle-class birth, during his most formative years Mishima was beset by contradictions, and the suffering they generated benefited his art, inextricable as it was from his life. His prose, for example, uses language that is vast in its range and of extraordinary aesthetic refinement, yet it is juxtaposed with images and scenes of extreme crudity and power.

It was during his teenage years, as he recalls in *Confessions of a Mask* (*Kamen no kokuhaku*, 1949), the novel that brought him success at the age of twenty-four, that he came across Guido Reni's painting of Saint Sebastian. It played a crucial part in forming his view of Eros and Thanatos, of ecstasy and martyrdom in the service of a loftier ideal – a concept of death which he continued to think and write about until he made it into a reality. Death must catch a man when he is in full possession of his intellectual faculties and physical strength. Rather than coming in the form of a demoralizing decline when all energy is gone, it must be like the severing of life by steel, like the death of a Greek hero on the battlefield, a samurai in a duel, a pilot in a kamikaze attack, the life force swept away like the froth of cherry blossom touched by a breeze.

His troubled soul's need for inner harmony began to grow, and in the figure of the passionate and ambivalent Etsuko, a female character in *Thirst for Love* (*Ai no kawaki*), published in 1950, Mishima described his own tormented condition – that of a man who searches anxiously for love only to reject it as soon as it is found. He does the same in the first part of *Forbidden Colours*, published three years later in 1953, where he attempts 'to express the conflicts and contradictions seething inside him, as represented by two separate "selves"'. These two selves, represented in the novel by an old misogynist intellectual, Hinoki Shunsuke, and a beautiful young man, Yuichi, never ceased to provoke violent conflicts within him, and they recur from time to time, in different guises, in later works.

Mishima spurned the literary world, preferring those of businessmen and soldiers. He said, 'My dislike of intellectuals was a reaction to my enormous, monstrous sensitivity. This is why I have wished to become a classic.' The only exception was Kawabata, the novelist who in his style and way of life differed from Mishima perhaps more than any other writer, but who, alone among leading literary figures, helped and supported him at the very beginning when he had been discouraged by other writers, such as Shiga Naoya (1883–1971). There was always a kind of tutor–pupil relationship between the two men, and in his last days Kawabata, who himself committed suicide almost two years after Mishima, used to say that he could hear his pupil's spirit urging him to join him.

Mishima's dream of classicism became a reality in 1952 when, at the end of a year-long journey through the Americas and France, he eventually arrived in Greece. There he fell in love with 'the blue sea and intense sky of that classical land' but, most importantly, he found the inspiration that helped him to find a path to some form of inner reintegration. As he later wrote in *My Wandering Years* (*Watakushi no henreki jidai*, 1963), 'In ancient Greece, I thought, spirituality did not exist. But there was equilibrium between body and intellect, between *soma* and *sophia*. "Spirituality," I thought, was a grotesque product of Christianity. In ancient times the Greeks had lost that equilibrium too easily. Yet their exertions and efforts to preserve it had helped to create beauty.' This is one of the keys to understanding Mishima the writer, playwright, actor and, above all, Mishima the man. His need was to lead himself, an individual torn apart within a disintegrated society, back to an inner unity where all aspects of life co-existed in harmony, rather than under the supremacy of the intellect – a medieval Christian legacy still alive and well, even in people who called themselves modern.

In 1954 there was a gentle interlude in his vast and tormented literary output: the story of the idyllic love between two star-crossed lovers, a young fisherman and a girl on a small island in the Japanese archipelago. In *The Sound of Waves* (*Shiosai*) the simple life, the purity of the sky, the power of the sea, the brightness of sunlight take the reader back to an earlier concept of life's values, where beauty and goodness merge within a single vision of reality. The novel was hugely successful and was even adopted as a text in schools. But the happy island of this Japanese Daphnis and Chloe, which Mishima had created in his heart and imagined for his soul — which so desperately yearned for peace — was soon submerged in the merciless tide of very different passions that smouldered within him.

Mishima spent those years struggling with his demons and searching for a physical and moral identity — a search that he pursued single-mindedly, by building up his puny body into a gymnast's perfect machine and delving into, exploring and interrogating the most hidden places of his personality in order to uncover its contradictions and, by making them public, come to know himself. These were the years of *The Temple of the Golden Pavilion* (*Kinkaku-ji*, 1959); of his relationship with the kabuki actor Nakamura Utaemon VI (1917–2001), a famous interpreter of female roles; of nō dramas revisited from a contemporary perspective; of explorations of theatrical forms, which led more than one critic to describe him as the leading Japanese playwright of the twentieth century. Mishima burst on to the international literary scene. He wrote novels that were translated into many languages, like *Kyōko's House* (*Kyōko no ie*, 1959), *After the Banquet* (*Utage no ato*, 1960), *The Sailor Who Fell from Grace with the Sea* (*Gogo no eikō*, 1963); and plays like *Madame de Sade* (*Sado kōshaku fujin*, 1965). He also published works on aesthetics, like *Sun and Steel* (*Taiyō to tetsu*, 1968), and pieces of literary criticism. He took punctilious care of his physical appearance and of social relationships; and he took every opportunity to turn himself into a celebrity — from the luxurious Western-style house he built after he married, with its great hall designed according to his 'dream, or nightmare, of Victorian opulence', to, I believe, his tiny army. Mishima tried to attract attention to himself by every possible means, while at the same time working on his most ambitious and large-scale project: his death.

It was in carrying out this final work that Mishima attained the degree of harmony between body and spirit, violence and refinement, horror and elegance that he had been pursuing all along through the expression of beauty in art and in life. He evoked and attracted his death, playing with it as a snake charmer plays with a snake, until he could force it to come when and how he wanted it. And he rehearsed it many times — in works like *Yūkoku* (*Patriotism*, 1961), where he describes in minute detail a young officer's *seppuku*; in the film of the same name, which he directed and acted in five years later; and also in *Hitogiri*, a film in which he played the part of a samurai who killed himself according to *seppuku*.

But it is almost as though his death was really evoked through an exhibition that dealt with his life. Using extensive photographic documentation displayed against a black background, Mishima divided it into four 'rivers' that told the story of his life from four different viewpoints: 'the river of writing'; 'the river of theatre'; 'the river of the body'; 'the river of action'. He was aware that, as indeed happened, most people would stop at just one of these 'labels' without attempting to understand the profound and unitary meaning of himself – and he personally prepared the labels for them. As he himself said, 'The visitor will be able to choose his preferred river and to avoid being dragged into those he does not like. I shall be grateful to those people who will follow all four of my life's rivers, but I doubt that there will be many who will.' The exhibition, which lasted for a week and attracted over a hundred thousand visitors, closed just a few days before his suicide.

It is impossible not to wonder why Mishima played his unbelievable, theatrical game with death throughout his life. Everyone must, sooner or later, accept this inexorable guide to their last journey. In Mishima's case it was he who forced it to come on a planned date, and who made sure it came, after jousting with it, and exploring, studying and experiencing its nature; after rehearsing this meeting over and over again, and describing it as if it were a performance, the greatest of all performances. He executed his most important work of art against a background of total indifference on the part of the public. In paying the highest price, he showed that he identified not so much with the mask of vanity and feverish excitement he had worn for years in order to hide his neuroses and insecurities, but with the inner demon that had constantly driven him to push himself beyond his contingent limits, alluring him with the mysterious and irresistible smiles on thousands and thousands of faces. To assert until the point of death his freedom to be a man.

Mishima in the Snow, 1969,
photograph by Yato Tamotsu

Ikkō: A Flash of Light

Light – intense, clear, revealing – is even more essential to the graphic work of Tanaka Ikkō (1930–2002) than are colour and line, the signature elements of his designs. He used light, balancing it, permeating the image with it, to imbue the values of his own culture with expressive forms typical of the twentieth century. He achieved this through his designs for posters, logos, brands, books, galleries, shops, exhibitions, packaging, calligraphy (including new characters), newspapers, magazines and textiles. For Tanaka, graphic art was a means of communicating the aesthetic values acquired by the Japanese through a centuries-long process of refining them and translating elements of external cultures and sources into their national idiom. It is in this capacity to create designs which, while steeped in tradition, strike an immediate chord in the contemporary collective imagination and can be visually appreciated regardless of social and cultural barriers, that the value of Tanaka's work lies – whether in Tokyo or Paris, Milan or Washington, Mexico City or London, São Paulo or Warsaw.

'Style' is a term to be used sparingly when talking about art, and even more so in a field like graphic art given the rapid succession of trends and the rise and fall of fashionable forms and stylistic features. Yet Tanaka is the one contemporary Japanese graphic artist whose work could not be described without resorting to the word 'style'. With his vast and diverse output, he lived through the traumas, upheavals and excitements of the decades after the Second World War, and was fully involved in every movement and every sudden shift. His passion for traditional forms is reflected in his images, the interplay of figures and script, the way in which colour is always applied to absorb or repel light within shapes that are carefully delineated and constructed with lines that are never tentative or vague, but clear and fluid. They are definitely Japanese in inspiration, but their compositional structure transforms them into archetypes of aesthetic qualities and values, which are universally identifiable and can be related to everyone's personal parameters.

From his debut in the 1950s, when Japan was stunned by defeat and its post-war situation, and when traditional forms were being rejected with iconoclastic fervour, Tanaka was an active participant in all the social and artistic upheavals that occurred in rapid succession during those years of change and innovation: the long process of recovery during the 1960s and 1970s, with the technological and urban explosion as evidenced by the Tokyo Olympics, the construction of the 'bullet train' line in 1964 and the Osaka Expo of 1970; and then the euphoria of the 'bubble economy' of the 1980s before the crisis of the 1990s.

'I was born in Nara,' Tanaka said of himself, 'an ancient city that is the repository of Japan's most ancient traditions. And I studied in Kyoto, another cradle of ancient thought. That is why I have never managed to sever the link with old traditions. In 1957, when I moved to Tokyo – by then a cosmopolitan city – I took with me everything my traditions had taught me.'[1]

Yet, despite this formative process, the traditional sources of Tanaka's inspiration must be sought in the art and culture of the Edo period (1615–1868) rather than those of previous eras – and even then it is only in a very small way that he was inspired by the great graphic works of the *ukiyo-e* tradition. His aesthetic concepts, his constructivist need for order and the architectural positioning of each element within the image, his way of grouping the rich blocks of colour he loved to use, his search for clear, rational graphic signs, point to other sources, the most significant of which is perhaps the Rinpa school. Tanaka was always interested in the Rinpa style. As he himself said,

> To me, Rinpa is a dangerous world. It comes close to you with various seductions. I say 'comes close' and that is not an exaggeration; Rinpa has a lingering fragrance that makes you long just to let yourself slip into its tender bosom, a warmth that is far too soppy – too 'Japanese' for me. It might be the oh-so-delicate sound of the *koto* [Japanese long zither] or might be those shrilly sighing melodies and intense rhythms of the flute, there's something in it that gets the average Japanese very worked up. The Rinpa's a style that's always infallibly elegant, free, generous, so wonderful, offering that oh-so-delicate warm touch that never flaunts its beauty obtrusively – like the early spring sun captured in a pond, delicately announcing, perhaps, the beginning of our moist seasonal round – so far removed from the severity of the climate of other continents that might be perennially deep in snow or desert. From our tougher contemporary point of view, the sense of self is always in stress and pushed to conflict. The Rinpa style purveys an idea of beauty that's far too far away from what we are. That's why I'm somewhat afraid of its overwhelming genorisity.[2]

There are formal elements in some of Tanaka's works that could justify regarding him as the last of the great Rinpa artists. An example is one of his most famous posters, *Japan*, created for the JAGDA (Japan Graphic Designers Association) graphics exhibition of 1986 and depicting a deer. It was inspired by an illustrated Buddhist text dating back to the twelfth century, the *Heike nōkyō*, kept in the Itsukushima shrine in Hiroshima. The original image of the deer was apparently retouched by Sōtatsu 500 years later. This and many of Sōtatsu's paintings

1 Gian Carlo Calza, *Tanaka Ikkō: Graphic Master*, London, Phaidon, 1997, p. 14.

2 Ibid., p. 15.

with the same style and subject matter (including the famous horizontal scroll known as the 'Deer Scroll', also reproduced above in the chapter called 'Nature's Magnificence' featuring Kōetsu's calligraphy and held in the MOA Museum of Art in Atami, and the one in the Seattle Asian Art Museum) share many stylistic aspects with both the *Heike nōkyō* and the *Japan* poster. Parallels can also be found between Tanaka's work and Kōrin's, as in the great irises in the posters he produced for his one-man show at the 'ggg' Gallery in 1990, or in the murals created in 1992 for Narita Airport. The flowers are reminiscent of those in Kōrin's screen, now in Tokyo's Nezu Art Museum, or the *Yatsuhashi* screen in New York's Metropolitan Museum – to mention only two works by the great seventeenth-century master that feature this particular subject. Other critics have preferred to draw similarities between Tanaka and Hon'ami Kōetsu and the circle of artists and craftsmen who gathered under him in Takagamine, a village north-east of Kyoto, after the death of the great tea-master Sen no Rikyū. This became an important and highly influential centre for the arts and culture of the day, a kind of precursor of the Bauhaus.

However, although comparisons with Kōetsu, Sōtatsu and Kōrin – three of the greatest ever artists and interpreters of Japanese aesthetics – could not have failed to gratify him, Tanaka preferred to be judged in his own right and without being categorized; his is an art that must be understood in itself and needs no external references to be appreciated. Clearly, critical definitions do not quite fit him: those who, like Ronald Labuz, have described him as a 'colourist' later had to include him in other categories. He himself emphasized his independence from any group or 'school', and dispelled any lingering doubts by describing himself as a *bake-yakusha*, or ghost actor, reviving a rare term that indicates the multiple-role masks used in nō theatre.

The leitmotif running through the tensions that set Tanaka relentlessly on his quest to free himself from past and present trends and mannerisms is an exquisitely spiritual reality. The 'spirit' contained in a design, and found within the forms in which it is expressed, is the same one that has kept Japanese culture alive even at those times (not infrequent in Japan's history) when it may have seemed lost – and is also the spirit that gives it inner life. The key to understanding the way Tanaka sees this spirituality extending to himself, as well as to Japanese art and design of all eras, is contained in one of his publications, *Simplification and Design* (*Tanjunka to design*). He also set out his thoughts and ideas on art and life in other articles and, above all, in his work. *Simplification*, however, brings them together so effectively that it is worth quoting a few of its passages at some length.

At the beginning of modern design there was an idea of 'simplicity' as a form of limitation in response to the needs of mass production, which was contrary to ostentation and so eliminated it. But recently objects have been appearing in which simplicity becomes nothing more than an alibi. This can be called Academic Modernism. [...]

The Stone Garden, the Tea Ceremony or the Nō theatre are examples of these declarations of the spirit, are based on abstracting a harmonious dialogue with Nature. But in the modern version of simplification there is no such elegant dialogue. Instead of the simplicity that symbolizes a multiplicity of meanings, we have a merely intuitive simplicity. If in the past the absence of embellishment stood for things that had been allowed to become completely forgotten, now 'simplicity' means only that there is nothing there. With the expansion of space/time and the rapid mechanization of urban life, artificial satellites and supersonic travel, it is Man himself who is becoming less and less important, and little by little traditional aesthetics are going the same way. [...]

The modern, intuitive, idea of 'simplicity' has a more direct, impulsive immediacy than Pop or Op. It cancels everything out as though the feverish state in which we live were ultimately aiming at a state of coldness. This creates the idea that beauty must be some sort of physical shock meant to happen in the body itself, some sort of blinding flash. Becoming a sensual experience it creates the impression that there is nothing to look at at all. Instead it directly 'zaps' all five senses, drowning out their separate sensibility and any need for passion or thought. Perhaps this is the idea of beauty as understood by modern intuitive simplicity: total transparency or essence. [...]

Modern communication can use this intuitive idea of simplicity. Rather than the distorting approach taken by Pop and Op Art, we can now communicate in fresher ways by developing a very clear concept of what the advertising message wants to say. I do think that if we have to have fireworks we might as well try to make them beautiful.[3]

Clearly, the subject matter Tanaka set out to explore in this essay was universal, rather than specifically Japanese, aesthetic values – his constant theme, even when he appears to be totally immersed in his own culture. This, as well as the formal quality of his work, is why his graphic output can be so easily accepted and appreciated across geographical and cultural borders. It was to the constant pursuit and preservation of spiritual freedom and its expression through

3   Ibid., pp. 16–17.

design (the indispensable condition, after all, for creating an individual style) that Tanaka devoted his artistic career. And, in keeping with his philosophy, he gave his quest a particular slant: identifying spiritual values, personally experimenting with them and then translating them, by means of images that reflect their quintessence, into archetypal forms. Here lies the key, simple yet extremely challenging, to his work.

Many factors enabled him to develop his style and keep it a constant, for so many years, and for these to become clearer it is necessary to look not only at his artistic and professional journey, but also at his life. Tanaka's quest was integral to his very existence, and not merely to his profession. Even the most mundane moments and occasions, seemingly unconnected with his work, were part of a constant, uninterrupted flow enriched by his capacity to draw something significant from each and every thing. A constant exchange between art and life, as evinced both by his many prizes (he won an award every single year, with the exception of 1962), and by his wide interests outside his profession from which most of the impetus for his work stemmed. All these factors seem to have been present right from the start.

Editorial graphics was a field that Tanaka considered very important both because of the complex nature of the end product, which has implications for a number of sectors, and for its cultural consequences, of which he was always acutely aware. He maintained that his activity in this aspect of design developed markedly during the 1960s and 1970s, only to decrease in the 1980s and 1990s as a result of publishers' growing interest in the mass market at the expense of books produced with particular attention to detail. Typically, his involvement in editorial graphics was 'total': from page make-up to layout, from the content of books to the creation and selection of images, from the study of fonts and characters to bookbinding. This work enabled Tanaka to realize his eternal dream, namely the creation of an ideal workshop that would include all arts and crafts, where the most diverse teams could work together as one.

His commitment to rediscovering the values of Japanese society and making them known both abroad and in Japan itself (where, as had happened with other values elsewhere in the world, their meaning had often been lost) goes well beyond the identification of forms and stylistic features. This was rightly pointed out by the graphic artist Nagai Kazumasa (b. 1929), whose long and deep friendship with Tanaka endows him with a unique perspective on his colleague's work:

> Tanaka was clearly very much affected by having grown up in Nara and
> Kyoto, and these influences are reflected in his design. But had he only used these

influences to work out his own approach, this would not have been so complete as it is. While he did not crucially depend on the fact that the traditions of ancient Japan ran in his veins, his cool gaze, as it fixed the present moment, allowed the thought to filter through. Had his modern thinking not been cultivated by this cool rational gaze I don't think he would have arrived at this sensibility, able to decode Japanese tradition within himself and reorganize it as his own.[4]

Rediscovering a subject that is part of his native culture, allowing his entire self to absorb it both through those 'cold rational eyes' and that blood tinted with the colours of Nara and Kyoto, allowing the spirit to merge with his own; and then, without being overpowered by it, re-presenting it in a contemporary idiom so that others can participate in it – this is what Tanaka did in the greater part of his work. It was mainly with Yoshida Mitsukuni, a friend and teacher from the Atelierza days, and later a lecturer at Kyoto University, that Tanaka developed his work in the area of books on Japanese culture. The 1968 set of volumes entitled *Motifs of Japan: Nature and Landscape* (*Nippon no mon'yō. Kachō fūgetsu*) demonstrate this constant, at times almost didactic, interest in deconstructing and reassembling properties and forms that belong to the past – in art, crafts, religion and nature – in order to transform them into images of the present.

During the 1980s Tanaka created a successful genre: the large human face. The first example was his poster for *Nihon buyō*, performances of Japanese dance given in 1981 at the Asian Performing Arts Institute (part of the University of California in Los Angeles). It featured the head of a female dancer, occupying the whole of the foreground, created by assembling flat, brightly coloured geometrical shapes. The result is a picture that is both highly evocative and optically striking. Tanaka took an image from tradition and turned it into an abstract concept full of visual meaning. 'Large heads', with dominant broken lines as in the example above, or curved ones as in *The New Spirit of Japanese Design* (a poster created for the cover of *Print* magazine), became a constant theme throughout Tanaka's work. In fact, they are not unlike the polychrome prints featuring half-bust 'large head' portraits (*ōkubi-e*) of kabuki actors, famous courtesans and beautiful women in their everyday lives, invented in the 1790s by some of the leading graphic artists in Japanese history. These had been an immediate success and contributed significantly to the fortunes of artists like Utamaro, Sharaku, Shunkō and Shun'ei, as well as those of their publishers – the inimitable Tsutaya Jūzaburō in particular. The genre was subsequently banned by the Tokugawa government, who considered it 'too luxurious' for the middle

4 Ibid., p. 24.

classes, who, although the wealthiest people in Japan, were at the bottom of the social hierarchy.

It was barely surviving in the twentieth century when Tanaka revived it with a critical energy comparable to that of his eighteenth-century predecessors – but in a totally new guise. As far as the earlier pictures were concerned, the greatest innovation had been to depict a true likeness of famous people of the period, so that everyone would recognize in the prints then circulating (not unlike today's gossip magazines) their fantasy role models: the handsome actor Segawa Kikunojō III, the famous courtesan Hanaōgi, or Ohisa, Okita and Toyohina, women who rivalled each other in beauty.

Tanaka revived this genre but totally changed the approach. His own giant, abstracted faces were sometimes full of wonderment, sometimes severe, sometimes amused, their flat colours set off against precisely geometricized outlines. In effect, they became a genre in their own right, breaking away from the lifelike portrait to develop the presentation of human activities as idealized images – a sort of portraiture of archetypes. With great interest, he is still exploring this theme: from the Sixth National Cultural Festival, Chiba 1991, to the 1994 exhibition for the bicentennial of Sharaku, 'Sharaku 200 Years', a book cover in 1995 for *A Terrible Taste* (*Osoroshii aji*), and *In Search of Elegance*, for the 1996 International Congress on Japanese Modern Art in Venice.

Unlike the fawn in the *Heike nōkyō* mentioned above, it would be misleading to say that in this case Tanaka had any particular precedent consciously in mind. It is more likely that stored in his genes was a vast wealth of traditional values, principles and styles, which he called on until they surfaced ready to be given a new life and a new form. While it would be incorrect to attribute precise references to the *ukiyo-e* artists in the case of Tanaka's portraits, it is undoubtedly true, as Nagai said, that *ukiyo-e* flowed in his blood and became apparent. A similar process must have taken place with the pictures of flowers that he began to create in the second half of the 1980s, although here the reference appears more explicit. The flowers are large and, depicted in the same way as the portraits, emerge boldly and powerfully from the background, the true protagonists of the blank surface. In the irises created for his 1990 exhibition 'Ikkō Tanaka Graphic Art Botanical Garden' there are clear references to the paintings by Kōrin mentioned earlier in this chapter, but here it is the individual flower itself that is placed at the centre of the visual focus – just like an 'idealizing' portrait. In some cases, Tanaka went so far as to treat flowers like anthropomorphic creatures, as in the pair of tulips in the poster designed for the 'First Japan Exposition in Toyama 1992'.

Was Tanaka extending ethology to include the plant world? Consciously or subliminally – it makes no difference – what emerges is an ancient thread of Buddhist thought interwoven with Shintō naturalism, according to which there is a level of consciousness not just in humans and animals but also in plants with the result that they, too, can achieve salvation. The flowers that Tanaka elevates to sublime dignity in the large murals at Tokyo's Narita Airport are, no doubt, symbols of the new universal interest in nature; what place more appropriate, then, than an intercontinental airport? But they are more than that; they symbolize a time-honoured, centuries-old religious and cultural practice that sees the whole of nature as a sacred place inhabited by gods. Images that are new yet linked to the past, they recall in spirit the famous *Large Flowers* series made by Hokusai in about 1830.

Here Hokusai depicted the flowers in the foreground with only their upper parts visible, thus revolutionizing the iconographic paradigms of the time, since, standing in front of them, observers have the impression that they are looking at true portraits. The flowers are the uppermost part of the plants bearing them: they could almost be called their 'faces'. And they are dazzling faces, conscious of their splendour, like those in *Iris and Grasshopper*: plants that symbolize the samurai because of their sword-shaped leaves and proud, erect stance. However, Hokusai added a grasshopper – and on the boldest (but also the most indented) blade. The devouring, parasitic insect and the no-longer-sharp blade: an allusion to the dying feudal system and the triumph of that most despised of social classes, the merchants? Or simply a juxtaposition of greens and browns and contrasting shapes?

In his flowers Tanaka revived this approach, and his irises, colder and more impersonal than Hokusai's, transmit a similar feeling as well, but in a manner more suited to the twentieth century – less involving, less emotional. According to some graphic designers, Tanaka seemed to possess a kind of sixth sense that enabled him always to remain in tune with the times and, notwithstanding a style so closely linked to tradition, to produce work that, constantly and without fail, responded to the needs of the contemporary collective imagination.

This is unquestionably an interesting theory. Looking at his output over the years and at his impact on Japanese culture, it is possible to believe that he anticipated that collective imagination, creating visions and situations capable of reflecting modern aspirations and the present-day need for values, both old and new. Tanaka's work seems to have been created specifically to stimulate people today, to sensitize, refine and orientate them, and, in the final analysis, teach them to appreciate forms and realities which, though previously ignored, soon become the expression of a set of coherent aesthetic values that have their roots in society: in a word, a style.

Through his way of experiencing his work physically as well as emotionally and intellectually, of re-presenting images from Japan's indigenous tradition and creatively reinterpreting and renewing them for the modern world, Tanaka provided his own answer to our current identity crisis. His exploration of routes other than graphic design, such as the tea ceremony and its aesthetics, ensured that his quest never lost its momentum and that, time and again, he went beyond any sort of newly found equilibrium. The aesthetic aspects of tea, combined with a profound interest in crafts and materials, led him to establish a research and work space that was in a way not unlike the one founded by Kōetsu in Takagamine. It was something of an art coterie, although, given the needs of the twentieth century, it was not based in a particular place but was spread over the length and breadth of Japan. Its users were artists and craftsmen, graphic designers and art directors, publishers and printers, potters and tea-masters, poets and intellectuals, photographers and calligraphers; and through his own work Tanaka often became the interpreter and disseminator of theirs. As a result, there was a radical narrowing of the ancient gap between graphic art and fine art, and between design and crafts. The fixed point of reference for this journey was nature in all its aspects, combined with a love of materials. Echoes, perhaps, of Shintō's animistic roots and profound respect for human labour, for the physical aspect of production – constant themes in Tanaka's approach to art and life. He was faithful to the meaning of his name: Tanaka Ikkō, 'a flash of light in the middle of a rice field'.

田中一光グラフィックアート植物園
IKKO TANAKA GRAPHIC ART EXHIBITION

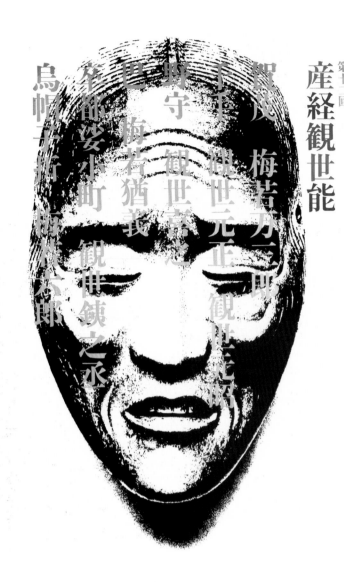

第十二回

産経観世能

観世左近

梅若万三郎

千五郎

観世元正

野守

観世寿夫

梅若猶義

卒都姿小町

観世鍊之丞

鳥帽子折

観世栄夫

昭和四十年二月二十八日（日）　大阪サンケイホール特設能舞台　主催・サンケイ新聞社　大阪新聞社

Previous page:
Tanaka Ikkō
One man exhibition poster,
1990

Left:
Tanaka Ikkō
Sankei Kanze no (XII),
performing arts poster, 1965

Right:
Tanaka Ikkō
Sankei Kanze no (V),
performing arts poster, 1958

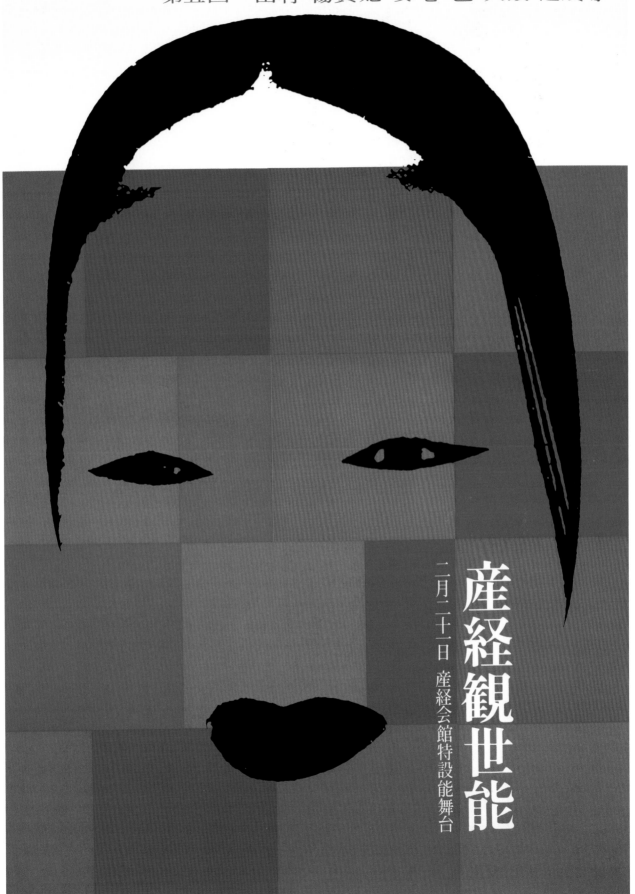

第五回　田村　楊貴妃　安宅　巴　天鼓　道成寺

産経観世能

二月二十一日　産経会館特設能舞台

281

Tanaka Ikkō
*The Discovery of the Kabuki
Theatre* (*Kabuki no hakken*),
book poster, 1974

歌舞伎の発見

誰でもわかる歌舞伎の見方　富田鉄之助 著　白金書房刊

助六由縁江戸桜勧進帳鳴神矢の根毛抜解脱不破嬲
暫不動象引寿曽我対面菅原伝授手習鑑神霊矢口渡
国性爺合戦蘆屋道満大内鑑嫗山姥小野道風青柳硯
仮名手本忠臣蔵平家女護島傾城反魂香義経千本桜
博多小女郎浪枕源平布引滝一谷嫩軍記壇浦兜軍記
奥州安達原鬼一法眼三略巻八陣守護城忍夜恋曲者
御所桜堀川夜討祇園祭礼信仰記加賀見山旧錦絵
本朝廿四孝鎌倉三代記妹背山婦女庭訓絵本太功記
敵討天下茶屋聚伊賀越道中双六近江源氏先陣館
恋女房染分手綱摂州合邦辻伽羅先代萩楼門五三桐
曾根崎心中近頃河原の達引桂川連理柵艶容女舞衣
天竺徳兵衛韓噺東海道四谷怪談双蝶々曲輪日記
女殺油地獄大経師昔暦恋飛脚大和往来新版歌祭文
生写朝顔話心中天網島伊達娘恋緋鹿子積恋雪関扉
夏祭浪花鑑伊勢音頭恋寝刃廓文章お染の七役茨木
京鹿子娘道成寺連獅子草摺引素襖落土蜘蛛紅葉狩
春興鏡獅子六歌仙容彩船弁慶壬生三番曳釣女藤娘
与話情浮名横櫛色彩間苅豆乗合船恵方万歳三社祭
四千両小判梅葉水天宮利生深川十六夜清心吉原雀
籠釣瓶花街酔醒神明裏和合取組五大力恋緘手習子
人情咄文七元結怪異談牡丹燈籠佐倉義民伝鳥羽絵
蔦紅葉宇都谷峠東海道中膝栗毛明烏花濡衣神田祭
天衣紛上野初花梅雨小袖昔八丈天一坊大岡政談黒塚
盲長屋梅加賀鳶巷談宵宮雨元禄忠臣蔵名月八幡祭
刺青奇偶桐一葉番町皿屋敷一本刀土俵入双面水照月
沓手鳥孤城落月鳥辺山心中修禅寺物語暗闇の丑松

Glossary

Akikonomu The daughter of Genji and the lady from Akashi with whom he had a relationship while exiled at Suma. She was adopted by the Prince and later became Empress.

Akutagawa Ryūnosuke (1892–1927) Among the most influential writers of the post-First World War period, his output consists chiefly of short stories, poetry and essays. He in turn was influenced by late nineteenth-century Western literature and the works of his contemporaries Natsume Sōseki and Mori Ōgai. His earliest published works were short stories written while he was still at university, and were based on Japan's traditional themes. Physically weak and psychologically fragile, he committed suicide at the age of 35, leaving behind a hundred or so short stories, some of which, like *Rashōmon* and *Kappa*, are held to be among the great masterpieces of Japanese literature.

Amaterasu Ōmikami The name of the highest deity in Shintō mythology. She is the Goddess of the Sun and of Light and is traditionally believed to be the progenitor of the Imperial Family. The Ise Temple, the foremost shrine of the Shintō religion, is dedicated to her.

Amida (in Sanskrit: *Amitābha*) Of the four Buddhas who preside over the four points of the compass, Amida is the ruler of the West and also, therefore, of the Paradise of Pure Land, believed to be located there. His cult, known as Amidism, is a branch of *mahāyāna* Buddhism, which developed in eastern Asia and is still widespread in Japan, where it became established through the activity of various sects.

aragoto The highly spectacular acting style of the kabuki theatre, very popular in Edo in the late seventeenth century. Initiated by Ichikawa Danjūrō I (1660–1704), it differed from the more restrained and refined *wagoto*, the dramatic style popular in Osaka.

Asai Ryōi (?–1691) Writer of short stories widely read by ordinary people (*kanazōshi*), he became one of the major interpreters of an emerging popular and middle-class culture. It was with his novel *Ukiyo monogatari* (*Tales of the Floating World*, 1661) that the term *ukiyo* came to assume a more mundane and ephemeral connotation, losing its Buddhist meaning of 'fleeting world'.

Ashikaga Powerful feudal dynasty which governed Japan from 1333 to the end of the fifteenth century, when a series of revolts weakened its authority, until it was finally overturned in 1568.

Atai A form of spiritual symbiosis, typical of certain primitive societies, between a human being and an element of nature, almost invariably an animal. A special sort of mutual dependence, both physical and spiritual, is formed between them and lasts for the rest of their lives.

Atelierza Student theatre group based at the Kyoto Fine Arts University, for which Tanaka Ikkō designed sets and make-up.

bakufu (military government, or 'government of the tent') The system of military government headed by a shōgun. The first *bakufu* was established by Minamoto no Yoritomo (1147–99), who, having emerged victorious from a feud with the Taira family, ruled over the city of Kamakura. His power was officially recognized in 1192, when he was awarded the title of shōgun. The second military government was that of the Ashikaga, which lasted from 1333 to 1568. The third, led by the Tokugawa, spanned over 200 years, from 1603 to 1867.

Bandō Mitsugorō VIII (1906–75) A kabuki actor specializing in male roles, mainly historical figures and warriors. He died tragically in Kyoto from *fugu* poisoning.

bijinga Term used to indicate paintings or prints whose exclusive or primary subject are beautiful women.

biwa Stringed instrument similar to the lute, originally from China or central Asia. The best-known types are those with four or five strings, which were commonly used during the Nara and Heian periods to accompany court music (*gagaku*). From the late eighth century it spread also in Kyūshū where it became the instrument commonly played by Buddhist monks to accompany the singing of the *sutras*. From the tenth century onwards, it became associated with the *biwa hōshi*, or blind itinerant singers, so called because of their habit of shaving their heads and wearing robes like monks.

bodhi (in Sanskrit: 'awakening') Term used to indicate the condition of the being who, having overcome the barriers of the world of phenomena, can finally know true reality. The route to this state is that set out by Sākyamuni, who thus became the Buddha.

Bodhidharma (sixth century AD; in Japanese: *Daruma*) Founder and First Patriarch of *chan* Buddhism, which he established in China, having arrived there from his native India around 520 AD. In Japan, where his Buddhist school assumed the name of Zen, Bodhidharma is considered one of its most popular historical-mythical figures.

bodhisattva (in Japanese: *bosatsu*) The one who has reached the Buddhist state of perfection immediately before that of Buddha. The name is given to those who have achieved salvation, but maintain a connection with the human world in order to alleviate its suffering. In traditional iconography, while the Buddha wears the robes of an Indian monk, the *bodhisattva* is depicted as a prince.

bonsai Dwarf trees typical of the Chinese and Japanese cultures. Their technical and philosophical tradition originated in China over a thousand years ago, and they were probably introduced into Japan during the Kamakura period, following the growth of Zen Buddhism. In Japanese culture, bonsai represents the highest form of natural beauty, obtained through artifice of the most sophisticated kind.

Buddha (sixth century BC) An Indian prince, born in Lumbini, near Kapilavastu, in present-day Nepal, who probably lived between 550 and 447 BC. His historical name was Siddhārtha of Sākya descent. He founded the religious school named after him and the method for achieving deliverance from the chain of reincarnations and attaining the ultimate self-annulment within the One. The term also applies to those who achieved such awakening (*bodhi*) before the coming of the historical Buddha. The subsequent doctrinal developments (see 'Buddhism') foretold the coming of a future Buddha, Maitreya, as well as of other Buddhas, like those, for example, who preside over the four points of the compass. Among these, Amitābha (in Japanese: Amida) acquired a particular importance in Japan, as the ruler of the West, where Paradise in located.

Buddhism Philosophical-religious system founded by the Buddha in the sixth century BC and based on his oral teachings. It has two major branches: the *hīnayāna*, or small vehicle, which is more faithful to the original tradition and is particularly widespread in Sri Lanka and Burma; and the *mahāyāna*, or large vehicle, which, by absorbing elements of other cults encountered in its expansion outside India, became a religion in the true sense of the word. The latter is the form that has spread from India to central Asia, China, Korea, Indochina and Japan.

bunraku Professional marionette theatre established, in its embryonic form, in the early seventeenth century. It developed rapidly and reached full maturity in the course of the following century. The word is of recent coinage.

calendar The traditional Japanese calendar, used in the country from 604 AD to 1872, originated in China. It followed the lunar cycle and divided the year into 12 months, each called large or small according to its duration. Each year, therefore, lasted either 354 or 355 days, and started when the sun entered the constellation of Pisces, that is to say some time between 20 January and 9 February. However, when the accumulated 'lost' days meant that the thirteenth lunar cycle no longer entered the constellation of Pisces to signal the start of the New Year, a thirteenth, 'intercalary' month was added. The months were, and still are, known by their ordinal numbers, so that even today January is called 'first month', February 'second month', and so on.

cha-bana ('tea flowers') A type of greatly stylized flower arrangement, normally consisting of a single blossom, displayed in the *tokonoma* of pavilions or rooms used for the tea ceremony.

Chōbunsai Eishi (1756–1829) Born in Edo to a samurai family of Fujiwara lineage, named Hosoda, he became a pupil first of Kanō Sukenobu (1671–1751), and later of Torii Bunryūsai (active in the late eighteenth century). He adopted the name of Eishi, given to him by shōgun Tokugawa Ieharu (1737–86), whom he served till the age of 30. His early works were in the Kanō style. After leaving the shōgun court, he devoted himself to *ukiyo-e*, specializing in prints of beautiful women (*bijinga*), in which he rivalled Utamaro. Despite the large number of prints he produced, he is also renowned as a painter, whose works are considered to be some of the finest ever produced by *ukiyo-e* artists.

Chōkyōsai Eiri (active 1790–1800) Little is known about Eiri. As a painter and maker of *ukiyo-e*, he used several different names. One of the works attributed to him is the famous portrait of the writer Santō Kyōden (1761–1816), himself an illustrator known under the name of Kitao Masanobu. The primary subject of his prints was feminine beauty; in his style, the female form was portrayed as extremely elongated, slender and almost disembodied.

chōnin Generic term in use during the Tokugawa period to indicate non-aristocratic city-dwellers, but mostly used of craftsmen and merchants. Although at the very bottom of the social hierarchy, it was the mercantile class that actually held the country's economic power. The *chōnin* played a crucial role in the development of new art forms that appealed to their tastes.

daiichiza ('the principal sitting place') Term indicating an important member of the Zen hierarchy. The 'principal place' it refers to is the one that, in the meditation room, is next to the Abbot (jūji), who holds the highest honorary rank in this hierarchy.

daimyō ('great name') Term deriving from the larger characters used on territorial maps for the names of members of the highest rank in the samurai class, who were to all intents and purposes feudal lords.

deigan ('applied eyes') A type of mask worn by the female lead during the first part of dramas about women's jealousy.

dengaku A dance style accompanied by music and acrobatics, popular during the Kamakura period. It developed from a form of popular performance staged at Buddhist temples, which had adopted the chants sung by peasants while working in the fields.

dhyāna Sanskrit term meaning 'meditation'. The practice of meditation is, in Buddhist philosophy, one of the most important means of achieving *bodhi*. Through it, the believer experiences a gradual path to perfection in Buddhist life, the apex of which is becoming a Buddha.

Edo The ancient name of Tokyo. Originally a small village, it grew out of all proportion from the seventeenth century onwards, after becoming the main centre of the dominant Tokugawa clan and the administrative state capital. It gave its name to the period immediately preceding the modern era.

edokko no kamisama (lit. 'idol worshipped by Edo citiziens') The name given to the most fashionable actors of the Edo period.

Ehon saishikitsū (*Illustrated Manual on Colouring*) Published by Hokusai at the age of 88, this is the work that contains the fundamental principles of the master's art, providing invaluable clues as to his style as well as detailed descriptions of technical aspects, such as

basic brush-holding and colour-making techniques. The many descriptions are always complemented by exhaustive explanatory illustrations.

Eikō Hosoe (b. 1933) Born in Yonezawa, in the Yamagata prefecture, he spent his childhood and adolescence at a Shintō shrine in Tokyo, his adopted city. He graduated from the Tokyo Institute of Photography in 1954, and in 1959 founded the group 'Vivo', bringing together the most significant avant-garde photographers in Japan. His world-famous collection entitled *Barakei* (*Ordeal by Roses*, 1963) was created for and with the writer Mishima Yukio.

emaki Illustrated scroll with the pictorial narrative unfolding horizontally and almost always accompanied by text.

Enma Ancient Indian deity introduced into Japan with the assimilation of Chinese Taoism and subsequently absorbed into the Buddhist pantheon. He was venerated as 'Lord of the Underworld' and presided over receiving and judging the dead.

Fugaku hyakkei (*One Hundred Views of Mount Fuji*) A three-volume collection of monochrome woodblock prints, published in 1834 and 1835 (the first two), and 1849 (the third). The principal subject of the images is Mount Fuji, Japan's sacred mountain, which sanctifies with its presence human life and nature itself. For the artist, depicting the mountain becomes an opportunity to create evocative pictures of the most varied themes: pure landscapes, aspects of nature, architectural structures, religious scenes, mythological subjects and, above all, ordinary people and their daily lives. It is one of Hokusai's masterpieces, as well as a masterpiece of the Japanese art of engraving.

Fugaku sanjūrokkei (*Thirty-six Views of Mount Fuji*) Considered the undisputed masterpiece of Hokusai's colour-print graphic works, this series was produced when the master was about 70 years old. Lack of documentation leaves some of the issues around it unresolved. There are

46 (not 36) prints. It is thought that 10 designs were added at a later stage, in response to the success the series enjoyed. There are also technical questions surrounding the engravings. The colour of the key-block varies: in some sheets the outlines are blue, in others black. The general consensus among critics is that Prussian blue was used on the key-block for the original *Thirty-six Views*, while the 10 additional prints and successive runs were made using the more usual black. No reference numbers or dates appear in this series.

Fujiwara An aristocratic family that exerted strong political influence on the court during the Heian period, and in particular from the tenth to the twelfth centuries. Originally in charge of imperial liturgical matters, its power became almost limitless. The most powerful among its members was Fujiwara no Michinaga (966–1028), who dominated the court by strengthening the ties between the Imperial Family and his own. He was the father of four Empresses and the grandfather of three Emperors. The Fujiwara also had considerable influence in the sphere of art and culture, so much so that the last three centuries of the Heian period are often called the 'Fujiwara period'.

furisode An elegant garment worn by adolescents, characterized by long, wide and open sleeves. On reaching 19, boys and girls, married or not, were required to sew the sleeves up.

futon A very thick quilt that can be laid down directly on floor mats. As bedding, the term can indicate both a light mattress and a blanket to lie under to protect oneself from the cold.

geiko The local term used in Kyoto for a geisha.

geisha A woman of the pleasure districts who, during the Edo period, used to entertain tea-house guests, often playing the *shamisen* to accompany the songs and dances of the courtesans. In more recent times they have taken on the role of courtesans. The most important among them formed semi-official relationships with men from the world of finance and politics, who would sometimes redeem and marry them.

Genji monogatari Masterpiece of classical Japanese literature, written in the early eleventh century by Murasaki Shikibu, a lady in service at the Heiankyō court, and considered as the first novel in the history of world literature. Of its 54 chapters, 42 tell of the life of prince Genji, called the 'Shining Prince' because of his extraordinary charm and elegance. The story follows the hero in life and beyond, recounting his many romantic adventures and his changing political fortunes. Genji is not only the novel's main character, but the symbol of the whole Heian era and culture, whose aesthetic ideals he embodies through his exceptional skills in the art of dance, song and poetry. Sophisticated and melancholy, and the ideal lover, he faces adverse fate with great dignity, conscious that the beauty of things is enhanced by their very transience. The story continues for 12 chapters after his death.

Genji monogatari emaki A series of horizontal scrolls, dating back to around 1140, constituting the earliest illustrations of *Genji monogatari*'s 54 chapters. Possibly consisting originally of 10 scrolls, the series comprised illustrated scenes alternating with exquisite calligraphy. The scrolls were taken apart in the seventeenth century for conservation purposes.

Ginkaku-ji ('Temple of the Silver Pavillion') It was built in 1474 by the shōgun Ashikaga Yoshimasa (1435–1490), who sought to emulate the golden Kinkaku-ji commissioned by his grandfather Ashikaga Yoshimitsu. It seems that the intention was to cover it in silver but the silver covering was never added on to it.

Gion A district of Kyoto near the Yasaka Shintō shrine. In ancient times it had been an isolated place, but, following the erection of several temples, numerous tea-houses sprang up in its proximity. There young girls, wearing the *furisode* and a red apron, served tea and entertained customers playing the *shamisen* and dancing. More intimate forms of entertainment were provided by slightly older women. Gion later became the pleasure district of Kyoto.

go A two-man game of strategy, originally from China, played on a large chequerboard with sets of black and white pawns.

gofun A white pigment, obtained by cooking and pulverizing oyster shells.

---

haboku ('broken' ink; in Chinese: *pomo*) A technique of painting in ink thought to have been invented by Wang Wei, poet and painter of the early Tang Dynasty, and further elaborated by Yu Jian, painter of the Song Dynasty (both in China). It involves breaking up uniform areas of ink wash by means of thicker brushstrokes. In other words, barely diluted ink is used over a surface still damp with previously applied thinner ink.

haikai no renga A poetic genre, usually called simply *haikai*, which originated in the early sixteenth century as a pastime for professional *renga* poets. It differs from the latter in its humorous purpose and use of colloquialisms, which were normally not permitted in literature. Having gained official recognition, it was codified by Matsunaga Teitoku (1571–1653), who gave it the rules that govern its structure.

haiku A short poetic composition, consisting of 17 syllables divided into 3 units on the pattern 5–7–5. Known also as *haikai*, it was a form favoured by great poets, such as Matsuo Bashō (1644–94), Yosa Buson (1716–84) and Kobayashi Issa (1763–1827).

hana ('flower') According to Zeami's aesthetics, it indicates the quintessence of an actor's skill in the performing arts.

haniwa Small clay figures, typical of the proto-historic phase of the Japanese civilization. Arranged around the grave of the sovereign or of other members of the Imperial Family, their purpose was to recreate the social circle of the deceased. They are a direct source of information about the customs of early inhabitants of Japan.

hannya The demon of female jealousy, at the centre of many dramas and stories. Its stage appearance is represented by two types of mask with terrifying expressions: the *aka* and the *shiro hannya*. The former (the 'red demon of jealousy') is used for more mature female characters, while the latter (the 'white demon of jealousy') indicates younger ones.

Hasegawa Tōhaku (1539–1610) Born in Nanao to a family of dyers, he was adopted by the Hasegawa clan. In 1570 he moved to Kyoto, where he studied the Kanō style and Chinese painting. Seeing himself as a direct heir to Sesshū Tōyō, he abandoned the Kanō school to found, within his studio, the Hasegawa school. He specialized in interior decoration and ink paintings inspired by the Zen style of the thirteenth century.

Heian-kyō ('capital of peace and serenity') The name given by Emperor Kanmu (737–806) to the new capital he built in 794, based on the design of Chang'an, the Chinese capital city of the Tang Dynasty. Just like Nara before it, the city was built on a perfect rectangular plan, with a grid of perpendicular streets. This pattern can still be seen in modern Kyoto.

Hishikawa Sōri III (active in late eighteenth and early nineteenth centuries) Sōri III was one of Hokusai's first pupils. As was customary in artists' studios of the period, it was the master who gave him the pseudonym Sōri, a name that he himself had used before discarding it in favour of the name Hokusai. His prints and paintings are heavily influenced by (and in some cases seem to be actual copies of) the master's works. It is likely that they were the result of exercises carried out by the pupil in order to learn the art of painting. It was common practice for pupils to learn techniques by copying their master's pictures.

hokkyō ('bridge of the [Buddhist] Law') Honorary Buddhist title of lower rank, awarded mainly to doctors and painters.

Hon'ami Kōetsu (1558–1637) Poet, painter, calligrapher, potter, garden designer, tea-master, lacquer artist and notable expert on swords, Kōetsu lived in Takagamine near Kyoto, where he founded an important community of artists. He was one of the greatest artistic figures bridging the Momoyama and Edo periods, and is credited today as the inspiration and the real founder of the Rinpa school, as well as being remembered for his long and creative artistic partnership with Sōtatsu.

hōshi ('master of the [Buddhist] Law') Honorary Buddhist title.

Hyakunin isshu uba ga etoki (*One Hundred Poems by One Hundred Poets Explained by the Nurse*) Dated circa 1835–6, it is considered Hokusai's last great series. It is based on one of the best-loved collections of poems in the entire Japanese tradition, the *Hyakunin isshu*, an anthology compiled in the twelfth century by Fujiwara no Sadaie (1162–1241). During the Tokugawa period the anthology became the educational text for *chōnin* women but, above all, it was used as the inspiration for the poetry competitions organized in celebration of the New Year. Hokusai's series consists of 27 prints, plus one print of the outlines matrix only, 55 preparatory drawings for unpublished works, 4 photomechanical reproductions of original drawings, 4 prints published in Kyoto by Satō Shōtarō in 1921, and two recently discovered drawings. Two factors might be responsible for the project's not being completed: on the one hand, the serious economic crisis which the country suffered during the Tenpō period (1830–44); on the other, the growing success of the landscapes painted by Hiroshige, which overshadowed the popularity of Hokusai's work. The prints are not, however, exact iconographic companions to the poems, but evocative images juxtaposed with the text.

Ichikawa Danjūrō VII (1791–1859) One of Edo's *kami-sama* of the first half of the nineteenth century and an actor of considerable skill and talent, he first appeared on stage at the age of 4, but made his official debut in 1796. Three years later he took over the reins of the school of the Ichikawa family. He forged links with Edo's artistic and literary world through specific productions. In 1842, a sumptuary law forced him to lower his high standard of living and, having left the capital, he moved to the provinces. His exile helped to turn him into a mythical figure throughout the country.

Ichikawa Danzō III (1719–72) The son of an assistant at the Morita Theatre in Edo, he became a pupil first of the actor Bandō Matakurō II (?–1734) and later of Ichikawa Danzō I (1684–1740). He specialized in the *aragoto* style, in which he played the role of samurai, a vassal loyal to his lord, in a strongly expressionistic acting style.

Ihara Saikaku (1642–93) Not much is known about this wealthy Osaka merchant who, following his wife's death, embarked on a life of pilgrimage. An author of *haikai* poems, after 1682 he devoted himself to writing fiction, quickly obtaining considerable popularity. He interpreted the burgeoning tastes of the middle classes, giving rise to a new literary genre, in which the *chōnin* were able to recognize their ideals: money, love affairs, life in the pleasure districts. With novels such as *Life of an Amorous Man* (*Kōshoku ichidai otoko*, 1682), *Life of an Amorous Woman* (*Kōshoku ichidai onna*, 1686), and, above all, *Five Women who Loved Love* (*Kōshoku gonin onna*, 1686), he reached the apogee of Floating World narrative.

ikebana ('living flowers') The art of arranging flowers.

iki (in Chinese: *sui*) One of the most intriguing and indefinable among the concepts of Japanese aesthetics. In its generic meaning, it was first commonly used in the seventeenth century, but, with the advent of the erotic literature of the Genroku period (1688–1704), it began to assume a more specific connotation, closely related to the sphere of erotic art. It was codified in the early nineteenth century, when it acquired the aesthetic characteristics that distinguish it. The concept does not, actually, correspond with a quality, but with a set of behaviours and a way of life.

Ise Peninsula on the Pacific south of Nagoya, and the site of the Shintō shrine of the same name. For Buddhists it is the equivalent of Mecca, since believers feel it is their duty to visit it at least once in their lifetime. Situated in today's Mie province, on the Kii peninsula, the shrine is also seen as the archetypal Japanese house. Tradition dictates that it is completely demolished and rebuilt every 20 years, following the original model and using the timber from the *kryptomeria* trees growing in the surrounding forest.

Ishikawa Toyonobu (1711–85) *Ukiyo-e* artist of the middle Edo period. A pupil of Nishimura Shigenaga (c. 1697–1756), his early works include numerous 'lacquered prints' (*urushi-e*). He specialized in portraying female figures and enjoyed considerable fame in the period before polychrome engravings became widespread. He subsequently lost favour among the public.

ja Mask, typical of the nō theatre, representing female jealousy. Similar to the one called *hannya*, but with exaggerated, more powerful features.

jinja A Shintō shrine.

jōruri Generic term for the ballads, mostly tinged with tragic overtones, normally performed by itinerant blind singers to the accompaniment of a *biwa*, the traditional lute originally from the mainland. They grew popular during the Edo period, and later became associated with marionette theatres (see *bunraku*). Here the term *jōruri* stands for the descriptive element of the drama, performed by a narrator (*gidayū*) to the accompaniment of a *shamisen*. The specific term for the visual element, represented by the marionettes' movements, is *jōruriningyō*.

junshi Suicide carried out in order to accompany one's master in death.

kabuki Characteristically lavish and spectacular theatre performance, originating in the seventeenth century as an expression of the new 'popular culture', which was beginning to flourish and to establish its own identity, separate from the classical one. Although today it is usually thought to have derived from the merging of different forms of entertainment, it seems to have originated from the traditional dances of Okuni, a priestess of Izumi who used to perform in Kyoto, dressed in male clothing. Because of the scandals surrounding actresses, in 1629 the government banned women from appearing on stage, and replaced them with young male actors, creating a new kabuki style, the *wakashū*. The consequent scuffles to vie for these boys' favours were no improvement on the previous disturbances, so that, from 1652, they too were banned from the stage. From then on, kabuki became increasingly professional, while remaining the exclusive domain of male actors.

kachō ('flowers and birds') A genre of Far Eastern painting, depicting images from nature, such as flowers, birds, fish and insects.

kake-kotoba Key words used, especially in poetry, to create a double meaning, because the way they fit together lends itself to more than one interpretation. When two words are identical in sound, their different meanings are usually identified by the different ideograms representing them. To achieve a *kake-kotoba*, therefore, it is necessary to use phonetic writing, which does not allow for this distinction. Because of the ambiguity they give rise to within the text, words of this kind are mainly used to express emotions and passions, which, in Japanese literature, are very seldom referred to explicitly.

Kamekura Yūsaku (1915–97) One of the major graphic artists of post-war Japan. His vision and leadership contributed to the systematization of his country's great tradition in graphic art, and his international perspective had a unique impact on its stylistic and professional renewal. In all his output, particularly significant in the fields of posters and branding, Kamekura always tried to combine the style and taste of the classical tradition with the aesthetic trends and commercial dictates of his day. He was ahead of his time in adopting innovative themes, such as Optical Art, and avant-garde techniques, including the use of photography.

kana Generic term indicating the graphic symbols contained in the syllabic system of Japanese orthography. They developed following the introduction of characters (*kanji*), because of the need to adapt the Chinese script to Japanese phonetics.

kanawa A type of mask in use in the nō theatre, representing a female character possessed by the demon, half way between a *deigan* and a *hannya*.

kanji ('Chinese character') Ideogram, pictograph.

Kanō Painting school and dynasty that flourished from the mid-fifteenth century. It combined the technique, Chinese in origin, of painting in China ink, with the indigenous method called *yamato-e*. Its foundation was laid by Kanō Masanobu (1434–1530), who was awarded the hereditary title of 'court painter' at the shōgun court of the Ashikaga. His successors were his son Motonobu (1476–1559) and grandson Eitoku (1543–1590). The latter painted the screens in the castles of Oda Nobunaga (1534–82) and Toyotomi Hideyoshi (1536–98). Later, the Kanō school split into two separate branches. One, led by Eitoku's grandson, Tan'yū (1602–74), moved to Edo (Edogano), where it enjoyed the patronage of the

Tokugawa; the other, led by Eitoku's adopted son, Sanraku (1559–1635), remained in Kyoto (Kiōgano). Both branches continued to enjoy the patronage of powerful rulers up to the nineteenth century and gave rise to 20 or so minor schools.

Kanō Eitoku (1543–90) Eitoku, whose personal name was Kuninobu, was the eldest son and pupil of Kanō Shōei (1519–92) and the grandson of Motonobu, thus representing the fifth generation of the principal branch of the Kanō of Kyoto. His painting style gave rise to a new type of highly ornamented decoration for interior walls, characterized by opulent gold backgrounds and brightly coloured painted details, combined with the use of strong ink brushwork. His patrons were Oda Nobunaga and Toyotomi Hideyoshi, the great leaders of the Momoyama period, for whom he created paintings and decorated castles. His sumptuous and vigorous style was a mirror of the times and was greatly favoured by the military elite.

Kanō Masanobu (ca. 1434–1530) The acknowledged father of the Kanō school of Japanese painting, which was founded during the Muromachi period and lasted until the early Meiji period. The official painter at the Ashikaga court, in 1490 he was awarded the ecclesiastic title of hokkyō, and in the following year assumed the pseudonym Masanobu. He became a Zen monk and so enjoyed the patronage not only of the bakufu of the time, but also of Buddhist temples, enabling him to lay the foundations for the future prosperity of the Kanō school.

Kanō Motonobu (1476–1559) Elder son of Masanobu, the founder of the Kanō school. After his father's death in 1530 he took over the role of official painter at the shōgun court. He also painted for the aristocracy and the Imperial Family, thus strengthening the school's links with the court. His distinctive style became particularly evident in his wall paintings and sliding panels, and laid the foundations of this genre for the subsequent Momoyama period. By

continuing to use the Chinese techniques adopted by his father, while at the same time assimilating the yamato-e techniques typical of the Tosa school, he created a new style, which combined the powerful compositional structure of Chinese paintings with the chromatic richness of Japanese tradition.

Katsukawa Shun'ei (1762–1819) Active during the Kansei period (1789–1801) and leading pupil of Katsukawa Shunshō, he was a master of ukiyo-e towards the end of the Edo period. Shun'ei was an artist of considerable talent and particularly outstanding for his portraits of actors, theatre scenes and sumō, in which he made use of free, flowing and lively brush strokes. Particularly powerful are his half-bust portraits of actors, stylistic precursors of the more famous portraits by Sharaku.

Katsukawa Shunkō (1743–1812) As a pupil of Shunshō, he continued the tradition of the Katsukawa school, producing prints of actors' portraits. Later in his career, he specialized in half-bust 'large-head' portraits (ōkubi-e), believed to have been his invention. He did not distance himself stylistically from Shunshō: the quality of the brushwork is similar, but his expressions are more powerful.

Katsukawa Shunshō (?1726–92) One of the major ukiyo-e artists of the second half of the eighteenth century. Having studied painting under Katsukawa Shunshui (active in 1744–64), he devoted himself to producing prints of actors' portraits, a genre that underwent a fundamental change thanks to him, as well as to the stylistic influence of Harunobu. His school flourished to the point that he was able to delegate the production of prints to his pupils and devote himself almost exclusively to painting, in particular, to the study of beautiful women. Some of his many pupils are among the most eminent names of ukiyo-e, such as Hokusai, Shun'ei and Shunkō.

Katsura The Imperial villa situated in the south-western area of Kyoto, near the river Katsura, from which it derives its

name. Built for the heir to the throne, Prince Toshihito (1579–1629), it was completed in 1620 and enlarged in 1642 by his son Noritada. One of the supreme examples of indigenous Japanese architecture, it displays a minimalist approach to structure in perfect harmony with its natural surroundings, and has been a major source of inspiration to some of the greatest modern architects of the Western world.

Katsushika Hokusai (1760–1849) One of the supreme ukiyo-e artists, Hokusai started his career as an apprentice to Katsukawa Shunkō, among the greatest masters of his day for both graphic and painted works, but he left the studio following the master's death. Hokusai assimilated not only the style of the ukiyo-e artists, but also those of the Kanō, Tosa and Rinpa schools, as well as certain elements of Western art. From a synthesis of all these, he developed a totally individual style, which places him among the world's greatest exponents of the art of painting. His life, like the legend surrounding it, is peppered with anecdotes describing rather eccentric behaviour. He moved house over 90 times and gave himself dozens of different names. His vast output can be divided into six periods, each corresponding with a different painting style and his principal pseudonyms. Unlike many ukiyo-e artists, he was as good an engraver as a draughtsman and painter. Series such as his Thirty-six Views of Mount Fuji had a huge impact on European art, especially on the French Impressionists.

Kawabata Yasunari (1899–1972) In 1968 he became the first Japanese writer to be awarded the Nobel Prize for Literature. From his debut, he devoted himself to an evocative style of narrative, imbued with lyrical and atmospheric qualities. From the time he was orphaned at the age of 3, he was raised by his blind grandfather in a world steeped in silence and ritual. Growing up in total solitude, he developed an extraordinary power of imagination, which he then transferred to his novels and short stories. The principal

theme of his work is the quest for subtle beauty, one that is never manifest or explicit, but can only be alluded to, and is so strikingly embodied in his remarkable female characters.

Keisai Eisen (1790–1848) The pseudonym of Ikeda Yoshinobu, a pupil of Eizan and of a minor member of the Kanō school. He was a prolific ukiyo-e artist, specializing in prints of beautiful women (bijinga), of landscapes and of erotic subjects. He worked with Hiroshige on the famous series Sixty-nine Stations of the Kisokaidō (Kisoji rokujūkyū tsugi no uchi, c. 1850).

ki (in Chinese: qi) An untranslatable concept signifying the spirit, or essence, of life. It is one of the loftiest and most indefinable concepts of Oriental philosophy.

Ki no Tsurayuki (c. 872–945) One of Japan's literary giants, an important figure at the Heian court and the compiler of the first Imperial anthology of poetry, the Kokin Wakashū. His preface in Japanese, where he expounds the essence of the country's poetic tradition, is in itself a masterpiece of deep philosophical thought and stylistic elegance, besides being Japan's first real work of literary criticism.

kibyōshi ('yellow cover') Illustrated books containing easy-to-read stories, originally written and illustrated by the same person. From 1775 onwards they started to overtake similar genres in popularity. After 1780, having developed from the cheapest form of vernacular fiction, they began to attract professional authors.

kijin (in Chinese: jiren, yimin) It indicates an extraordinary person and, in a less complimentary sense, an eccentric. The term was used for authors and artists whose ideas and behaviour were out of the ordinary.

Kikugawa Eizan (1787–1867) From 1800 until 1830, the year of his retirement, Toshinobu Eizan was one of the pre-eminent makers of prints featuring beautiful women and erotic subjects. He initiated the so-called Kikugawa style, and his work anticipated the imminent decline of *ukiyo-e*.

Kinkaku-ji ('Temple of the Golden Pavilion') One of the masterpieces of Japanese architecture, erected in 1398 for shōgun Ashikaga Yoshimitsu (1358–1408). In 1950 a monk obsessed with the pavilion's perfect beauty destroyed it by setting it on fire. This dramatic event inspired Mishima Yukio's wonderful novel *The Temple of the Golden Pavilion* (1959).

Kitagawa Utamaro (1754–1806) Utamaro was one of the most prominent figures in the art world during the Edo period. As a pupil of Toriyama Sekien (1712–88), he was given by the master the name of Toyoaki, which he changed to Utamaro in 1781. Discovered by fashionable publisher Tsutaya Jūzaburō, he achieved fame thanks to his innovative style, characterized by elongated, graceful figures: tasteful, refined and elegant. The theme throughout his work is the life of women, both in the pleasure districts and in their private homes. He also produced a large number of *ōkubi-e*. Utamaro's art flourished from the 1780s, when he started working for Tsutaya, until the time of the latter's death in 1797, when the quality of his work suffered a certain decline, especially from the technical point of view.

kocho The term given by Tanaka Ikkō to a new set of characters which he designed, drawing inspiration, so he claimed, from the capital letters in Bodoni's type, which he much admired for their elegance and formal rigour.

koto A 13-string musical instrument, which could be described as a horizontal harp.

Kuki Shūzō (1888–1941) Born in Tokyo to a family belonging to the Meiji oligarchy, he studied philosophy at Tokyo's Imperial University, despite being destined by his father for the diplomatic service. In 1921 he left for a study trip in Europe, where he remained until 1929. There he met Heinrich Rickert, Henri Bergson and Martin Heidegger, with whom he

continued to pursue his studies. The years he spent researching enabled him to refine and perfect his knowledge, and inspired him to undertake an in-depth study of the concept of *iki*, which he later expounded in his book *The Structure of Iki* (*Iki no kōzō*, 1930).

kyōgen ('crazy words') Short farces performed between two nō dramas. The term also indicates the actors who play minor roles in nō performances, such as servants, messengers, and so on.

kyōka ('crazy poems') Humorous poetic composition consisting of 31 syllables. It is a comic variation on the *waka* and contains many of *kake-kotoba*.

Ma Xia Painting style attributed to Ma Yuan (in Japanese: Baen) and Xia Gui (in Japanese: Kakei), who flourished in China during the Southern Song Dynasty. The style also took root in Japan, and can be identified in paintings of landscapes, as well as in *kachō* pictures.

maiko ('dancer') Young women instructed in the art of entertaining through dance. In today's Kyoto, they occupy the social rung immediately below that of the *geiko*.

manga A generic term meaning 'sketch' or 'drawing'. The most famous are those featured in Hokusai's *Manga*, a collection of the master's sketches divided into 15 volumes. Started in 1814, during his lifetime he was able to complete it up to the thirteenth volume (1849–50). Volumes 14 and 15 were published posthumously and may be apocryphal. The collection is an encyclopaedia of drawing, containing the most diverse types of subjects normally reproduced in figurative art forms. The sketches display a great sense of irony and may often seem like caricatures, but are unique and invaluable tools for understanding Japanese life and traditions of the time. *Manga* was the collection that in the nineteenth century secured Hokusai's success in the West. From the Meiji period onwards, the term *manga* has come to indicate Japanese comic books.

Maruyama Ōkyo (1733–95) Born in a village in the district of Tanba, in the region of present-day Kyoto, Ōkyo studied Chinese and Kanō painting in Kyoto itself. Among his most important developments were paintings with no contour lines (*tsuketate*), as well as the use of 'chiaroscuro' and other techniques imported from the West, such as the *megane-e*. His very individual style, where Japanese and Chinese traditions meet those of Western perspective and 'chiaroscuro', is particularly evident in his large-scale works. He founded the school of painting that carries his name. (see also Shijō).

Matsuo Bashō (1644–94) Bashō was the pseudonym assumed in middle age by Matsuo Jinshichirō. Born in Ueno, a town in the Iga province, to a low-ranking samurai family, at the age of 9 he was placed in the service of Yoshitada, the young son of the local *daimyō* and a lover of *haikai*. Following the death of his feudal lord, Bashō left politics to devote himself to poetry. With him, *haikai* acquired a high technical quality and gained appreciation on a par with classical poetry. In 1684 he undertook the first of his many pilgrimages to the country's most celebrated places. His evocative accounts of these journeys are held to be among the masterpieces of Japanese literature.

megane-e ('eyeglass pictures') Reproductions in the form of small woodcuts, characterized by exaggerated perspective and the application of colour by hand. They were first reflected in a mirror, then enlarged through a glass viewer – a Dutch invention – similar to a present-day slide projector, which gave the image a three-dimensional effect.

meisho-e Paintings of places renowned for their beauty or for being the site of some important event. They also feature people and animals, as well as visual references to the seasons. The earliest examples were usually accompanied by a *waka*.

Mingeikan The museum founded in 1936 by Yanagi Sōetsu (1889–1961). Its aim

was to raise awareness and appreciation of the popular art form, which he called *mingei*, that features objects used in everyday and religious activities. They included *ema* (votive pictures dedicated to temples), *ōtsue* ('souvenir' pictures produced in Ōtsu, near Kyoto), as well as textiles, garments, pottery, baskets and objects crafted in wood, stone, paper and leather. The current Director of the museum is Sōetsu's son, the designer Yanagi Sōri.

Miroku (in Sanskrit: Maitreya) The *bodhisattva* anticipated as the Future Buddha. One of the first Buddhist deities to be known in Japan, by the seventh century he had become one of the best loved and venerated. Around the twelfth century, his cult was overshadowed by that of Amida, who, thanks to the cult of the Pure Land sect, became the most popular among Japanese Buddhist deities.

Mishima Yukio (1925–70) Pseudonym of Hiraoka Kimitake, one of the most controversial figures in modern Japan. A prolific and versatile writer, he devoted his entire life to self-expression and the transformation of his own reality according to the classical concept of 'harmony'. Writer, poet, playwright, theatre director and actor, he committed suicide in the prime of his life, after being the dominant figure on Japan's cultural scene.

miyako ('capital') The term used in Japan to indicate present-day Kyoto, the seat of the Imperial Court. See also Heian-kyō.

Mizoguchi Kenji (1898–1956) One of the fathers of modern Japanese cinema, he began his career in 1922. A constant theme in all his films is the contrast between tradition and the realities of contemporary Japan, seen mainly through the eyes of his female characters. Humiliated and wounded by society, these women allow the audience to enter a small world, punctuated by the rhythms of daily life – a world that appears gentle, even lyrical, but also distressing.

mono no aware A fundamental concept in Japanese aesthetics. Over the centuries, and with new ideas about life and mores, its meaning has changed considerably. In the Heian period, the term indicated subtle melancholy and was used in relation to unusual beauty associated with deep emotions. In the eighteenth century, it acquired the meaning of 'sensitivity to things'.

Mori Ōgai (1862–1922) An important writer of the Meiji period. Having initially devoted himself to fiction, he later pursued the study of medicine, especially while based in Germany with the army, where he reached the highest ranks, only to return to literature. His most famous stories are those written early in his career, following his time abroad, and his later historical works.

Mu Qi (1200?–1270?) The greatest *chan* monk and painter of the Chinese late Southern Song Dynasty, he was responsible for some of the finest masterpieces of Chinese painting in ink. Some of his works were quick to reach Japan and had a huge impact on that country's painting style.

Murasaki The name of both the author of *Genji monogatari* and one of the novel's characters. The author (978?–1016?) was the daughter of the poet Fujiwara no Tametoki and a lady at the court of Emperor Ichijō, and became one of the figures that best represented the culture of the time, her writing perfectly reflecting the spirit of the Fujiwara period. The character is a young girl adopted by Genji and who was brought up by him as his female alter ego and later his life's companion. He helped her grow the qualities aspired to by the ideal woman of that specific time, the Heian period, when every aspect of a person's behaviour was guided by a developed aesthetic sense.

Muromachi An old district of Kyoto used, after 1378, to house the shōgun palace and the main administrative offices of the Ashikaga government. For this reason, the Ashikaga period is also known as the Muromachi period.

Nagai Kazumasa (b. 1929) Born in Osaka, he is one of Japan's most prominent graphic artists. His style, originally characterized by cold, abstract geometrical shapes, has changed direction and is now more concerned with environmental issues. His artistic output is extremely varied, consisting of posters, logos and advertising images, as well as prints and drawings of different kinds, and has been featured in exhibitions at home and abroad.

Nakamura Utaemon VI (1917–2001) One of the late twentieth-century kabuki actors who specialized in female roles (*onnagata*). In 1951 he was given the name that made him famous, and in 1973 he was awarded the title of 'national human treasure' (*ningen kokuhō*) for his art and his extraordinary impersonation of women, from young girls to courtesans and great ladies. He was a close friend of Mishima, who chose him to act in several of his plays.

nanga Painting school founded in Japan at the end of the seventeenth century, in reaction to the conventional quality of traditional styles, in particular those of the Kanō school. It drew inspiration from the school and style of southern China.

national human treasure As well as works of art, the Japanese government elevates as 'national treasures' (*kokuhō*) individuals (*ningen*) whose lives centre on a creative activity. Among those awarded are nō and kabuki actors, potters, weavers, dyers and so on.

Natsume Sōseki (1867–1916) A leading figure in Japan's literary world of the early twentieth century, his works bear witness to the difficulties experienced in attempting to adjust to the country's new reality. In a world where tradition was fast being replaced with new values, Sōseki explored the restless spirit of a modern hero, who found no alternative to his own isolation.

nengō A historical period lasting a variable number of years. It was determined either by the accession to the throne of an Emperor, or by a portentous event, auspicious or otherwise. The division of Japanese history into *nengō* was started by Emperor Kōtoku (596–654) in 645, the first year of the Taika period. Since 1868, a *nengō* has been made to correspond to the reign of a single monarch.

Nishida Kitarō (1870–1945) A prominent exponent of philosophical studies in modern Japan, for many decades he devoted himself to the study of Western thought, in order to understand its methodology. He devised a personal philosophical system based on oriental religion and Buddhism in particular.

Nisshinjōma (*The Daily Exorcisms*) Sketches created by Hokusai between the eleventh lunar month of 1842 and the twelfth lunar month of 1843 (i.e. 1844) and designed to exorcise sickness and death. About 220 examples of these drawings are known. Executed in black ink (*sumi*), each one portrays a *shishi*, the mythical lion of Chinese tradition, often drawn by the master as a fantastical portrait of himself and his emotions or moods.

nō A classical form of Japanese theatre originating in the period straddling the fourteenth and fifteenth centuries. Its roots can be found in certain popular dance forms and sacred performances, while it also includes music and dance elements imported from continental Asia. It is a very complex theatrical form, with profound implications of a philosophical and symbolic kind.

nōmen The generic term for the mask worn in nō performances.

nō schools A great number of acting schools have been founded over the centuries, and have been responsible for training the majority of nō actors, in particular those destined to play the lead role (*shite*). There are five principal schools, the so-called 'classical schools': Kanze, dating back to Zeami, Hōshō, Konparu, Kita and Kongō. The first four are in Tokyo, the last in Kyoto. A sixth school, the Umekawa, acquired some autonomy towards the end of the nineteenth century and managed to keep the genre alive at a time when it seemed doomed. It was the period after the Meiji Restoration (1868) when Japan, in its frantic rush to westernize, began to repudiate anything that represented the past.

---

obi The long sash made of heavy silk, used to tie a kimono around the waist. Besides being functional, it also complements the kimonos, especially those worn by women, and it often constitutes their most important aesthetic element. A smaller version made of plainer material is also worn by men. There are other versions of obi, such as the light-weight or cotton ones worn in summer and the informal ones worn with casual robes (*yukata*).

Ogata Kōrin (1658–1716) Kōrin, whose personal name was Ichinojō, was born in Kyoto and lived in Edo, where he became one of the leading exponents of the Rinpa school. In 1687, after his father's death, he and his brother found themselves heirs to a colossal fortune, which Kōrin squandered in a matter of a few years. In 1696 he decided to devote himself entirely to art. Besides painting, he flourished also in the field of lacquer work, pottery and textiles. Having studied the Kanō style, his main inspiration, however, was Sōtatsu (?–1643?), whose decorative qualities he adopted and developed. In Kōrin's more mature style, Sōtatsu's emphasis on colour is combined with the strong compositional characteristics of the Kanō school.

Okakura Kakuzō (1862–1913) He was born in Yokohama to a family of merchants. While at university, he forged a close relationship with Ernest F. Fenollosa, with whom he studied Buddhism. They travelled together throughout Japan on government missions whose aim was to revive traditional art forms and obtain for them the appreciation they deserved, not just in Japan but in the world at large. 1889 saw the opening of the Tokyo School of Art, with Okakura as president from its inauguration until 1898. In 1904 he went to the United States to work at the Museum of Fine Art, Boston, as consultant on Japanese painting and sculpture. It was there that, in 1906, he published his famous small volume called *The Book of Tea*. He continued to devote his time to study and travel in the USA, Europe and China. Having left Boston for good as late as 1913, he returned to Japan, where he died not long afterwards.

ōkubi-e ('pictures of large heads') The term used to indicate the portrait format, typical of the late eighteenth century, in which kabuki actors, famous courtesans and beautiful women are depicted from the chest up and occupy most of the foreground. This style achieved immediate success.

Onō no Komachi (active in the second half of the ninth century) A *waka* poetess, named by Ki no Tsurayuki as one of the *rokkasen*, or the six poetic geniuses. A lady at the Heian-kyō court between 850 and 869, she became a legendary figure in Japanese tradition, famous for her extraordinary beauty, acumen and elegance, as well as for her many suitors. She inspired various works of literature, especially nō dramas, many of which told of her life and loves.

Ōshima Nagisa (b. 1932) This giant of international cinema was born in Kyoto, the son of a government official of samurai descent. Growing up in postwar Japan, under the crushing weight of American political and military control, he found in films the opportunity to vindicate his entire generation. Always critical of the State, his work focuses on the most contradictory and hidden aspects of both Japanese society and the individual. Powerful examples of this include some of his masterpieces, such as *In the Realm of the Senses* (*Ai no koriida*, 1976), *Furyō – Merry Christmas Mr Lawrence* (*Senjo no merii*

kurisumasu – Furyō, 1983) and *Taboo* (*Gohatto*, 1999).

renga A poetic composition with 'linked' lines. With its earliest examples dating back to the twelfth century, it is a unique form, consisting of several linked hemistichs, forming lines composed alternately by different poets. At first, renga was seen as a kind of pastime for court poets, but it was later accepted as one of the official poetic genres. This led to the canonization of its compositional rules, which are vital to both the harmony of the whole poem and the independence of each individual verse.

Rinpa ('school of Rin') The painting style initiated by Tawaraya Sōtatsu and Hon'ami Kōetsu (1558–1673) and revived by Ogata Kōrin (1658–1716). The name of the school was coined in the Meiji period by putting together the second syllable of the name Kōrin and the word for 'school'. Sōtatsu's style was a genuinely new departure, in which monochrome ink images took second place to new compositions that featured strong colours applied flatly over the whole surface. Their overall effect, particularly on large areas such as screens and walls, was very evocative.

sakura A species of Japanese cherry tree bearing small inedible fruit, but prized for its blossom. *Sakura* parks are famous, and attract large numbers of Japanese visitors, who sometimes undertake long journeys in order to admire the magnificent sight. Many pages of literature have been written extolling the beauty of the pink froth created each spring by the mass of blossoms on the Kyoto hills and in many other locations throughout Japan. The temporary nature of its magic makes the *sakura* a perfect metaphor for the transience of beauty and life itself. Logically, therefore, the cherry blossom symbolizes youth and its passing; it is also the symbol of the samurai, who can be cut from the tree of life as easily as petals can be detached from the *sakura* by the faintest breeze.

samurai A generic term indicating members of the military aristocracy. The latter was divided into two categories: the *daimyō* (literally 'great names'), who were, to all intents and purposes, feudal lords; and the samurai, who, in the strict sense of the word, were subordinates, vassals or mere soldiers in the service of the *daimyō*. At the top of the military hierarchy was the most powerful of the *daimyō*, namely the shōgun, whose family was the country's de facto ruler, although nominated, if only formally, by the Emperor. When, for whatever reason, a samurai found himself without a master – through expulsion from his clan or the extinction or destruction of his lineage – in theory he was not allowed to serve under any other. He would then become a *rōnin*, a wandering swordsman, literally a 'wave man', frequently taking up the life of an outlaw.

sankin kōtai The law issued in 1634 by shōgun Tokugawa Iemitsu (c. 1603–51), which decreed that all *daimyō* should divide their time between residing in their domains and in Edo for periods of a duration proportional to the distance between the two places. Moreover, when going to their domains it was their duty to leave their wives and children in the capital. This was a way for the *bakufu* to try to ensure its supremacy: by exerting absolute control over the *daimyō*, it precluded any alliances among them and any strengthening of their economic and military power. The law was repealed in 1862.

sarugaku A type of choreographed performance, precursor of the nō theatre. It was livelier and more 'plebeian' than the traditional dramatic forms favoured by the aristocracy. Kan'ami transformed it into something quite new by introducing into it elements borrowed from *dengaku* and other types of performance. It was Zeami who later developed it further and gave it the new name of *sarugaku no nō*, literally 'the talent of the sarugaku'. In time, most of the name was dropped, leaving in use only the term nō.

satori (in Chinese: *wu*) Key Buddhist concept, which indicates the 'awakened' condition achieved by the Buddha. With the introduction of Zen theory, however, it acquired different connotations. At the basis of this doctrine is the attainment of a new viewpoint from which to observe oneself and reality. It can only be achieved by abandoning all previous patterns of thought. This attainment is what Zen masters call *satori*.

Sei Shōnagon (c. 965 to c. 1017) Famous writer of the Heian period, author of the *Pillow Book* (*Makura no sōshi*) and responsible, with Murasaki Shikibu, for making the literature of the time widely celebrated. Sei Shōnagon was not, however, her real name, but the title under which she was known at court. She is considered the creator, as well as the leading exponent, of the literary style known as *zuihitsu*.

seirō ('green houses') Courtesans' homes, also synonymous with pleasure districts.

seppuku ('stomach-cutting') Ritual suicide carried out by members of the samurai class when, for reasons valid or otherwise, they have broken the code of honour on which their conduct was based, or if they have been deeply offended by a superior. It was also the type of capital punishment reserved for the samurai. Every aspect of the ritual followed a precise protocol, reinforcing the sacred aura that surrounded such a dramatic gesture. The weapon, usually a dagger, was thrust into the stomach where, according to Japanese tradition, the spirit is located. The ceremony took place in the presence of witnesses and an assistant (*kaishakunin*), whose duty it was to intervene if death was not instantaneous. In that case, he was required to sever the man's head with a blow of his sword, making sure he did not detach it completely from the trunk. In the West this ritual is better known as hara-kiri.

Sesshū Tōyō (1420–1506) The pre-eminent exponent of the art of painting in ink. Having joined the order of the monks of the Shōkoku temple at an early age, he was able to study painting there under the painter-monk Shūbun. In 1467 he joined a commercial expedition to China, where he remained until 1469. During this prolonged stay, he studied Ming painting, which at the time was still unknown in Japan. Drawing inspiration mainly from the landscape paintings of the Northern Song Dynasty, he created some of the most outstanding masterpieces of Japanese art.

shamisen An instrument similar to the lute. It has three strings, and its size may vary according to the type of music played. It can be played with a plectrum (*bachi*), also of different sizes, or by plucking the strings with the fingers. It was used by geishas to entertain their clients, and also during *jōruri* and kabuki performances to accompany the spoken parts. Later it was also played in other kinds of musical performance. Its origin can probably be found in a string instrument imported from the Ryūkyū Islands, itself possibly hailing from China or central Asia.

shibui A concept in aesthetics based on sobriety and refinement. It is primarily associated with art and the aesthetics of the tea ceremony.

Shiga Naoya (1883–1971) He was the author of short stories and one of the pre-eminent writers of the 'autobiographical novel' (*watakushi shōsetsu*), an early twentieth-century literary genre which grew out of Japan's 'naturalistic' style. His stories had an autobiographical flavour and, through an alter ego, the author described events from his own life. Shiga Naoya was well known also as an expert on traditional gardens.

Shijō The painting school founded by Matsumura Goshun (1752–1811). Its name is that of the Kyoto district where the master's studio was situated. Developed as an offshoot of the Maruyama school, the Shijō style differed in its more delicate approach to landscape and *kachō* prints.

shinja A particular type of mask used in *hannya* and *ja* nō.

shinjū A test of love, varying in intensity from mild to extreme, when it refers to a suicide pact.

Shintō An indigenous Japanese religion, according to which the Emperor, as a direct descendant of the goddess Amaterasu, belongs to a divine lineage. Its roots are found in the animistic cults and purification rites whose aim was to achieve a harmonious relationship between man and the cosmos. The Emperor is its supreme priest.

shite The term given to the leading role in nō theatre. In fact, in most plays the *shite* is not just the protagonist, but the only real character in the story, with the others playing no more than a supporting or evocative role. He assumes the name of *maejite* or *nochijite* when appearing in the first and second parts of the play respectively.

shōgun Abbreviated form of the term '*sei i tai shōgun*' (literally 'great general subduing barbarians'), an ancient army rank that later became the highest political-military title in Japan. He was usually the most powerful feudal lord, who established a ruling dynasty working alongside the Emperor's merely nominal one. The shōgun was therefore a kind of dictator who governed the country on behalf of the Emperor. The latter's role and responsibilities were limited to ritual matters. The last shōgun belonged to the powerful Tokugawa dynasty and was deposed in 1868 during the Meiji Restoration.

shōji The sliding door, made of paper and wood, which in traditional interiors separates the inside from the outside or one room from another.

Shokoku meikyō kiran (*Rare Views of Famous Japanese Bridges*) Hokusai's series of 11 prints in landscape format, published around 1834. The bridges are mainly imaginary, although some are based on actual material. In this series, the artist gives prominence to architectural structures and their relationship with the landscape, where man is merely complementary.

Shokoku taki meguri (*A Tour of Japanese Waterfalls*) Hokusai's series of eight prints, published between 1833 and 1835. It was created in portrait format in order better to emphasize the featured landscapes. In it Hokusai tackled a new theme, namely water, making it the focus of the series. The innovative and bold painting techniques employed by Hokusai give these pictures an unprecedented power. He treats the depiction of waterfalls in the same manner as portraits of famous people, by making his subjects fill the whole space. Another key factor is his choice of colours, usually contrasting, which creates the impression of movement.

Shūbun (active 1414–63) Also known as Tenshō Shūbun, he was a great innovator, especially in the field of landscape painting and the Shino-Japanese painting style (*karayō*). As a monk at the Shōkoku Zen temple in Kyoto, he taught the great painter Sesshō, passing on to him the technique of painting in ink.

signs of the zodiac Alongside the traditional calendar (see 'calendar') and the system of dating by period (see *nengō*), Japan has another system, originating in China, based on sexagesimal dating. In it the years are grouped in cycles of 60 and named according to particular combinations based on the 10 celestial symbols of the 5 elements (earth, metal, water, wood and fire), each counted twice (once as 'elder brother' and once as 'younger brother'), and the 12 symbols of time and the zodiac (rat, ox, tiger, hare, dragon, snake, horse, goat, rooster, dog and wild boar). Thus, starting from the first combination, we have the 'year of the rat elder brother of the earth', followed by 'year of the ox younger brother of the earth', and so on, until a 60-year cycle is completed.

Sōami (c. 1455–1525) A *suiboku* painter and the last of the three 'ami': Nōami (1397–1471) and Geiami (1431–85). Like his father Geiami before him, he became the official curator of the collection owned by shōgun Yoshimasa (1436–90), restoring and cataloguing his paintings.

He achieved fame also as garden designer, tea-master, art critic and poet.

Sōen (active 1489–1500) A Zen monk who lived for a time at the Engaku-ji Temple in Kamakura. In 1495 he travelled to the Suō Province in order to study with Sesshū, soon becoming the master's favourite pupil. After returning to Kamakura, he made the master's style known throughout the Kantō district.

Sorayama Hajime (b. 1947) Famous illustrator born on the island of Shikoku. Since 1978 he has concentrated on his 'sexy robots', to which he owes his notoriety.

suiboku A painting technique used during the Muromachi period in particular, and in works inspired by Zen. It consists of painting in black ink on paper or silk, with the occasional addition of lightly applied coloured brushstrokes. Paintings created in this style are grouped in a genre known as *suibokuga*.

sukiyaki A dish consisting of thin strips of beef served raw, which each guest then cooks in a frying-pan placed over a fire at the centre of the table. The pan contains a soy broth into which pieces of vegetables can also be dipped.

Sumiyoshi The Sumiyoshi school of painting was founded in 1662 by Tosa Hiromichi (1599–1670), elevated by Emperor Gosai (1637–85) to the position of principal painter at the Sumiyoshi shrine in Osaka. He later moved to Edo to work mainly as the shōgun's official painter. The school followed the *yamato-e* style and the classical themes typical of the Tosa school from which it originated, with added Kanō influences.

surimono Prints, often containing poetic verses, created using a particularly refined technique. They had no commercial use, but were given as greetings cards within a limited circle of people. They varied considerably in size and often incorporated precious metals, such as gold and silver.

Susano-o no mikoto In Shintō mythology he was a male deity and the brother of the goddess Amaterasu. Violent and unruly, his ill deeds led to his exile in Izumo. He contaminated Amaterasu's palace with the blood-soaked hide of a horse, upsetting her so deeply that she sought refuge in a cave, thereby plunging the universe into darkness. The gods tricked her into coming out of the cave and there was light in the world again. Susano-o is held to be the progenitor of the Izumo line and is worshipped as the god of storms and the moon.

Suzuki Harunobu (1725–70) One of the first masters of *ukiyo-e* to develop polychrome engravings, in 1765. Using the new technique, he produced a large number of prints, mainly of women – young girls or alluring courtesans – in which the subjects were depicted in a delicate and sophisticated style. He also produced erotic prints (*shunga*).

Taito II (active 1810–53) A pupil of Hokusai, born in Edo to a samurai family from Kyūshū. In 1820 the master passed on to him the name of Taito, which he himself had been using as a pseudonym since 1810. As well as working with Hokusai on the second volume of the *Manga*, he was a prolific illustrator of books.

Takizawa Bakin (1767–1848) A writer of popular books and a pupil of Santō Kyōden (1761–1816), one of the most popular authors of the late eighteenth century. He belonged to a low-ranking samurai family but, following a period of severe difficulties that seriously reduced the family's finances, he renounced his status and lived as an ordinary citizen, earning a living from writing. Particularly successful was his historical novel containing the famous tale called *Biography of Eight Dogs* (*Nansō satomi Hakkenden*, 1814–42).

tan'e ('red-orange pictures') Prints in which only the outlines of the figures were engraved. They were then hand-coloured using predominantly the reddish orange *tan* (lead oxide).

Tanaka Ikkō (1930–2002) World-famous graphic designer, whose name has been associated with many cultural fields, such as exhibitions, stage performances, musical events, book publishing. He used

shape and colour to communicate the values and principles of a better quality of life, infusing his art with a strong social and cultural meaning.

Tanizaki Jun'ichirō (1886–1965) Modern novelist, whose books are among the Japanese works of fiction best known in the West. His mature novels are famous worldwide, such as *The Makioka Sisters* (*Sasameyuki*, 1948), *The Key* (*Kagi*, 1956) and his last novel *Diary of a Mad Old Man* (*Fūten rōjin nikki*, 1961–1962). In his essay *In Praise of Shadows* (*In'ei raisan*, 1933), he compares East and West and highlights, above all, the different sensibilities of the two worlds. With a great sense of irony he pushes this process to its paradoxical limit, by comparing daily objects, places and environments and using them as a basis for reflection on his aesthetic tradition.

tanzaku Vertical print format measuring at least 12x34 cm. The name derives from the long vertical strips on which brief poems were often written.

tarashikomi The technique of applying colour over a still-damp wash, so that the new colour spreads forming an irregular shape. The decorative effect thus obtained is particularly successful in the rendering of mosses and lichens. This technique was first developed by Sōtatsu and the Rinpa school.

Tawaraya Sōtatsu (?–1643?) Sōtatsu, whose exact dates of birth and death are uncertain, flourished in Kyoto during the Momoyama period and in the early years of the Edo period. He took his surname from the fan and screen workshop with which he was associated. He devoted himself to studying both Chinese ink painting and the traditional Japanese *yamato-e*, and frequently collaborated with Hon'ami Kōetsu (1558–1637). In 1630 he was awarded the title of *hokkyō* and in the same year the Emperor entrusted him with the decoration of some screens. Sōtatsu painted in ink and in colour and made use of gold and silver; his individual style was in great favour at the Imperial court of the time. He had a particularly marked influence on the painting style of Ogata Kōrin, the central figure of the Rinpa

school; the school itself, in fact, is usually thought to have its direct roots in Sōtatsu.

tempura Dish featuring fish and vegetables, coated in a flour and water batter, deep fried in oil and then dipped in soy sauce. The term is believed to have come from Portuguese 'tempero'.

tenmoku A type of stoneware tea bowl with a wide rim and small circular turned foot, first developed in the Chinese southeastern Province of Fujian, in the small market town in Jianyang county during the Song Dynasty. It takes its name from the mountain temple in China (*tianmu*, in Japanese *tenmoku*) where iron-glazed bowls were used for tea. These objects are considered very precious, especially by lovers of tea, and are typically glazed in patterns known as 'oil spot' and 'hare's fur', among others.

teppō A low-class prostitute offering her services in the disreputable districts of town or in the so-called 'floating houses', which were barges moored on waterways and used as brothels.

teriyaki A method of cooking chicken, beef or fish on a grill, using sugar as an ingredient. This helps to achieve the glossy quality indicated by the term.

Tōkaidō Famous trunk road linking Edo and Kyoto, punctuated by 53 stations consising of porter stations and horse stables as well as lodgings, food and other places a traveller may visit. During the Tokugawa period it was the most important communication route, thus assuming a key role in the social life of the time. It came to be part of the collective lore and one of the subjects most in demand for *ukiyo-e* prints. Many series focused on it, the most famous being the one created by Hiroshige. It was also the location of the comic novel *Tōkaidōchū hizakurige* (*Walking Along the Tōkaidō*, or *Shanks's Mare*, 1802–22), by Jippensha Ikkū.

tokonoma A niche or alcove, usually located in the most important room in the home, for displaying a painted vertical scroll or a piece of calligraphy and an arrangement of flowers according to the season.

Tokugawa The name of the feudal family descended from a branch of the Minamoto Dynasty. It rose to the highest position after Ieyasu succeeded in gaining control over the whole of Japan, thus founding the last of the shōgun dynasties to rule the country (1603–1868).

Tosa A school of painting that developed in the early Muromachi period, although its name had already been used during the first half of the twelfth century, with Tsunetaka (active in the late twelfth or early thirteenth century). It drew inspiration from the traditional *emaki* paintings of the Heian and Kamakura periods.

Tōshūsai Sharaku (active in 1794–5) Hardly anything is known about this artist, who flourished in the field of *ukiyo-e* for the duration of just one theatre season (from the fifth month of 1794 to the end of 1795). He produced mainly portraits of kabuki actors, painted either in the *ōkubi-e* style, or full-length, in the *tanzaku* format. The refinement and high quality of his work are signs of his great skill and proof that he was not a novice. Who he really was, however, is a mystery, although many theories have been put forward as to his identity: various outstanding artists of the period have been suggested, including Hokusai, a nō actor, and even Tsutaya Jūzaburō, the famous publisher who is supposed to have used a pseudonym when creating his own work. None of these hypotheses has been confirmed.

Toyohara Kunichika (1835–1900) He is numbered among Utagawa Kunisada's pupils, despite not using the name of his school. The subjects of his prints are those most frequently portrayed at that time: actors, landscapes and historical subjects. His work marks the end of one of the most brilliant periods in Japanese print-making and shows an impoverishment in colouring techniques.

Toyotomi Hideyoshi (1537–98) Hideyoshi completed the process of unification of Japan, which had been started by Oda Nobunaga in the second half of the sixteenth century. A man of humble origins, he became an extremely able strategist, who opposed the growth of Christianity and ensured that the Jesuit missionaries were forced to leave the country. He saw them and their faith as potentially capable of breaking up the centralist power. His attempted invasion of the mainland came to an abrupt end almost immediately, with the failed occupation of Korea.

Tsurezuregusa (*Essays in Idleness*, c. 1331) A literary work by Kenkō (c. 1283–c. 1352), consisting of 243 essays introduced by a short preface. It is one of the most refined examples of the *zuihitsu* style, in which the lack of formal structure results from a free and deliberately casual organization. The essays in the book are miscellaneous and extremely varied in length and focus, moving frequently from one subject to another. What links them all is their acting as a starting point for reflection on human life. Many, in fact, are the passages that refer to the precarious nature of human existence, to the need to maintain a solid sense of tradition, and to a vision of life with a clearly Buddhist perspective.

Tsutaya Jūzaburō (?–1797) One of the most prestigious *ukiyo-e* publishers, responsible for some of the most refined prints in the genre. He surrounded himself with a circle of men of letters and visual artists, some of whom, such as Utamaro, actually lived in his house.

ukiyo ('floating world') Initially, this term expressed a fundamental principle in Buddhist philosophy: the transient nature of the world and all its phenomena. During the Edo period it came to signify what is most impermanent in life, in particular the world of pleasure.

ukiyo-e Paintings or prints depicting the aspects of the Floating World, best loved by the urban classes: beautiful women, the theatre world, erotic scenes, famous landscapes, images taken from nature and popular traditions.

urushi-e ('lacquered images') The hand-coloured type of *ukiyo-e* print that followed after the *tan-e* exemplars. The bright and vivid colours of the *urushi-e* were obtained by applying ink mixed with a large amount of glue, resulting in a shiny layer similar to lacquer (*urushi-nuri*), which was then dusted with a mixture of copper and mica.

Utagawa Hiroshige (1797–1858) Hiroshige was born in Edo, the son of a shōgun government official in charge of fire control. Studying under Utagawa Toyohiro (1773–1828), he initially painted beautiful women and actors, and later devoted himself entirely to painting and in particular to engraving, having passed on to his adopted son the profession he had inherited from his father. He also studied at the Kanō, Shijō and *nanga* schools. From around the year 1831 he embarked on the series entitled *Famous Places of the Eastern Capital [Edo]* (*Tōto meisho*) and, drawing inspiration from things seen and heard during a trip to the Kansai on official business, he created the collection of prints called *Fifty-three Stations of the Tōkaidō* (*Tōkaidō gojūsan tsugi no uchi*). These earned him enduring fame and became a benchmark in the genre of landscape prints. Late in life he introduced a novel style within the 'flowers and birds' and 'animals and plants' genres.

Utagawa Kunisada (1786–1864) A pupil of Utagawa Toyokuni (1769–1825), whose name he adopted as his pseudonym. He worked both as a painter and as a graphic artist during the final phase of *ukiyo-e*, focusing mainly on book illustrations, erotic scenes, portraits of actors and courtesans.

Utagawa Kuniyoshi (1797–1861) Kuniyoshi was the most important and creative pupil in the Utagawa studio. He tried his hand at many styles, including Western painting, and was therefore a precursor of later artistic developments in Japan. While his early prints appear simple and recall Hiroshige's work, in particular his background landscapes, later on his style grew more individual and his work more complex. He devoted himself to painting historical themes, especially portraits of warriors, and figurative ones, such as portraits of actors.

Utagawa Toyoharu (1735–1814) After studying painting at the Kanō school in Kyoto, in 1763 he moved to Edo, where he embarked on print-making under the influence, in particular, of Ishikawa Toyonobu's style. He is the founder of the Utagawa school and, between 1780 and 1790, he devoted himself to painting and depicting perspective landscapes derived from Dutch and German engravings.

Utagawa Toyohiro (1773–1828) He joined Toyoharu's studio in 1782 as his pupil, and specialized in prints featuring landscapes, taking the genre forward. He also devoted himself to portraying feminine beauty, mainly following Eishi's elegant style. He was Hiroshige's master.

Utagawa Toyokuni (1769–1825) An eclectic artist, he tried his hand at various painting and print-making genres, but specialized in portraits of actors, depicted in their stage personas and in their private lives, and in *bijin*. He studied under Toyoharu and was also influenced by his contemporaries, such as Utamaro; he, in turn, had many famous pupils.

Utagawa Yoshitora (active in 1850–80) A pupil of Utagawa Kuniyoshi and minor *ukiyo-e* artist, who specialized in famous views of Edo and of foreign places, the latter based on Western pictures.

Uzume One of Shintō's earliest deities, whose whirling dance enticed the goddess Amaterasu out of the cave where she had hidden. Uzume is the goddess of dance and music.

waka Traditional Japanese poetry genre consisting of 31 syllables arranged according to the 5–7–5–7–7 pattern, typical of aristocratic poetry of the period from the eighth to the twentieth centuries. It was the customary format for any poem not in the Chinese style (*kanshi*).

yamato-e Paintings based on native Japanese, rather than Chinese, style. They differ from the latter both in subject-matter and in the technique of applying clearly outlined flat areas of intense colour over the entire surface. Artists belonging to the Tosa school are particularly representative of this style. The term emphasizes the strictly Japanese inspiration of these works: the word *yamato*, in fact, refers to the name of the region near Nara, which is considered the cradle of national Japanese culture.

Yatsuhashi ('the eight-planked bridge') Famous literary location found in the tenth century's anonymous classic *Tales of Ise* (*Ise monogatari*), which has remained an inexhaustible source of inspiration for the Japanese artistic imagination.

yin–yang Taoist principle and iconographic symbol, representing the unity of male and female, earth and sky, darkness and light.

Zeami (c. 1364 to c. 1443) Together with his father Kan'ami (1334–84), Zeami is considered the founder of nō theatre. He was a playwright, actor and theorist of this form of drama. The bulk of the surviving plays were, in fact, written by him. He also left several treatises, in which he explores the different aspects of the performance: from the role of actors, to musical accompaniment and even elements of set design. Having enjoyed for a long time the protection and patronage of the Ashikaga, in later life he was inexplicably exiled to the island of Sado.

Zhuangzi The classic text of Taoism, the Chinese philosophy based on man's harmonious and spontaneous relationship with nature. It consists of a number of different writings from the period between the fourth and second century BC. The constant blurring of the boundary between history and legend means that few details about the author, Zhuangzi, can be established with certainty. Probably from northern China, he was a man of boundless wisdom and the initiator of a process of renewal in classical Chinese thought.

zuihitsu Literary genre consisting of short essays and scattered writings composed by an author in a spontaneous style and with no formal structure. Highly personal, the *zuihitsu* reveals the most intimate aspects of the writer's life and, just like a diary, presents modern readers with a privileged window on to aspects they would not have otherwise known. In the Tokugawa period it was generally used by scholars of the classics and haiku poets.

Bibliography

Abegg, Lilly, *The Mind of East Asia* (*Ostasien denkt anders*), London, Thames and Hudson, 1952

Andō Tadao and Richard Pare, *The Colours of Light*, Phaidon, London, 1996

Araki Nobuyoshi, *Self Life Death*, Phaidon, London, 2005

Artaud, Antonin, *The Theatre and Its Double*, trans. M. C. Richard, Grove Press, London, 1994

Asano Shūgo and Timothy Clark, *The Passionate Art of Kitagawa Utamaro*, 2 vols., British Museum, London, 1995

Calza, Gian Carlo, *Tanaka Ikkō: Graphic Master*, Phaidon, London, 1997
– *Hokusai*, London, Phaidon, 2003
– *Ukiyo-e*, London, Phaidon, 2005
– *L'incanto sottile del dramma nō. La principessa Aoi*, Scheiwiller, Milano, 1975 (2nd ed., *Il fiore nel emonde. L'incanto sottile del dramma nō*, Editoriale Nuova, Milano, 1983)

Canetti, Elias, *Crowds and Power*, Farrar, Straus and Giroux, New York, 1984

Cassirer, Ernst, *An Essay on Man*, Yale University Press, New Haven, 1944

de Becker, Joseph Ernest, *The Nightless City; or, the History of Yoshiwara Yūkwaku*, Z. P. Maruya & Co., Yokohama, 1899

de Goncourt, Edmond, *Hokousaï*, Bibliothèque Charpentier, Paris, 1896

Dewey, John, *Art as Experience*, Minton, Balch & C., New York, 1934

Grotowski, Jerzy, *Towards a Poor Theatre*, Odin Teatrets, Forlag, Denmark, 1968

Heisenberg, Werner, *Physics and Philosophy*, Harper & Brothers, New York, 1958

Herrigel, Eugen, *Zen in the Art of Archery*, Routledge & Kegan Paul, London, 1953

Hokusai (Katsushika Hokusai), *One Hundred Views of Mount Fuji* (*Fugaku hyakkei*), Thames and London, London, 1988

Iijima Kyoshin, *Katsushika Hokusai den*, *Hōsūkaku*, Tokyo, 1983

Jung, Carl Gustav, 'The Spiritual Problem of Modern Man' in *The Collected Works of C. G. Jung, Vol. 10: Civilization in Transition*, ed. and trans. Gerhard Adler and R. F. C. Hull, Princeton University Press, Princeton, 1983

Kassner. Rudolf, *Gli elementi dell'umana grandezza*, Bompiani, Milano, 1942

Kawabata Yasunari, 'Jōjōka, Lyric Poem', trans. F. Mathy, *Monumenta Nipponica*, 26 (3–4) 1971
– *Beauty and Sadness* (*Utsukushisa to kanashimi to*), trans. Howard Hibbett, Secker and Warburg, London, 1975
– *House of the Sleeping Beauties, and other stories* (*Nemureru bijo*), trans. E. G. Seidensticker, Quadriga Press, London, 1969
– *The Master of Go* (*Meijin*), trans. E. G. Seidensticker, Secker and Warburg, London, 1973
– *The Old Capital* (*Koto*), trans. J. M. Holman, Northpoint Press, San Francisco, 1987
– *Palm-of-the-Hand Stories* (*Tanagokoro no shōsetsu*), trans. Lane Dunlop and J. Martin Holman, Picador, London, 1989
– *Snow Country* (*Yukiguni*), trans. E. G. Seidensticker, Secker & Warburg, London, 1957

Keene, Donald, 'The Vocabulary of Japanese Aesthetics I', in W. T. De Bary, *Sources of Japanese Tradition*, Columbia University Press, New York, 1958
– *Nō: The Classical Theatre of Japan*, Kodansha, Tokyo and Palo Alto, 1966
– *Seeds in the Heart: Japanese Literature from Earliest Times to the Late Sixteenth Century*, Henry Holt & Co., New York, 1993
– *Twenty Plays of the Nō Theatre*, Columbia University Press, New York, 1970

Kenkō Yoshida, *Essays in Idleness*, trans. D. Keene, Columbia University Press, New York, 1967

Ki no Tsurayuki (ed.), *Kōkin wakashū, Kokinshū: A Collection of Poems Ancient and Modern*, trans. L. R. Rodd and M. C. Henkenius, Cheng & Tsui Co., Boston, Mass., 1996

Kuki Shūzō, *The Structure of 'Iki'*, trans. J. Clark, John Clark, London, 1980

Labuz, Ronald, *Contemporary Graphic Design*, Van Nostrand Reinhold, New York, 1991

Lane, Richard, *Images from the Floating World*, Oxford University Press, Oxford, 1978

Maraini, Fosco, *Meeting with Japan*, Hutchinson, London, 1959

Marinotti, Marcella, *La Rivoluzione del Paesaggio in Sesshū*, unpublished dissertation, Milan, 2001

Mishima Yukio, 'Patriotism' ('Yūkoku') in *Death in Midsummer and other stories*, Secker & Warburg, London, 1967
– *After the Banquet* (*Utage no ato*), trans. Donald Keene, Secker & Warburg, London, 1963
– *Confessions of a Mask* (*Kamen no kokuhaku*), trans. Meredith Weatherby, Peter Owen, London, 1960
– *Death in Midsummer and other stories* (*Manatsu no shi*), Secker & Warburg, London, 1967
– *The Decay of the Angel* (*Tennin gosui*) (*The Sea of Fertility*), trans. E. G. Seidensticker, Secker and Warburg, London, 1975
– *Forbidden Colours* (*Kinjiki*), trans. Alfred. H. Marks, Secker & Warburg, London, 1968
– *Madame de Sade* (*Sado kōshaku fujin*), trans. Donald Keene, Peter Owen, London, 1968
– *Runaway Horses* (*Honba*) (*The Sea of Fertility*), trans. Michael Gallagher, Secker & Warburg, London, 1973
– *Spring Snow* (*Haru no yuki*) (*The Sea of Fertility*), trans. Michael Gallagher, Secker & Warburg, London, 1972
– *Sun and Steel* (*Taiyō to tetsu*), trans. John Bester, Secker & Warburg, London, 1971
– *The Sailor who Fell from Grace with the Sea* (*Gogo no eikō*), trans. J. Nathan, Secker & Warburg, London, 1966
– *The Sound of Waves* (*Shiosai*), trans. M. Weatherby, Secker & Warburg, London, 1957
– *The Temple of Dawn* (*Akatsuki no tera*) (*The Sea of Fertility*), trans. E. Dale Saunders and C. Segawa Seigle, Secker & Warburg, London, 1974
– *The Temple of the Golden Pavilion* (*Kinkaku-ji*), trans. I. Morris, Secker & Warburg, London, 1959
– *Thirst for Love* (*Ai no kawaki*), trans. Alfred H. Marks, Secker & Warburg, London, 1970

Murasaki Shikibu, *The Tale of Genji* (*Genji monogatari*), trans. A Waley, Modern Library, New York, 1960
– *The Tale of Genji* (*Genji monogatari*), trans. E. G. Seidensticker, Harmondsworth, Penguin Books, London, 1981

Murase Miyeko, *Images of the Tale of Genji*, Weatherhill, New York, 1983

Nakamura Hajime, *The Ways of Thinking of Eastern People*, University of Hawaii Press, Honolulu, 1964

Nara Hiroshi, *The Structure of Detachment: The Aesthetic Vision of Kuki Shūzō with a Translation of Ikino Kōzō*, University of Hawaii Press, Honolulu, 2004

Natsume Sōseki, *Kusamakura*, trans. E. McCelellen as *The Three-cornered World*, Arrow Books, London, 1984

Needham, Rodney, *Exemplars*, University of California Press, Berkley, 1985

Nogami Toyoichirō, *Japanese Noh Plays*, Kegan Paul International, London, 2005

Okakura Kakuzō, *The Book of Tea*, Charles E. Tuttle, Tokyo, 1964

Otto, Rudolf, *The Idea of the Holy*, trans. John W. Harvey, Oxford University Press, New York, 1958

Péri, Noël, *Le Nô*, Maison Franco-Japonaise, Tokyo, 1944

Philippi, Donald L. ed. *Kojiki*, Tokyo University Press and Princeton University Press, Tokyo, 1968

Revon, Michel, *Étude sur Hoksaï*, Lecène, Oudin et Cie, Paris, 1896

Rivetta, Pier Silvio, *Bellezza e* curiosità *della lingua nipponica. IV Il fascino dell'inespresso.* Yamato I (4) April 1941

Sei Shōnagon, *The Pillow Book of Sei Shōnagon* (*Makura no sōshi*), translated and edited by Ivan Morris, Oxford University Press, London, 1967

Serizawa Kōjirō, *Nihon bunka kenkyū kokusai kaigi-gijiroku*, International Conference of Japanese Studies – Report, Nihon PEN Club, Tokyo, 1973, 4 vols.

Suzuki, Daisetz T., *Zen and Japanese Culture*, Bollingen Series, New York, 1959

Tanizaki Jun'ichirō, *In Praise of Shadows*, (*In'ei raisan*), trans. T. J. Harper and E. G. Seidensticker, Cape, London, 1991

Terrasse, Antoine, 'Degas à travers ses mots', *Gazette des Beaux Arts*, série 6, 86, 1975

Weil, Simone, *Imitations of Christianity among the Ancient Greeks*, translated and edited by Elisabethe Chase Geissbuhler, Routledge & Kegan Paul, London, 1957

Yourcenar, Marguerite, *Mishima: A Vision of the Void*, trans. Alberto Manguel, Farrar, Straus & Giroux, New York, 1986

Zeami, *Il segreto del teatro nō*, ed. R. Sieffert, Adelphi, Milano, 1966

Zhuangzi jishi, ed. Guo Qingfan, Zhonghua Shuju, Beijing, 1978, 4 vols.

Acknowledgements and Personal Remarks

The idea for this book arose directly out of a series of lectures on Japan that I gave at the Centro Coscienza, Milan, at the time of the Hokusai exhibition, and I am grateful to the centre; by offering me that opportunity it indirectly prompted me to write Japan Style. Many of the deepest and most personal insights that I was able to gain and to express sprang from my long association with the centre's cultural and social environment, and the stimulation it has provided.

In addition to the material presented in those lectures, I planned to do no more and no less than ransack my own archive, and to select a number of texts from it. But in the event, partly because the various elements had to be given a connecting thread, partly because they had to be updated, but above all because I could not resist the allure of the subject matter, in the end I revised (several times, in fact) all my articles and essays, old and new.

Japan Style was thus the result of a set of related causes, and was inspired by a number of people who said things like, 'Why don't you collect some of the essays and articles you have written over so many [too many?] decades and turn them into a book? Otherwise they'll be lost, and it would be a terrible shame [a touch of flattery!]. They're full of interesting and useful thoughts, even after all this time [ouch!].' My thanks therefore go to the editors of those publications, both popular and scholarly, that offered me the opportunity to write them.

Richard Schlagman, who took on responsibility for this new international edition, encouraged me, from the time of the Milan exhibitions on Hokusai and ukiyo-e – for which he also produced the international editions – with a tenacity and friendliness that have always been a great support. Emilia Terragni followed in his footsteps in wanting this book to be published, and the careful translation by Imogen Forster and Irena Hill and the editorial contribution of Diego Garcia Scaro and Cameron Laux helped me turn the uncertainties of my solitary labours into a stimulating team exercise.

But without Martina Fuga's helpfulness and her unswerving powers of persuasion I would have found it difficult indeed to assemble and revise these texts. At the Hokusai Centre, Stefania Piotti helped me to prepare the manuscript for the publisher and to trace some apparently lost texts and many illustrations; her scholarly oversight of this new edition was invaluable.

These essays are also the fruit of 35 years' work at Ca' Foscari University, in Venice, reflecting my teaching and dialogue with students in classes and seminars. More specifically, I am grateful to a number of colleagues and friends in the Department of East Asian Studies. In particular, I am indebted to Maurizio Scarpari for some subtle thoughts on

Zhuangzi. Several valuable pointers came from Bonaventura Ruperti's passion for kabuki, and Federico Marcon provided a number of linguistic glosses on classical Japanese.

At the same time, the book owes a great deal, if indirectly, to Fosco Maraini, his work and way of life.

Among the many friends throughout the world who have helped me to penetrate the world of Japan, its art and its soul, I should like to mention above all Donald Keene, my friendship with whom goes back almost 50 years, and John Rosenfield, on whose support and stimulation I have always been able to rely.

Nevertheless, responsibility for this book is mine alone. My awareness of this led me to think how nice it would be to write the story of the way a book was conceived, how it took shape and matured, how it was altered, refined and rewritten more than once, and how it was finally completed more through the determination of others than through one's own conviction, and then to have the strength of mind to throw it way and just keep the story.

I do not have it.

But I realize that I am being inconsistent with my own often-expressed assertions on the supremacy of the creative act over the object created, but so it is; I shall always remain a westerner, even if an 'nipposinindianized' one.

All in all, *Japan Style* is a book of reflections on the art, literature, theatre, aesthetics and culture of the Rising Sun, also touching on religious ideas, especially those of Shintō. It was written in such a way that its connecting thread consists of the spirit of the people, objects, events and customs of Japan that have fascinated and stimulated the West in general, as well, obviously, as myself. Its central theme is the cult of beauty, understood both as harmony and discord, which dominates the first section, 'Irregular Beauty'. It is a conception of beauty based on a specific relationship with nature, set out in the second section, 'The Feeling of Nature', and embodied in the third, 'Masters of Art', in the direct experience of certain individuals who made works of art of their own life and work. Each section is separated from the next by an 'intermezzo', slightly jocular in tone, designed to relieve the overall seriousness, a bit like the *kyōgen* farces that break up a day of nō drama.

This book, therefore, does not claim to be strictly academic, but, I hope, cultural, and definitely personal: it aspires, however uncertainly, to be written in the way a landscape might be painted in ink, with misty areas and clear ones, some parts full of detail, others consisting of emptiness. It aims only to provide a stimulus for knowing ourselves through the 'other'. It should therefore not be taken too seriously, and certainly not literally, but cautiously, and then absorbed, modified, reinterpreted personally, freely.

Index

Credits

Phaidon Press Limited
Regent's Wharf
All Saints Street
London N1 9PA

Phaidon Press Inc.
65 Bleecker Street
New York, NY 10012

www.phaidon.com

First published 2007
Reprinted in paperback 2015
© 2007 Phaidon Press Limited

ISBN 978-0-7148-7055-7

Text published in Italian by Giulio
Einaudi Editore, 2002

A CIP catalogue record for this book
is available from the British Library

Translated by
Imogen Forster and Irena Hill

Designed by
Philippe Apeloig

Printed in China

To Donald Keene
forty-eight years of friendship